Integrating Microsoft® Office XP

Illustrated Introductory

Integrating Microsoft® Office XP
Illustrated Introductory

Beskeen/Duffy/Reding

COURSE TECHNOLOGY
THOMSON LEARNING

Australia • Canada • Mexico • Singapore • Spain • United Kingdom • United States

Integrating Microsoft Office XP - Illustrated Introductory

Beskeen/Duffy/Reding

Managing Editor:
Nicole Jones Pinard

Production Editor:
Anne Valsangiacomo

QA Manuscript Reviewers:
John Freitas, Ashlee Welz, Alex White, Harris Bierhoff, Serge Palladino, Holly Schabowski, Jeff Schwartz

Product Manager:
Emily Heberlein

Developmental Editors:
Katherine T. Pinard, Rachel Biheller Bunin, Barbara Clemens

Text Designer:
Joseph Lee, Black Fish Design

Associate Product Manager:
Emeline Elliott

Editorial Assistant:
Christina Kling Garrett

Composition House:
GEX Publishing Services

COPYRIGHT © 2002 Course Technology, a division of Thomson Learning™. Thomson Learning™ is a trademark used herein under license.

Printed in the United States of America

4 5 6 7 8 9 BM 05 04 03

For more information, contact Course Technology, 25 Thomson Place, Boston, Massachusetts, 02210.

Or you can visit us on the World Wide Web at www.course.com

ALL RIGHTS RESERVED. No part of this work covered by the copyright hereon may be reproduced or used in any form or by any means - graphic, electronic, or mechanical, including photocopying, recording, taping, Web distribution, or information storage and retrieval systems - without the written permission of the publisher.

For permission to use material from this text or product, contact us by
Tel (800) 730-2214
Fax (800) 730-2215
www.thomsonrights.com

Trademarks
Some of the product names and company names used in this book have been used for identification purposes only and may be trademarks or registered trademarks of their respective manufacturers and sellers.

Microsoft and the Office logo are either registered trademarks or trademarks of Microsoft Corporation in the United States and/or other countries. Course Technology is an independent entity from Microsoft Corporation, and not affiliated with Microsoft in any manner.

ISBN 0-619-04537-X

The Illustrated Series Vision

Teaching and writing about computer applications can be extremely rewarding and challenging. How do we engage students and keep their interest? How do we teach them skills that they can easily apply on the job? As we set out to write this book, our goals were to develop a textbook that:

- teaches students how to use their Office XP skills to create integrated projects
- provides varied, flexible and meaningful exercises and projects to reinforce skills
- serves as a reference tool
- makes your job as an educator easier, by providing resources above and beyond the textbook to help you teach your course

Our popular, streamlined format is based on advice from instructional designers and customers. This flexible design presents each lesson on a two-page spread, with step-by-step instructions on the left, and screen illustrations on the right. This signature style, coupled with high-caliber content, provides comprehensive yet manageable coverage of integrating Microsoft Office XP - it is a teaching package for the instructor and a learning experience for the student.

AUTHOR ACKNOWLEDGMENTS

David Beskeen It has, once again, been a pleasure working with all the talented people at Course Technology. I would like to especially thank Katherine Pinard who has worked hard on my chapters to make them better and easier to understand. I would also like to thank my family, Karen and the three J's, for being so understanding during the long hours of writing.

Jennifer Duffy I wish to express particular thanks to Pam Conrad for her tireless help and keen editorial sensibilities. I am also deeply grateful for the support of my husband, Fred Eliot, and our daughter, Isabella, who patiently waited to be born until this book was nearly finished.

Elizabeth Eisner Reding Creating a book of this magnitude is a team effort: I would like to thank my husband, Michael, for putting up with my ridiculous mood swings, Emily Heberlein, the project manager, and my development editors, Barbara Clemens and Kitty Pinard, for their insightful suggestions and corrections. I would also like to thank the production and editorial staff for all their hard work that made this project a reality.

Thanks to all the reviewers who provided invaluable feedback and ideas to us, especially Diane Blaney, Anne Burchardt, and Janis Cox.

Preface

Welcome to *Integrating Microsoft Office XP—Illustrated Introductory*. Each lesson in this book contains elements pictured to the right.

▶ How is the book organized?

The book is organized into sections, illustrated by the brightly colored tabs on the sides of the pages: One unit on Introducing Office XP, followed by seven Integration units. In these units, students explore using their application skills to create integrated projects involving Word, Excel, Access, PowerPoint, and Internet Explorer.

▶ What kinds of assignments are included in the book? At what level of difficulty?

The lessons use MediaLoft, a fictional chain of bookstores, as the case study. The assignments on the blue pages at the end of each unit increase in difficulty. Project files and case studies, with many international examples, provide a great variety of interesting and relevant business applications for skills. Assignments in each unit may include:

- **Skills Reviews** provide additional hands-on, step-by-step reinforcement.

- **Independent Challenges** are case projects requiring critical thinking and application of the unit skills. The Independent Challenges increase in difficulty, with the first one in each unit being the easiest (most step-by-step with detailed instructions). Independent Challenges within each unit become increasingly open-ended, requiring more independent problem solving.

- **E-Quest Independent Challenges** are case projects with a Web focus. E-Quests require the use of the World Wide Web to conduct research to complete the project.

- **Visual Workshops** show a completed file and require that the file be created without any step-by-step guidance, involving independent problem solving.

Each 2-page spread focuses on a single skill.

Concise text that introduces the basic principles in the lesson and integrates the brief case study (indicated by the paintbrush icon).

Unit C Integration

Embedding an Excel Chart into a PowerPoint Slide

You can easily embed an Excel chart into a PowerPoint presentation. Because it is embedded, you can double-click a chart to edit it using Excel tools. The original Excel chart object remains unchanged. Maria decides to include in her presentation an Excel chart that she received from the Accounting Department. She wants to format the chart after she adds it to her presentation, so she embeds it.

Steps

1. Click the **Slide 3 thumbnail** on the Slides tab, click the **Other Task Panes list arrow** on the task pane title bar, click **Slide Layout**, then click the **Title Only layout** under Text Layouts

2. Click **Insert** on the menu bar, then click **Object**
   The Insert Object dialog box opens.

   QuickTip
   You can reposition the chart on the slide by dragging it.

3. Click the **Create from file option button**, click **Browse**, select the file **INT C-3.xls** from the location where your Project Files are stored, click **OK**, then click **OK** in the Insert Object dialog box
   The Excel chart appears on the slide. Compare your screen to Figure C-5.

4. Click the **Fill Color list arrow** on the Drawing toolbar, then click the **light purple** square (labeled Follow Title Text Scheme Color)
   The chart text would be more readable if it were larger.

   Trouble?
   If the Chart toolbar does not appear, click View on the menu bar, point to Toolbars, then click Chart.

5. Double-click the **chart object**
   The PowerPoint menu bar and toolbars are replaced with the Excel menu bar and toolbars, and the Excel Chart toolbar appears.

6. Click the **Chart Objects list arrow** on the Chart toolbar, click **Chart Title**, click the **Format Chart Title button** on the Chart toolbar, click the **Font tab**, click **28** in the Size list, then click **OK**
   The change in the Excel chart is reflected in the embedded object in PowerPoint. Because this is an embedded object, editing the object does not alter the original Excel file.

TABLE C-1: Embedding vs. Linking

action	situation
Embed	You are the only user of an object, and you want the object to be a part of your presentation.
Embed	You want to access the object in its source program, even if the source file is not available.
Embed	You want to update the object manually while working in PowerPoint.
Link	You always want your object to have the latest information.
Link	The object's source file is shared on a network or where other users have access to the file and can change it.
Link	You want to keep your presentation file size small.

▶ INTEGRATION C-6   INTEGRATING WORD, EXCEL, ACCESS, AND POWERPOINT

Hints as well as troubleshooting advice, right where you need it — next to the step itself.

Quickly accessible summaries of key terms, toolbar buttons, or keyboard alternatives connected with the lesson material. Students can refer easily to this information when working on their own projects at a later time.

Every lesson features large, full-color representations of what the screen should look like as students complete the numbered steps.

Brightly colored tabs indicate which section of the book you are in.

▶ **What distance learning options are available to accompany this book?**

Visit www.course.com for more information on our Distance Learning materials to accompany Illustrated titles. Options include:

MyCourse.com

Need a quick, simple tool to help you manage your course? Try MyCourse.com, the easiest to use, most flexible syllabus and content management tool available. MyCourse.com offers you brand new content, including Topic Reviews, Extra Case Projects, and Quizzes, to accompany this book.

WebCT

Course Technology and WebCT have partnered to provide you with the highest quality online resources and Web-based tools for your class. Course Technology offers content for this book to help you create your WebCT class, such as a suggested Syllabus, Lecture Notes, Practice Test questions, and more.

Blackboard

Course Technology and Blackboard have also partnered to provide you with the highest quality online resources and Web-based tools for your class. Course Technology offers content for this book to help you create your Blackboard class, such as a suggested Syllabus, Lecture Notes, Practice Test questions, and more.

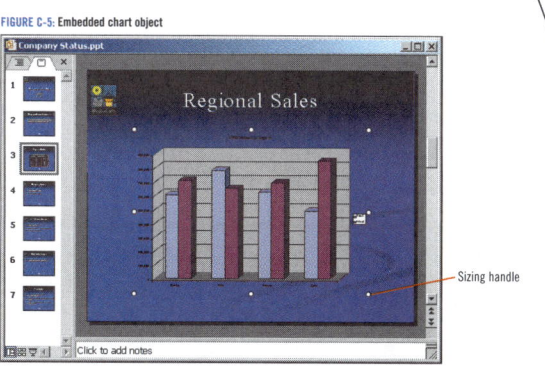

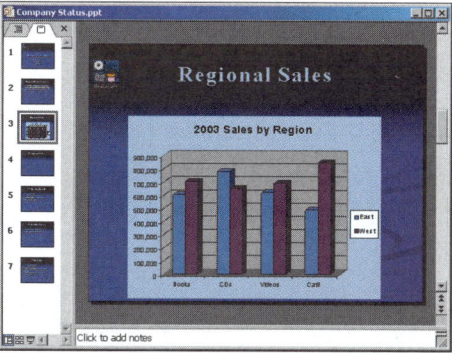

Clues to Use boxes provide concise information that either expands on the major lesson skill or describes an independent task that in some way relates to the major lesson skill.

The pages are numbered according to section and unit. Integration indicates the section, C indicates the unit, 7 indicates the page.

Instructor Resources

The Instructor's Resource Kit (IRK) CD is Course Technology's way of putting the resources and information needed to teach and learn effectively into your hands. All the components are available on the IRK, (pictured below), and many of the resources can be downloaded from www.course.com.

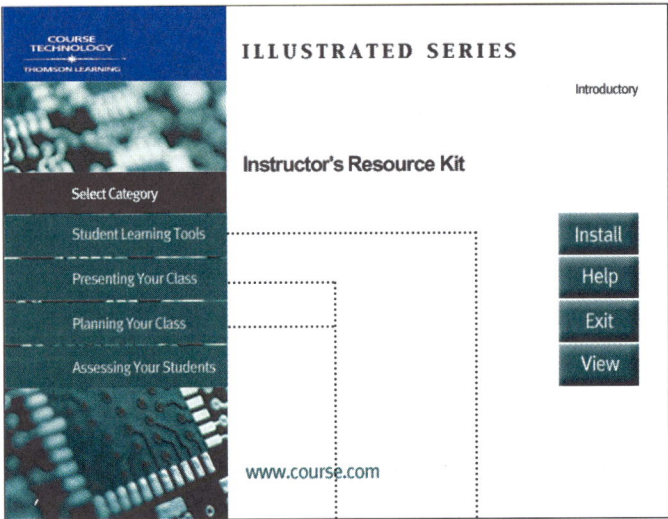

ASSESSING YOUR STUDENTS

Solution Files
Solution Files are Project Files completed with comprehensive sample answers. Use these files to evaluate your students' work. Or, distribute electronically or in hard copy so students can verify their own work.

ExamView
ExamView is a powerful testing software package that allows you to create and administer printed, computer (LAN-based), and Internet exams. ExamView includes hundreds of questions that correspond to the topics covered in this text, enabling students to generate detailed study guides that include page references for further review. The computer-based and Internet testing components allow students to take exams at their computers, and also saves you time by grading each exam automatically.

PRESENTING YOUR CLASS

Figure Files
Figure Files contain all the figures from the book in .jpg format. Use the figure files to create transparency masters or in a PowerPoint presentation.

STUDENT TOOLS

Project Files and Project Files List
To complete most of the units in this book, your students will need **Project Files**. Put them on a file server for students to copy. The Project Files are available on the Instructor's Resource Kit CD-ROM, the Review Pack, and can also be downloaded from www.course.com.

Instruct students to use the **Project Files List** at the end of the book. This list gives instructions on copying and organizing files.

PLANNING YOUR CLASS

Instructor's Manual
Available as an electronic file, the Instructor's Manual is quality-assurance tested and includes unit overviews, detailed lecture topics for each unit with teaching tips, comprehensive sample solutions to all lessons and end-of-unit material, and extra Independent Challenges. The Instructor's Manual is available on the Instructor's Resource Kit CD-ROM, or you can download it from www.course.com.

Sample Syllabus
Prepare and customize your course easily using this sample course outline (available on the Instructor's Resource Kit CD-ROM).

Brief Contents

The Illustrated Series Vision   V
Preface   VI

Office XP	Introducing Microsoft Office XP ....OFFICE A-1
Integration	Integrating Word and Excel ....INTEGRATION A-1
	Integrating Word, Excel, and Access ....INTEGRATION B-1
	Integrating Word, Excel, Access, and PowerPoint ....INTEGRATION C-1
	Integrating Office Applications with Internet Explorer ....INTEGRATION D-1
	Integrating Word and Excel ....INTEGRATION E-1
	Integrating Word, Excel, and Access ....INTEGRATION F-1
	Integrating Word, Excel, Access, and PowerPoint ....INTEGRATION G-1

Project Files List   1
Glossary   8
Index   11

Contents

The Illustrated Series Vision   V
Preface   VI

Office XP

Introducing Microsoft Office XP — OFFICE A-1

Defining the Office XP Suite ....OFFICE A-2
Creating a Document with Word 2002 ....OFFICE A-4
Building a Worksheet with Excel 2002 ....OFFICE A-6
Managing Data with Access 2002 ....OFFICE A-8
Creating a Presentation with PowerPoint 2002 ....OFFICE A-10
Browsing the World Wide Web with Internet Explorer ....OFFICE A-12
Integrating Office Information ....OFFICE A-14
Managing Office Tasks with Outlook 2002 ....OFFICE A-16

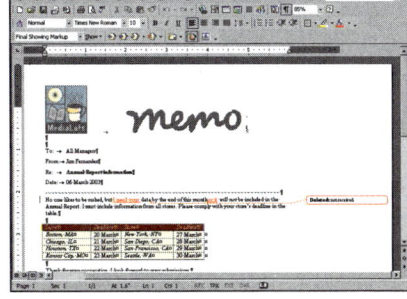

Integration

Integrating Word and Excel — INTEGRATION A-1

Understanding Integration ....INTEGRATION A-2
Opening Multiple Programs ....INTEGRATION A-4
   Using shortcut keys to switch between open programs ....INTEGRATION A-5
Copying Word Data into Excel ....INTEGRATION A-6
Independent Challenges ....INTEGRATION A-8

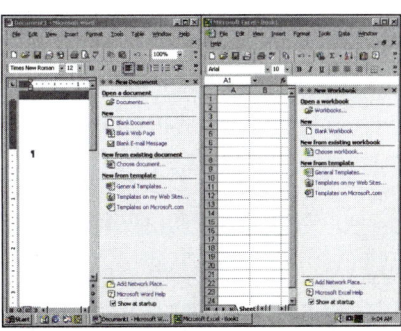

Contents

Integrating Word, Excel, and Access — INTEGRATION B-1

Merging Data Between Access and Word ...... INTEGRATION B-2
Using Mail Merge to Create a Form Letter ...... INTEGRATION B-4
Exporting an Access Table to Excel ...... INTEGRATION B-6
   Exporting an Access table to Word ...... INTEGRATION B-7
Independent Challenges ...... INTEGRATION B-8

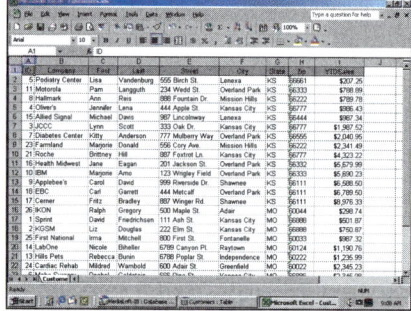

Integrating Word, Excel, Access, and PowerPoint — INTEGRATION C-1

Understanding Embedding and Linking ...... INTEGRATION C-2
Inserting a Word Outline into a PowerPoint Presentation ...... INTEGRATION C-4
Embedding an Excel Chart into a PowerPoint Slide ...... INTEGRATION C-6
   Embedding objects using Paste Special ...... INTEGRATION C-7
Linking an Excel Worksheet to a PowerPoint Slide ...... INTEGRATION C-8
Updating a Linked Excel Worksheet in PowerPoint ...... INTEGRATION C-10
   Updating links ...... INTEGRATION C-11
Exporting a PowerPoint Presentation to Word ...... INTEGRATION C-12
Independent Challenges ...... INTEGRATION C-14

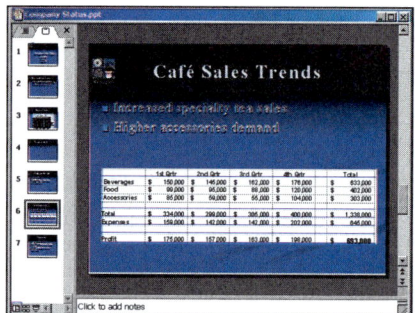

Integrating Office Applications with Internet Explorer — INTEGRATION D-1

Planning a Web Publication ...... INTEGRATION D-2
Creating a Web Page ...... INTEGRATION D-4
   Choosing Web page content and style ...... INTEGRATION D-5
Formatting a Web Page ...... INTEGRATION D-6
Creating a Web Page from a Word Document ...... INTEGRATION D-8
Creating a Web Page from an Access Table ...... INTEGRATION D-10

Using Access to create static and dynamic Web pages	INTEGRATION D-11
Creating a Web Page from an Excel Workbook	INTEGRATION D-12
Creating Web Pages from a PowerPoint Presentation	INTEGRATION D-14
Using frames	INTEGRATION D-15
Adding Hyperlinks	INTEGRATION D-16
Publishing your Web pages	INTEGRATION D-17
Skills Review	INTEGRATION D-18
Independent Challenges	INTEGRATION D-20
Visual Workshop	INTEGRATION D-24

Integrating Word and Excel — INTEGRATION E-1

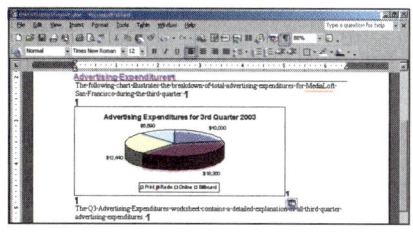

Linking an Excel chart to a Word document	INTEGRATION E-2
Embedding an Excel worksheet into a Word document	INTEGRATION E-4
Inserting a hyperlink to an Excel file in a Word document	INTEGRATION E-6
Independent Challenges	INTEGRATION E-8

Integrating Word, Excel, and Access — INTEGRATION F-1

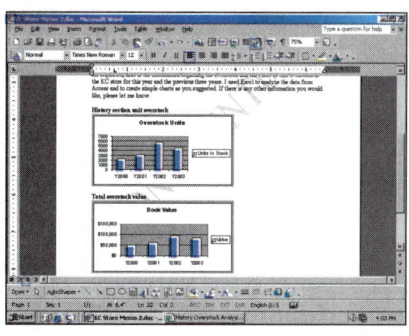

Copying an Access Table into a Word Document	INTEGRATION F-2
Copying an Access Table to Excel	INTEGRATION F-4
Embedding an Excel Chart into a Word Document	INTEGRATION F-6
Independent Challenges	INTEGRATION F-8

XIII

Contents

Integrating Word, Excel, Access, and PowerPoint — INTEGRATION G-1

Creating a PowerPoint Presentation from a Word Outline .... INTEGRATION G-2

Embedding a Word Table and Excel Worksheet into a Presentation .... INTEGRATION G-4

Creating a Relationship in an Access Database .... INTEGRATION G-6

Analyzing Access Data in Excel .... INTEGRATION G-8

Inserting Excel Data in a Word Document .... INTEGRATION G-10

Importing Excel Data into a PowerPoint Presentation .... INTEGRATION G-12

Independent Challenges .... INTEGRATION G-14

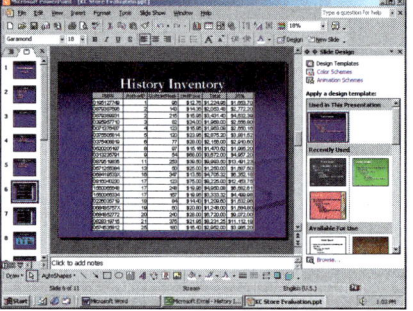

Project Files List — 1
Glossary — 8
Index — 11

Read This Before You Begin

Software Information and Required Installation

This book was written and tested using Microsoft Office XP - Professional Edition, with a typical installation on Microsoft Windows 2000, with Internet Explorer 5.0 or higher. In Unit D, depending on your Office installation, the templates and themes available to you may differ. Tips are included in the lessons and Instructor's Manual for this situation.

Tips for Students

What are Project Files?

To complete many of the units in this book, you need to use Project Files. You use a Project File, which contains a partially completed document used in an exercise, so you don't have to type in all the information you need in the document. Your instructor will either provide you with a copy of the Project Files or ask you to make your own copy. Detailed instructions on how to organize you files, as well as a complete listing of all the files you'll need and will create, can be found in the back of the book (look for the yellow pages) in the Project Files List.

Why is my screen different from the book?

1. Your Desktop components and some dialog box options might be different if you are using an operating system other than Windows 2000

2. Depending on your computer hardware capabilities and the Windows Display settings on your computer, you may notice the following differences:
   - Your screen may look larger or smaller because of your screen resolution (the height and width of your screen)
   - The colors of the title bar in your screen may be a solid blue, and the cells in Excel may appear different from the purple and gray because of your color settings

3. Depending on your Office settings, your toolbars may display on a single row and your menus may display with a shortened list of frequently used commands. Office menus and toolbars can modify themselves to your working style by displaying only the most frequently used buttons and menu commands, as shown here.

Toolbars on one row

To view buttons not currently displayed, click a Toolbar Options button at the end of either the Standard or Formatting toolbar. To view the full list of menu commands, click the double arrow at the bottom of the menu.

In order to have your toolbars display on two rows, showing all buttons, and to have the full menus display, you must turn off the personalized menus and toolbars feature. Click tools on the menu bar, Click Customize, select the show Standard and Formatting toolbars on two rows and Always show full menus check boxes on the Options tab, then click Close. This book assumes you are displaying toolbars on two rows and full menus.

Toolbars on two rows

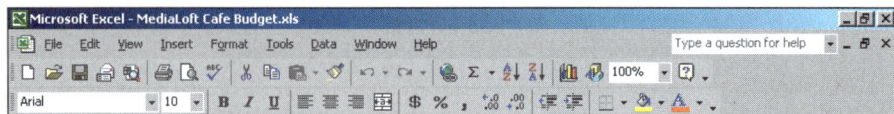

Office XP

Introducing
Microsoft Office XP

Objectives

- Define the Office XP Suite
- Create a document with Word 2002
- Build a worksheet with Excel 2002
- Manage data with Access 2002
- Create a presentation with PowerPoint 2002
- Browse the World Wide Web with Internet Explorer
- Integrate Office information
- Manage office tasks with Outlook 2002

Microsoft Office XP is a collection of software programs designed to help you accomplish tasks quickly and efficiently. Each Office program is designed to complete specific tasks and has similar buttons and commands to make switching among the programs easy and seamless. The Microsoft Office programs are supplied together in a group called a **suite** (although you can also purchase them separately). Suite programs are designed so that you can easily transfer information among them.

This unit introduces you to the Microsoft Office suite programs, as well as to MediaLoft, a nationwide chain of bookstore cafés that sells books, CDs, DVDs, and videos. By exploring how MediaLoft uses Microsoft Office components, you will learn how each program can be used in a business environment.

Defining the Office XP Suite

Microsoft Office XP is a collection of software programs known as **business productivity software** because it helps business people work efficiently. Office is available in several configurations, and the most commonly used programs are Word, Excel, Access, PowerPoint, and Outlook. Internet Explorer is a Web browser that comes with Windows and can be downloaded from the Web. The Office programs have a similar "look and feel," and are designed to exchange information seamlessly. All MediaLoft employees use Office programs to create business documents, communicate with associates, and access the Internet. See Figure A-1 for an overview of MediaLoft's stores and Figure A-2 for sample Office documents.

▶ The basic tools: Microsoft Office XP Suite components

The Office suite components work individually and with each other to help people accomplish tasks and work together. **Microsoft Word** lets you create powerful text documents. Isaac Robinson, the marketing director of the MediaLoft Chicago store, uses Word to create letters, reports, faxes, and flyers. You can automatically calculate and analyze data with **Microsoft Excel**. Jim Fernandez, MediaLoft's office manager, uses Excel to create budgets, financial statements, and payroll summaries. **Microsoft Access** lets you organize, track, and update complex data. Kelsey Lang, a MediaLoft marketing manager, uses Access to create and maintain a customer information database. You can create powerful visual presentations using **Microsoft PowerPoint**. Maria Abbott, MediaLoft's general sales manager, uses PowerPoint to create a slide show summarizing the company's performance; she will show it at an annual meeting of store managers. You can easily track contacts, appointments, and e-mail with **Microsoft Outlook**. Marketing manager Alice Wegman uses Outlook to stay in touch with MediaLoft employees around the world.

Internet Explorer lets you stay in touch with information on the Internet and World Wide Web. Alice Wegman, a MediaLoft marketing manager, uses Internet Explorer to find out about competitors in geographic areas the company is considering as sites for expansion.

▶ Working together: Program compatibility and integration

Because the Office suite programs have a similar "look and feel," you can use your knowledge of one program's tools in other suite programs. For example, you can use the same commands and icons for common tasks such as printing and saving. Office documents are **compatible** with one another, meaning that you can easily place, or **integrate**, an Excel chart into a PowerPoint slide, or you can insert an Access table into a Word document. You can specify that information in one file be automatically updated whenever information in another file changes. The Office programs also share a common dictionary, so that special words you use often can be used consistently across all of your Office documents. And you can use the Office Clipboard to easily transfer up to 24 entries between any Office programs.

▶ Supporting collaboration and teamwork: The new business model

Office supports the way people do business today, which emphasizes communication and knowledge sharing within companies and across the globe via company intranets and the Internet. All Office programs include the ability to share information over the Internet—called **online collaboration**. Employees can share documents, schedule online meetings, and have discussions over the World Wide Web. Office supports teamwork by allowing people to share documents and team members' feedback that can all be incorporated in one place.

FIGURE A-1: MediaLoft stores

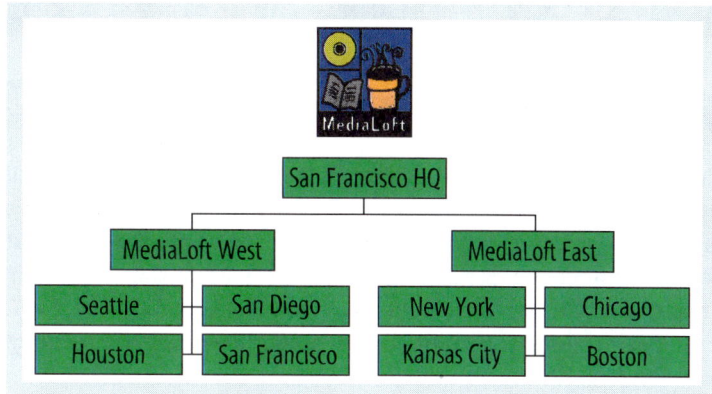

FIGURE A-2: Office documents created by MediaLoft employees

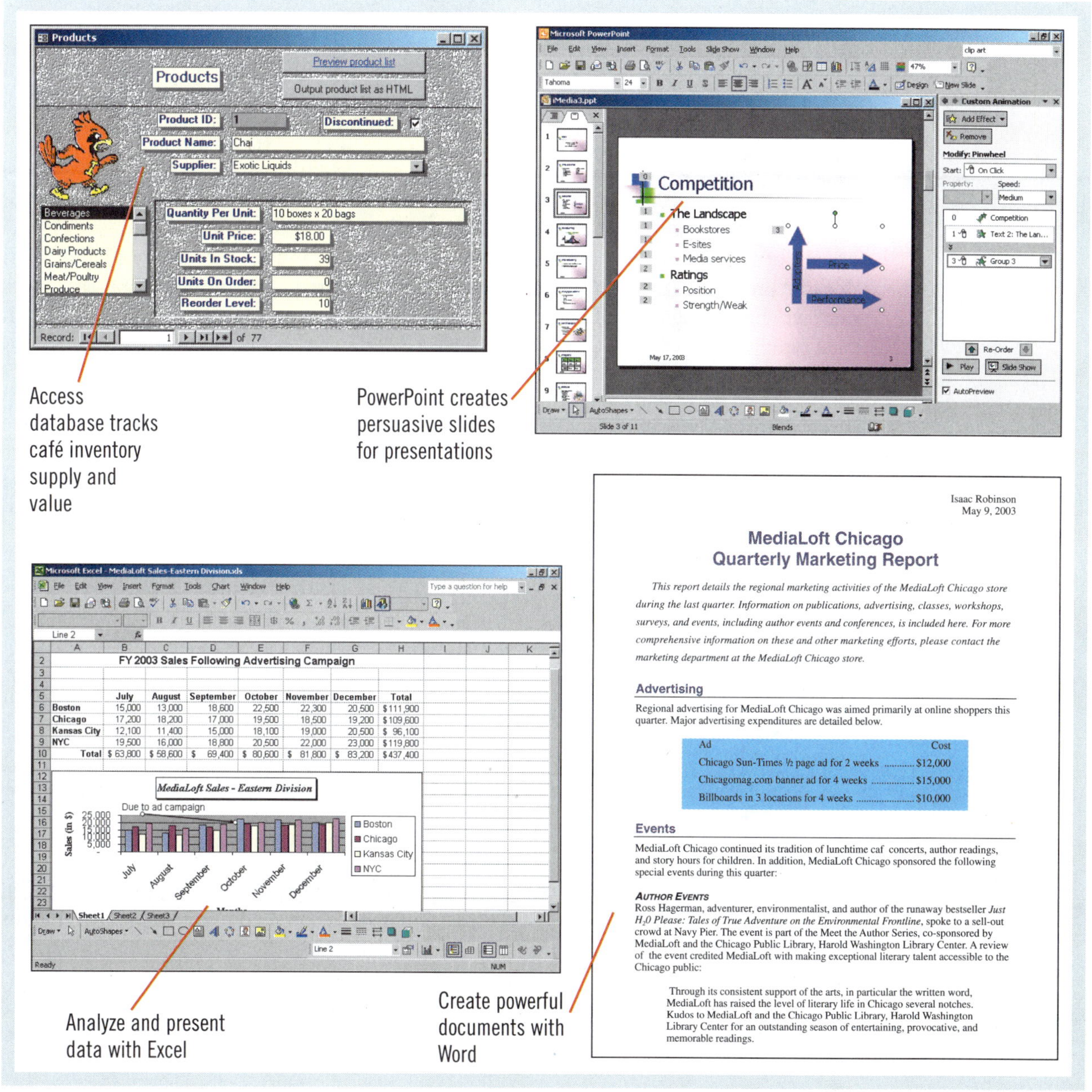

Access database tracks café inventory supply and value

PowerPoint creates persuasive slides for presentations

Analyze and present data with Excel

Create powerful documents with Word

INTRODUCING MICROSOFT OFFICE XP

Creating a Document with Word 2002

Microsoft Word 2002 is a **word processing** program that allows you to create and edit text documents. You can also format text with characteristics such as bold and italics to make text information easier to understand and to make important information stand out. You can use a word processor to create reports, memos, or letters that contain text, tables, and graphics. Sophisticated text-handling tools, such as an electronic thesaurus, indexes, and footnotes make Word ideal for long and complex text documents such as books. MediaLoft employees use Word to create documents for the company's Annual Report. The memo requesting information for the report is shown in Figure A-3. The memo contains the kinds of elements that make a document readable and professional looking.

The following are some of the benefits of using Word:

▶ **Enter text quickly and easily**
Word makes it easy to enter and edit text. Rather than having to retype a document, you can rearrange and revise the text on-screen. Bullets or numbers can make lists more attractive and easier to understand. When you move items in a numbered list, Word automatically corrects the numbers to reflect the new order.

▶ **Organize information in a table to make it easier to read**
Some information is easier to read in rows and columns, and it's easy to create and modify a table in Word. Once you create a table, you can edit its contents and modify its appearance using your own formatting or predesigned formats. You can always sort table data without any additional typing.

▶ **Create error-free copy**
You can use the Word spelling checker after you finish typing to help you create error-free documents. It compares each word in a document to a built-in dictionary and notifies you if it does not recognize a word. The Word AutoCorrect feature can automatically correct misspelled words as you type them. Word provides entries for commonly misspelled words, and you can also add your own.

▶ **Combine text and graphics**
Using Word, you can combine text and graphics easily in the same document.

▶ **Communicate with others**
You can use special Word features to communicate with teammates. For example, you can insert **comments** within a document that coworkers can see. You can use the **tracking** feature to keep a record of edits and view edits others make in a document. Figure A-3 shows a Word document containing tracked changes, text, and graphics as they look on the screen; Figure A-4 shows the printed memo.

▶ **Add special effects**
Word lets you create columns of text, drop caps (capital letters that take up two or three lines), and WordArt (customized text with a three-dimensional or shadowed appearance), adding a polished quality to your documents.

FIGURE A-3: Memo created in Word

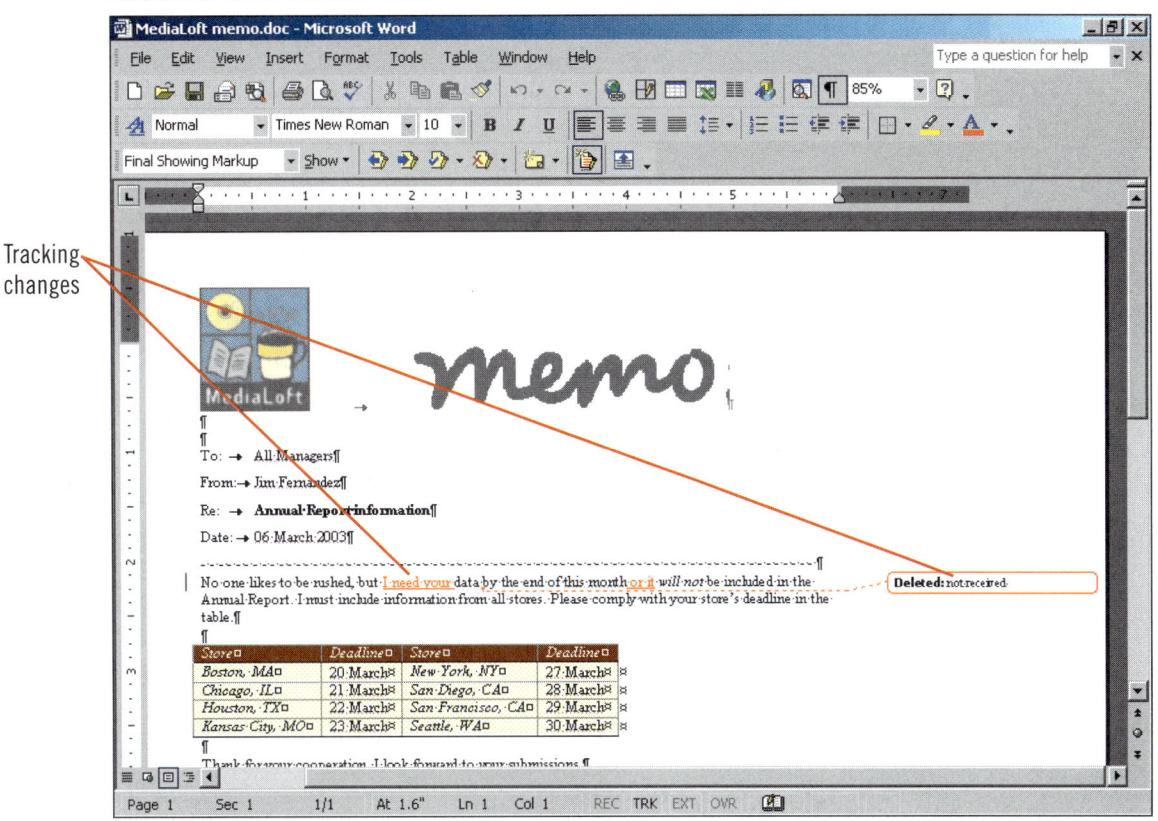

FIGURE A-4: Printout of completed memo

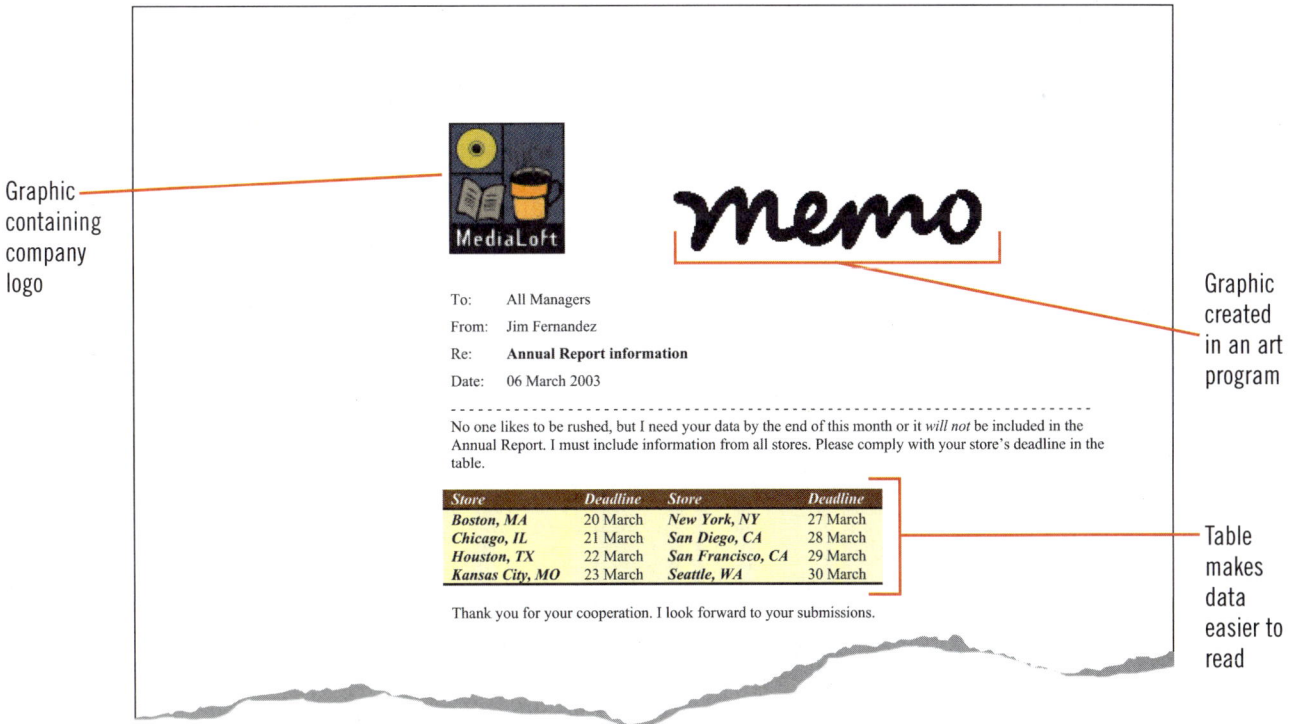

INTRODUCING MICROSOFT OFFICE XP

Building a Worksheet with Excel 2002

Microsoft Excel 2002 is a **spreadsheet** program you can use to analyze data, perform calculations, and create charts. Excel performs numeric calculations rapidly and accurately. Like traditional paper-based spreadsheets, this electronic spreadsheet contains a **worksheet** area that is divided into columns and rows that form individual cells. **Cells** can contain text, numbers, formulas, or a combination of all three. MediaLoft employees use Excel to store and analyze sales data as well as other numeric information they have collected. They can then format the data for insertion into the Annual Report.

The following are some of the benefits of using Excel:

▶ **Calculate results quickly and accurately**
With Excel, you can enter data quickly and accurately using formulas. Excel then calculates the results.

▶ **Recalculate easily**
Excel recalculates data easily by updating information automatically when you change or correct an entry.

▶ **Perform what-if analysis**
Because Excel automatically recalculates formulas when data changes, you can ask "what-if?" and create a variety of business scenarios, such as, "What if the interest rate on a corporate credit card changes?" Anticipating possible outcomes helps you make better business decisions.

▶ **Complete complex mathematical formulas**
Using Excel, you can easily complete complicated mathematical computations by using built-in formulas. The program tells you what data to enter, then you fill in the blanks, saving you valuable time.

▶ **Communicate with others**
In today's offices it is common for a group of people to review the same document. Readers can use the Comments feature to attach explanatory comments to worksheet cells. You can also keep track of changes others make to your worksheets by using powerful change-tracking tools.

▶ **Create charts**
Excel makes it easy to create charts based on worksheet information. With Excel, charts are automatically updated as worksheet data changes. The worksheet in Figure A-5 shows a bar chart that illustrates sales revenue for the eight MediaLoft stores over a three-year period.

▶ **Analyze worksheet data**
Worksheets containing data in a long list are easy to summarize and analyze quickly using the PivotTable feature. Once you create a PivotTable, you can chart its output. Without the PivotTable feature, it would be very difficult to analyze lengthy Excel data.

▶ **Create attractive output**
You can enhance the overall appearance of numeric data by using charts, graphics, and text formatting, as shown in Figure A-5. Figure A-6 shows the printed worksheet.

FIGURE A-5: Worksheet created in Excel

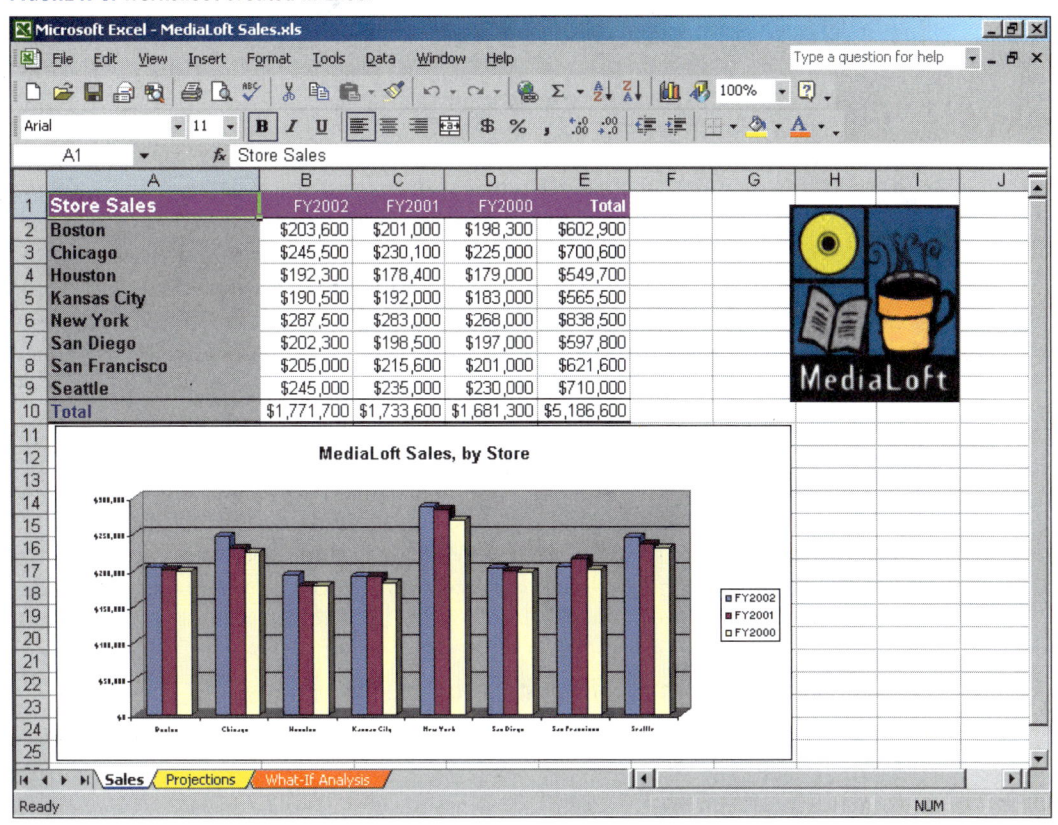

FIGURE A-6: Printout of annual revenue data with corresponding chart

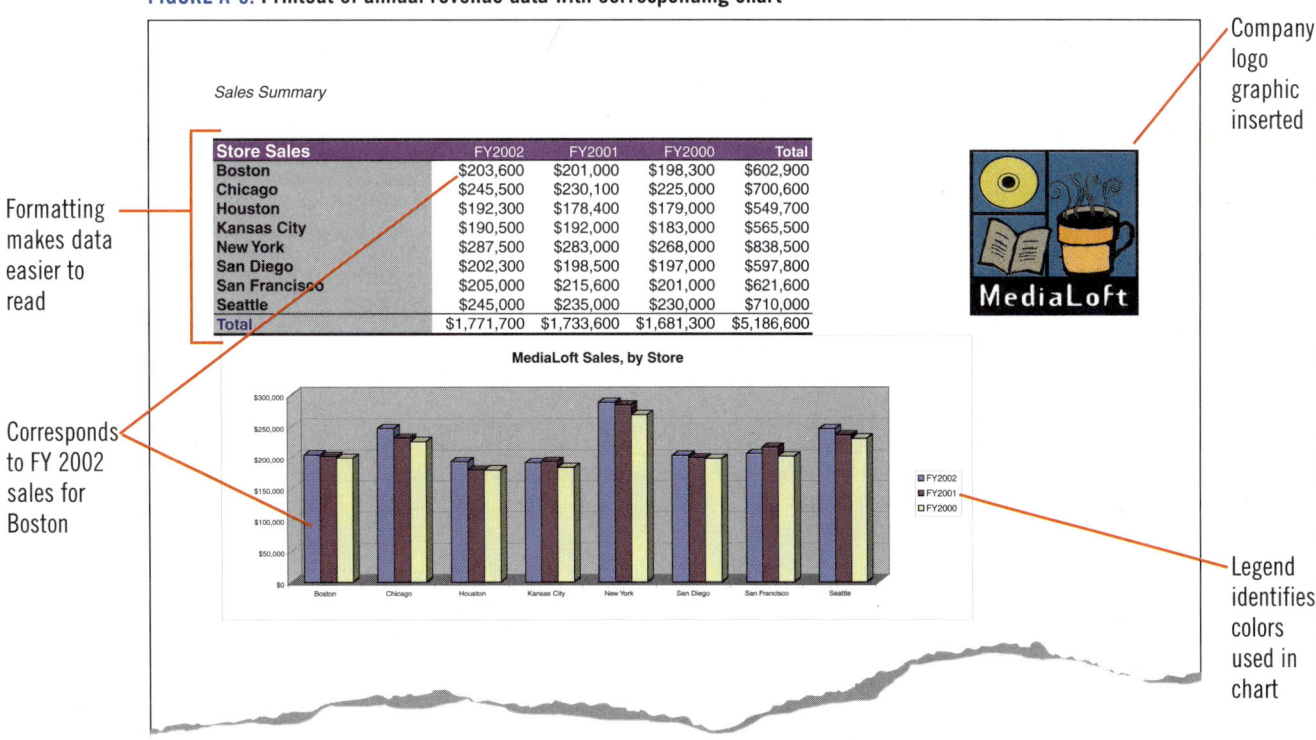

Formatting makes data easier to read

Corresponds to FY 2002 sales for Boston

Company logo graphic inserted

Legend identifies colors used in chart

INTRODUCING MICROSOFT OFFICE XP   OFFICE A-7

Managing Data with Access 2002

Microsoft Access 2002 is a database management system. A **database** is a collection of related information such as a list of employees, their Social Security numbers, salaries, and vacation time. A **database management system** organizes databases and allows you to link multiple groups of information. With Access, you can arrange and analyze large amounts of data in grids called **tables**, such as an inventory of products, or the members of a sales department. The tables in a database are related to one another by a common piece of information, such as a product number, which makes the database a powerful information retrieval tool. You can rearrange and combine the information in the tables in a variety of ways. For example, an inventory database might be listed alphabetically, by stocking location, or by the number of units on order. You might use a salesperson's name from a Sales Rep table and a product description from a Products table to create a sales report. A powerful database program like Access lets you use your data in a wide variety of ways. MediaLoft stores use Access databases to keep track of inventory. Information from these databases is used to generate inventory lists and data for the Annual Report.

The following are some of the benefits of using Access:

▶ **Enter data easily**
Employees can enter data in an existing table as the database grows or changes. Because Access organizes the data for you, the order in which you enter items is not a concern.

▶ **Retrieve data easily**
Access makes it easy for you to specify **criteria**, or conditions, and then produce a list of all data that conforms to those criteria. You might want to see a list of products by supplier or a list of discontinued products. Figure A-7 shows an inventory table containing music sold at MediaLoft's stores.

▶ **Create professional forms**
You can enter data into an on-screen form that you create in Access. Using a form makes entering data more efficient, and you'll be less prone to making errors. Figure A-8 shows a screen form that the MediaLoft music department uses for data entry.

▶ **Create flexible, professional reports**
You can create a report that summarizes any or all of the information in an Access table. You can create your own layout, and add summaries of data within the report. For example, a MediaLoft inventory report could include all the information in the Music Inventory table, then be subtotaled by music category.

▶ **Add graphics to printed screen forms and reports**
Forms and reports can contain graphic images, text formatting, and special effects, such as WordArt, to make them look more professional.

FIGURE A-7: List of inventory items in Access

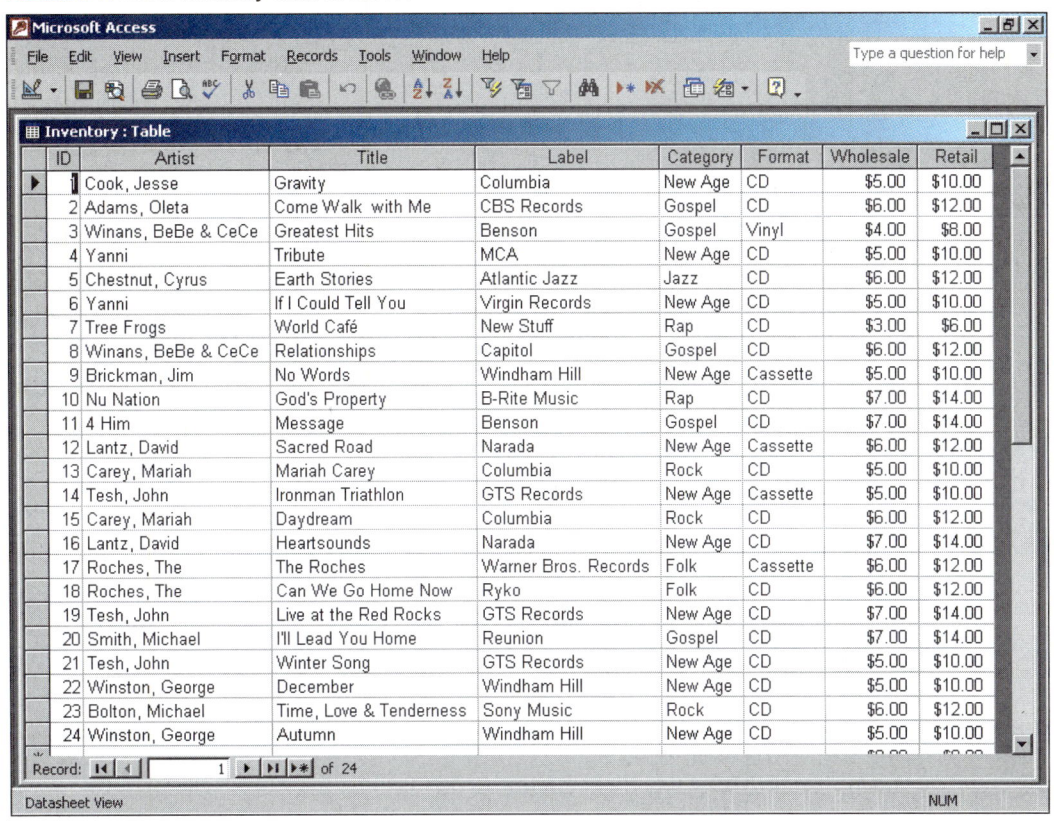

FIGURE A-8: On-screen Access data entry form

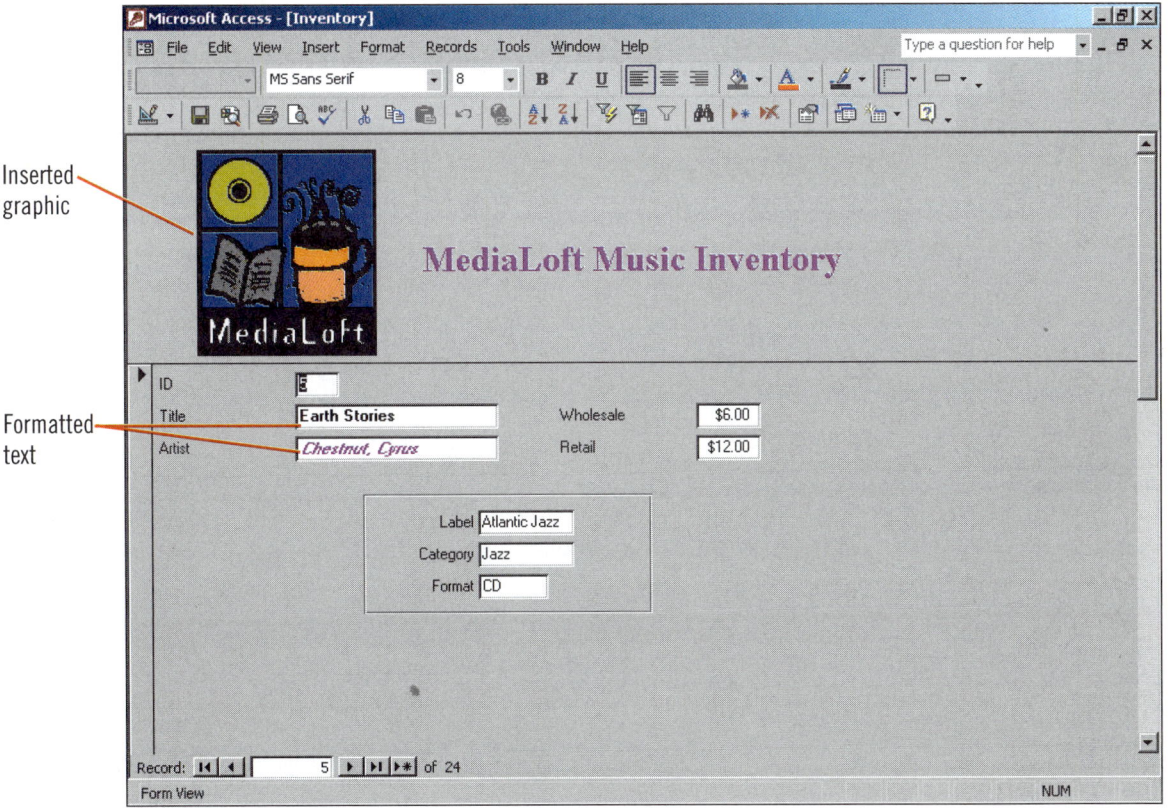

INTRODUCING MICROSOFT OFFICE XP

Creating a Presentation with PowerPoint 2002

Microsoft PowerPoint 2002 is a **presentation graphics** program you can use to develop slides and handouts for visual presentations. In PowerPoint, a **slide** is a "page" in an on-screen display called a **slide show**, in which consecutive images appear on a computer screen. The computer can be connected to a projector so a roomful of people can see the presentation. You can then use your on-screen slide content to create handouts, outlines, notes and 35-mm slides. Store managers present highlights of the Annual Report to MediaLoft executives using a slide show and notes created in PowerPoint.

The following are some of the benefits of using PowerPoint:

► **Create and edit slides easily**

You can enter text directly on a PowerPoint slide, enabling you to see how your slide will look. After you have learned how to edit text in Word, you can use the same techniques in PowerPoint. You can cut, copy, paste, and move slide text quickly and easily.

► **Combine information from Office programs**

You can use data you create in Word, Excel, Access, and other Office programs in your PowerPoint slides. This means that you can easily insert a worksheet you created in Excel, for example, without having to retype the information.

► **Add graphics**

Predesigned images called **clip art**, an Excel chart, or a corporate logo can further enhance any presentation. PowerPoint comes with many clip art images and accepts the most commonly available graphic file formats. PowerPoint also allows you to create your own shapes and enhance text with special effects using WordArt. Figure A-9 shows a slide containing a chart created in Excel and a graphic image of a corporate logo.

► **Print a variety of presentation materials**

In addition to being able to print out a slide, you can also create many other types of printed materials. Notes printed with each slide can contain hints and reminders for the speaker or for the audience members, who might receive printed copies of the presentation slides. Figure A-10 shows notes in PowerPoint. You can also print other types of handouts for presentation attendees that contain a reduced image of each slide and a place for handwritten notes.

► **Communicate with others**

In many businesses, employees share information and often contribute to others' work. You can use the Comments feature to insert explanatory comments on a slide. This makes communication more efficient, because co-workers can point out areas that are unclear or particularly effective.

► **Add special effects**

You can create slides that use special transitions from one slide to the next. Animation effects allow you to determine how and when slide elements appear on the screen and which sound effects accompany them. You can add audio and video clips to make your presentation look professional.

FIGURE A-9: Slide created in PowerPoint

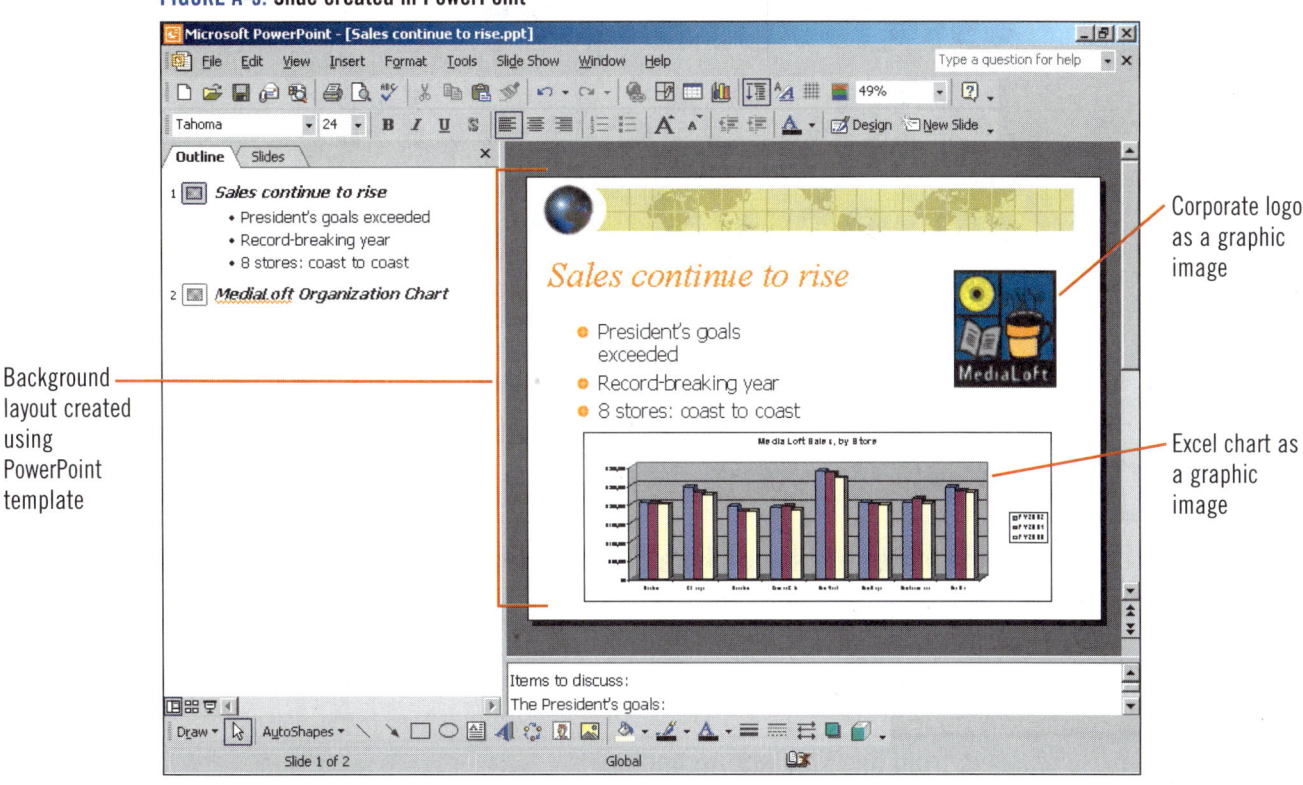

FIGURE A-10: Notes created in PowerPoint

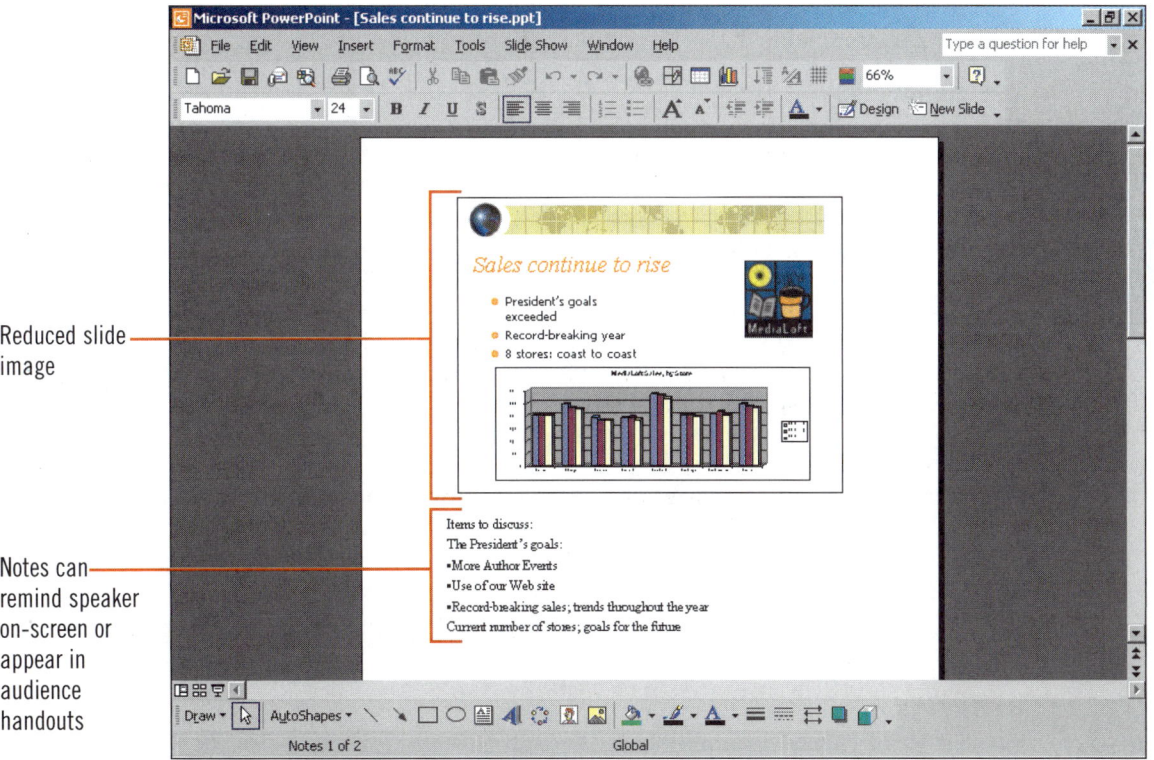

Browsing the World Wide Web with Internet Explorer

The **World Wide Web**—also known as the **Web**—is the part of the Internet that brings text, graphics, and multimedia information to your desktop. Internet Explorer is a **browser**, a program designed to help you view the graphic images and multimedia data on the Web. Many Web sites let you move to other sites with the click of your mouse using **links**, special areas that take you to different Web site addresses. MediaLoft employees keep informed on the latest trends and research competitors by using Internet Explorer.

The following are some of the benefits of using Internet Explorer:

▶ **Display Web sites**
Once you're connected to the Internet, you can view interesting and informative Web sites from all around the globe.

▶ **Move from one Web site to another**
Web page links let you effortlessly move from site to site. You can easily find information related to the topic in which you're interested.

▶ **Save your favorite Web site locations**
Once you've located interesting Web sites, such as the one shown in Figure A-11, you can save their Web site addresses so you can return to them later without performing another search. Internet Explorer makes it easy to compile a list of your favorite locations.

▶ **Use multimedia**
Web pages frequently contain video and audio clips. Internet Explorer allows you to experience the multimedia capabilities of the Web.

▶ **Communicate with others**
You can use your browser to participate in online discussions with other users.

▶ **Incorporate Web information**
Internet Explorer makes it easy to combine the immediacy of the Web with the power of Office suite programs: import data—whether it is text, graphics, or numbers—from the Web and edit it in the Office program you select, such as Word or Excel.

▶ **Print Web pages**
As you travel the Web, you may want to print the information you find. You can easily print an active Web page—including its text and graphics.

FIGURE A-11: Browsing with Internet Explorer

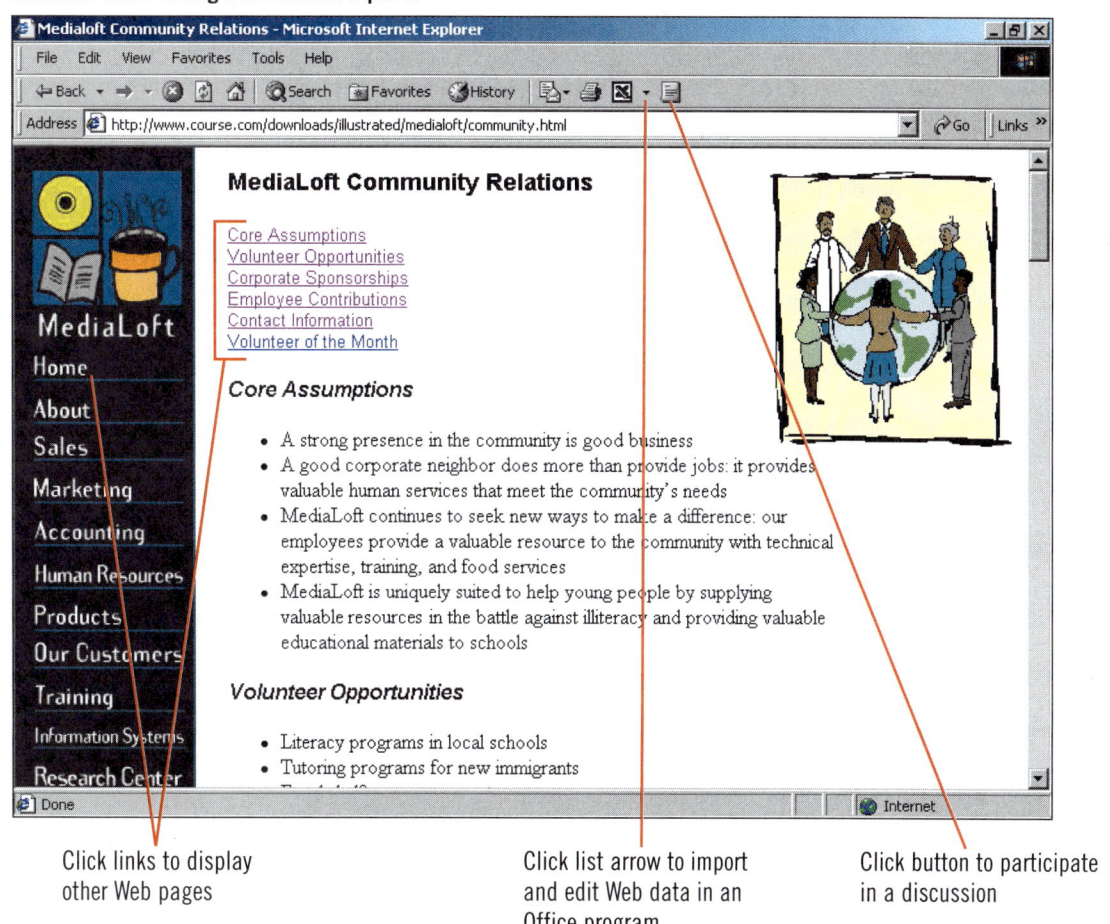

Click links to display other Web pages

Click list arrow to import and edit Web data in an Office program

Click button to participate in a discussion

Integrating Office Information

Information created in one Office program can be used in another. This means that a chart created in Excel can be used in Word without having to be retyped or reentered. Information in an Access table can be exported to Excel and analyzed, or pasted into a Word document. An outline created in Word can be imported into PowerPoint, saving you time and allowing you to work more efficiently. Using Office, integrating information is easy and can be accomplished in many ways. ✐ MediaLoft employees use integration as a means of working efficiently.

The following are some of the benefits of using integration:

► **Create information once**
It is not necessary to retype information each time you want to use it in another document or program. For example, an Excel chart can be pasted into a Word document and a PowerPoint slide, as shown in Figure A-12. Because you can copy information into the Office Clipboard, it is easy to paste it into any other Office program. Data can also be linked, so that when the original document is changed, the pasted data is changed too.

► **Merge data**
In addition to simple copy-and-paste techniques, Office programs offer more sophisticated processes, such as merging Access data with Word. This feature makes it possible to combine information in a database with text in a letter. The result is that you can easily create form letters with the click of a few buttons.

► **Export data**
Data in an Access table can be exported to Excel. Once in Excel, the data can be further analyzed and charted. Or, a PowerPoint presentation can be exported to Word, where you can save and edit the document to create special handouts to accompany the presentation. See Figure A-13.

► **Create hyperlinks**
With so many interrelated documents being used in business, it's helpful to know that Office lets you link on-screen documents. You can click on specially formatted text or graphics called **hyperlinks** and automatically be transferred to another area of your current document, or to another document entirely.

FIGURE A-12: Excel chart used in Word document and PowerPoint slide

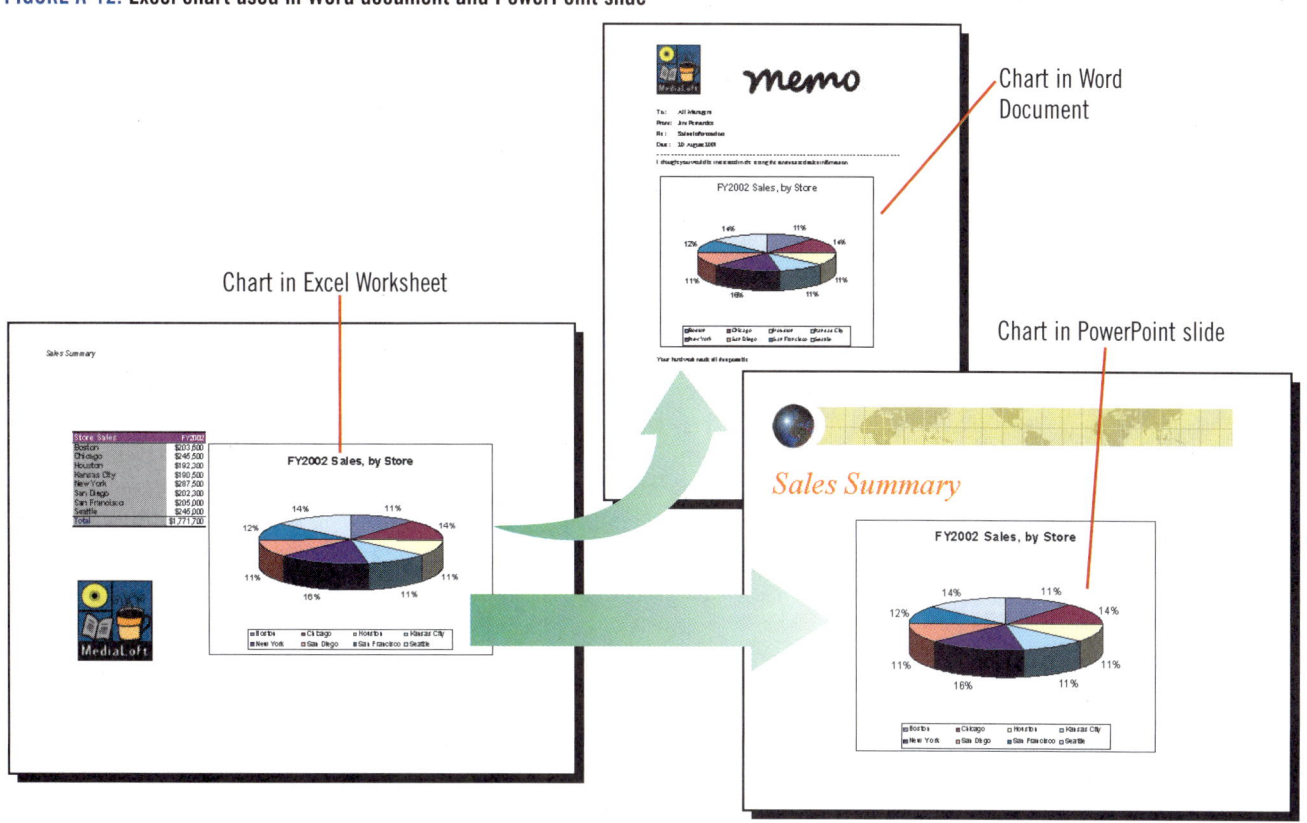

FIGURE A-13: PowerPoint presentation in a Word document

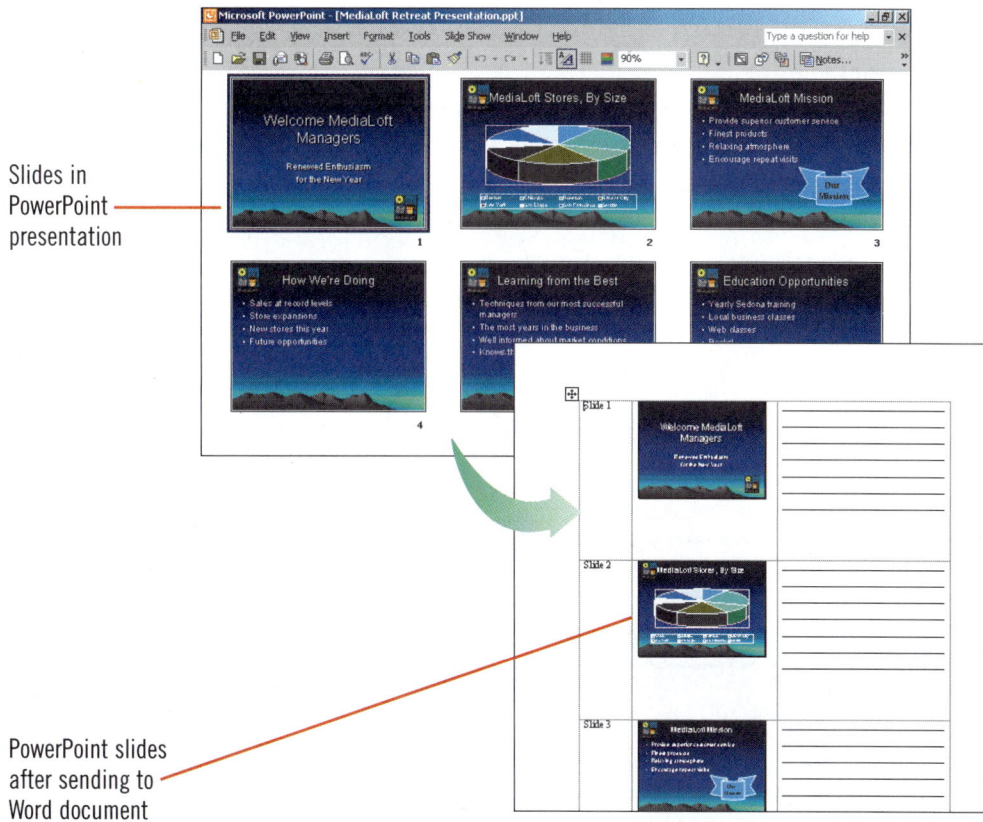

Managing Office Tasks with Outlook 2002

There's more to office work than creating documents, worksheets, databases, and presentations. Microsoft Outlook 2002 is an electronic **personal information manager** that helps you manage a typical business day. You can use it to schedule appointments, keep track of contacts, and send e-mail and files to people on your local network or intranet, as well as across the Internet to anyone with an Internet address. For example, using the Inbox, you can send electronic mail messages—or **e-mail**—to anyone with an e-mail address. Table A-1 describes tasks you can perform with Outlook. MediaLoft employees work more efficiently by using Outlook to send messages between stores, schedule appointments, and keep track of deadlines.

The following are some of the benefits of using Outlook:

► **Process mail**
Use the Inbox to read, forward, reply to, and create e-mail. The Inbox displays unread messages in bold text, so you can tell which messages still need to be read.

► **Create an address book**
Keep track of e-mail addresses in an address book so that you don't have to type an e-mail address each time you create a new message. You can also create distribution lists so that you can easily send messages to a group of people with whom you communicate frequently, without having to enter each e-mail address over and over.

► **Send attachments**
In addition to the actual content of a message, you can attach individual files to an e-mail message. This means you can send a colleague a spreadsheet created in Excel, for example, along with an explanatory message.

TABLE A-1: Additional Outlook tasks

task	description
Manage appointments	Use Calendar to make appointments, plan meetings, and keep track of events
Manage tasks	Use Tasks to keep track of pending jobs, set priorities, assign due dates, and express completion expectations for tasks
Track contacts	Use Contacts to record information such as names, addresses, phone numbers, and e-mail addresses for business and personal associates
Maintain a journal of your activities	Use Journal to track project phases, record activities, and manage your time
Create reminders	Use Notes—an electronic equivalent of yellow sticky notes—to leave reminders for yourself

Integration

Integrating
Word and Excel

Objectives

- ▶ Understand Integration
- ▶ Open multiple programs
- ▶ Copy Word data into Excel

Now that you have experienced the power of Word and Excel, it is time to learn how to integrate these two programs. When you integrate programs, you combine information from the output of the programs without retyping anything. Alice Wegman is a marketing manager for MediaLoft, a nationwide chain of bookstore cafés that sells books, CDs, and videos. Five of the MediaLoft stores noticed that they had an increase in sales soon after they started promoting MediaLoft's participation in a national literacy program. Alice collected the spring quarter sales data for the five stores and compiled this information in a Word document. She decides she wants to communicate this data graphically using Excel charts, so she needs to copy the data to an Excel workbook.

Understanding Integration

Programs in Microsoft Office are designed to work together. The ability to use information across multiple programs, or **integration**, makes it possible to share data among documents and between coworkers. The file from which the information is copied is the **source file**. The file that receives the copied information is the **destination file**. For example, charts created in an Excel worksheet, the source file, can be copied to and edited in a Word document or a PowerPoint presentation, the destination file. Alice decides to review some of the ways that data can be integrated among the Office suite programs and with other programs.

You can use Microsoft Office integration features to:

▶ **Copy and paste data**

You can copy information—whether it's text, values, or objects—created in one program into another program using the Copy and Paste commands. You can copy and paste one item at a time using the Windows clipboard, or, if the Office Clipboard task pane is open, you can copy and store up to 24 items. See Figure A-1.

▶ **Drag and drop data**

You can also copy selected text, values, or objects into other programs by using the drag-and-drop method. Once the files are opened and the program windows are arranged so that both the source and destination files are visible, you can press and hold [Ctrl] and drag a selection from the source file into the destination file.

▶ **Link and embed objects**

If you include data that is subject to change in multiple files, you should link the object you want to copy. A **linked** object maintains a connection to the source file so that the linked objects in both the destination file and the source file are updated when the data is changed in the source file. An **embedded** object maintains a link to the source program, but not to the source file. You can double-click an embedded object to open the source program and edit the object. The source file remains unchanged, however.

▶ **Import and export text and graphics**

You can also use files created in programs that are not part of the Office suite by using **filters**, programs built into the Office suite that convert files created in another format.

▶ **Create hyperlinks**

You can include hyperlinks in your files to other places in your files, other files, or a location on the Internet. Figure A-2 shows the Insert Hyperlink dialog box, which is used to create a hyperlink. When you click a hyperlink, the file or Web page that the hyperlink is connected to opens.

▶ **Work efficiently using Office eServices**

Microsoft maintains a Web site that offers a variety of tools—many of them free—that makes it easy to get the most out of Office, including sharing information. This site, shown in Figure A-3, changes often and offers many exciting features.

▶ **E-mail files**

You can share Office files by sending them as attachments to an e-mail message. By clicking the E-mail (as Attachment) button on the Standard toolbar. This opens your e-mail client and attaches the file to the e-mail message. By sending a file and using Office tools such as Tracking and Comments, you can easily incorporate input from your coworkers into your documents.

▶ **Collaborate online**

E-mail is one form of online collaboration. You can also use Office program features to share and review documents accessed by multiple users, and you can hold online discussions.

FIGURE A-1: Entries in Office Clipboard

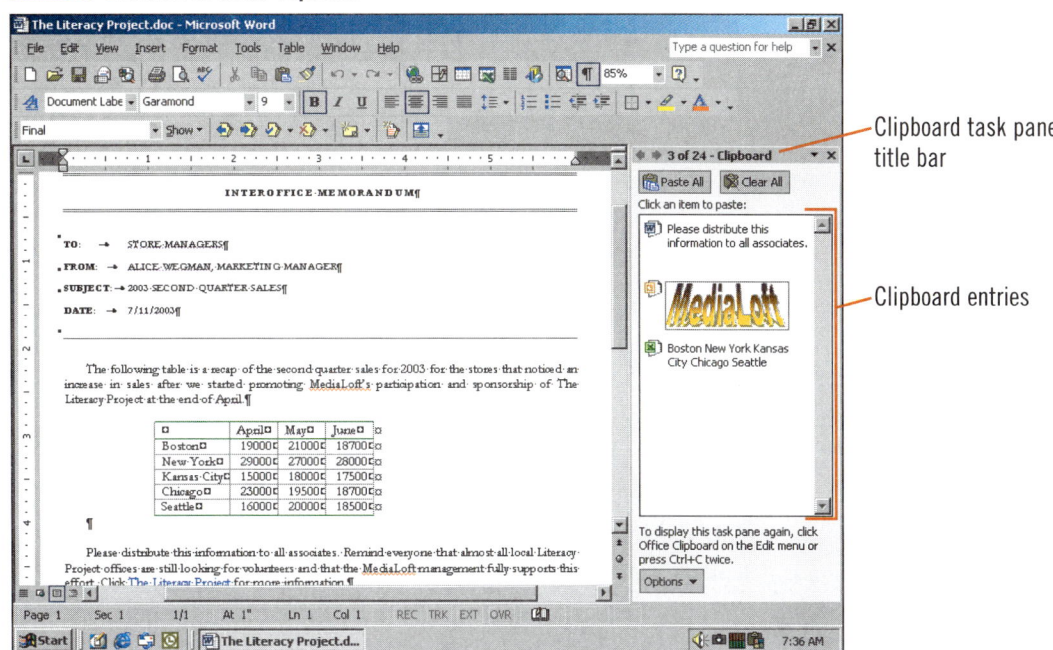

FIGURE A-2: Insert Hyperlink dialog box

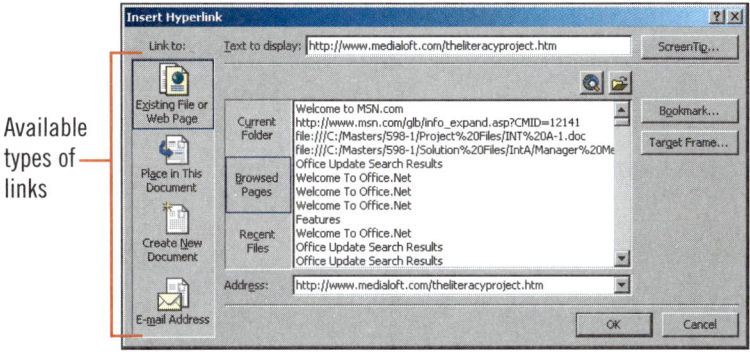

FIGURE A-3: Microsoft eServices on the Web

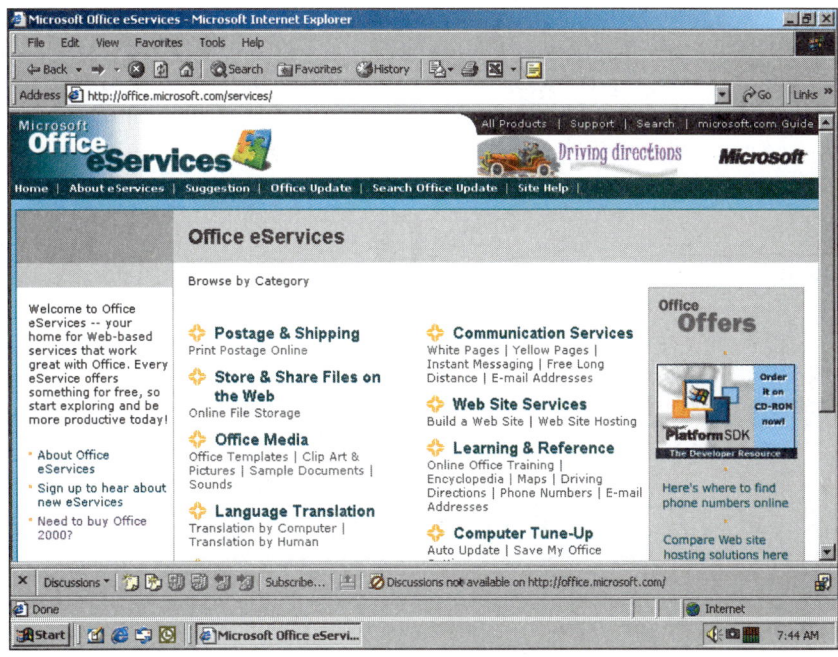

Opening Multiple Programs

When you are integrating information from one program into another, it is often necessary to have more than one file in more than one program open at the same time. The Windows environment gives you the ability to have more than one program open at a time, and to view them on the same screen simultaneously. This ability is sometimes called **multitasking**. Before integrating the data, Alice starts both Word and Excel. To make integrating the data easier, she aligns each program window side by side on the screen.

Steps

1. Click the **Start button** on the taskbar, point to **Programs**, then click **Microsoft Word** in the Program list
   A blank Word document opens.

   > **QuickTip**
   > It is not necessary to minimize a program window before you start another program.

2. Click the **Minimize button** in the program window
   The Word program window shrinks into a program button on the taskbar. Sometimes the taskbar is hidden.

3. If necessary, move the mouse pointer to the bottom of the screen
   The taskbar appears.

4. Click **Start** on the taskbar, point to **Programs**, then click **Microsoft Excel**
   A blank Excel workbook opens. The taskbar displays program buttons for Word and Excel, and the button for Excel is a lighter gray, as shown in Figure A-4. The light gray color of the Excel program button indicates that Excel is the active window.

5. Click the **Word program button** on the taskbar
   The Word window is maximized and Word becomes the active program. The Excel window is still open, but it is not active. You want to see both windows at the same time.

6. Right-click a blank area on the taskbar
   The taskbar shortcut menu appears.

7. Click **Tile Windows Vertically** on the shortcut menu
   The two program windows each occupy half the screen. Compare your screen to Figure A-5. The title bars of both windows are gray, and both program buttons on the taskbar are dark gray, indicating that neither program window is active.

FIGURE A-4: Excel workbook active and Word document inactive

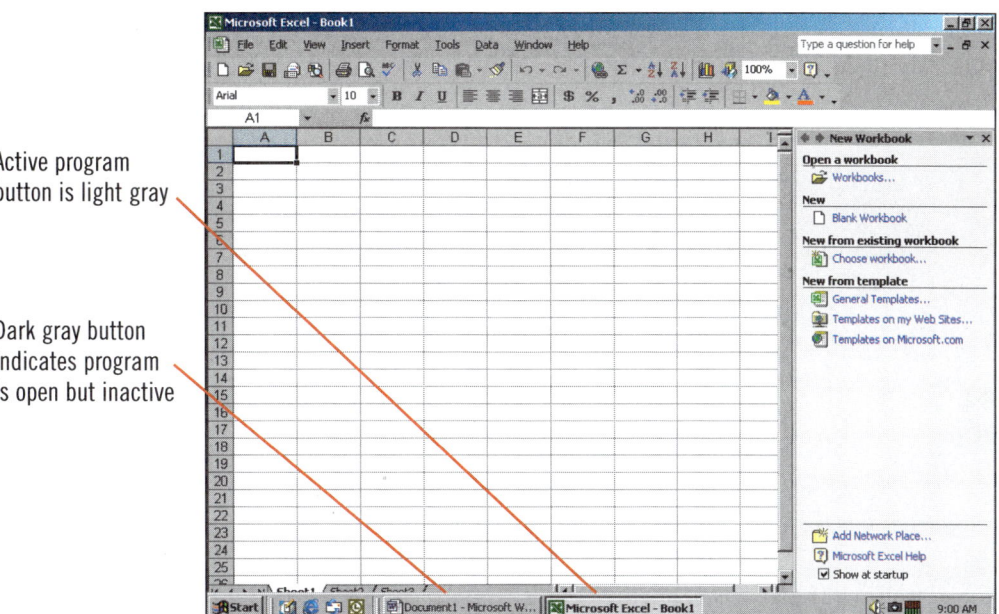

Active program button is light gray

Dark gray button indicates program is open but inactive

FIGURE A-5: Word and Excel windows open

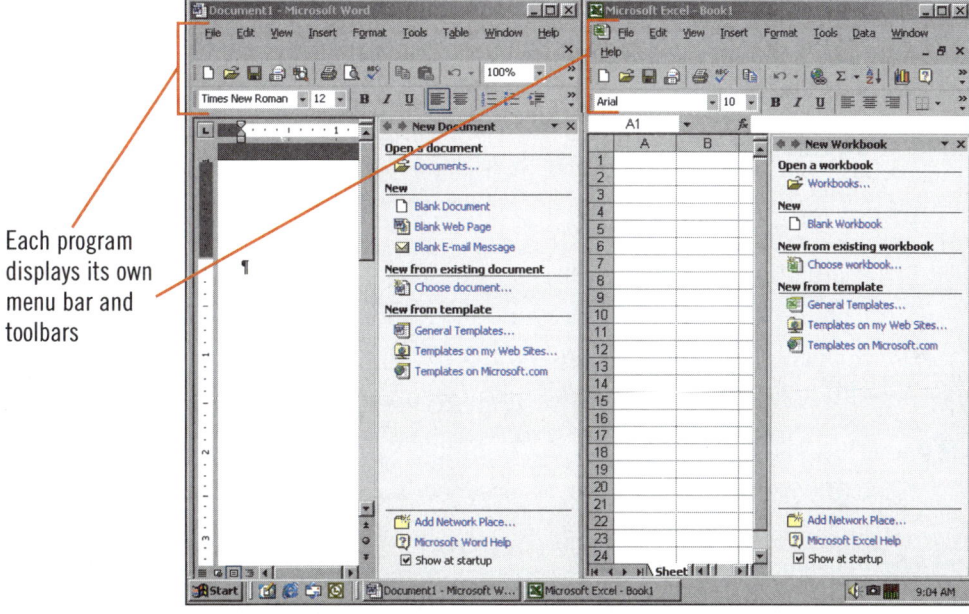

Each program displays its own menu bar and toolbars

Using shortcut keys to switch between open programs

You can switch between open programs by clicking the program buttons on the taskbar or by using the shortcut key combination [Alt][Tab]. Pressing [Alt][Tab] causes the icons and names of open programs (whether or not they are minimized) to appear in the center of the screen, as shown in Figure A-6. To see this on the screen, press and hold [Alt], then press and release [Tab]. If more than one program is open, press and release [Tab] again while still holding down [Alt] to move the selection box to the next icon in the center of the screen. When the program you want to activate is selected, release [Alt].

FIGURE A-6: Using [Alt][Tab] to switch among open programs

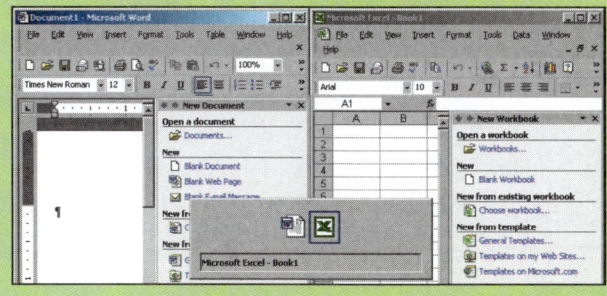

INTEGRATING WORD AND EXCEL

Copying Word Data into Excel

Moving or copying information from one program to another is just like moving or copying information within a single program. You can use the Cut, Copy, and Paste commands; buttons on the toolbars; or the drag-and-drop method to move or copy information. Alice typed a memo to the five store managers that includes a Word table containing the spring quarter sales data for all five stores. Alice wants to copy the data from the Word table into an Excel workbook. Later, Alice will be able to create the charts she needs once the data is copied into Excel.

Steps

1. **Click anywhere in the Word program window to make it active**
   Clicking in a window makes the window active.

2. **Open the file INT A-1 from the drive and location where your Project Files are stored, then save it as Manager Memo**
   Once the document is open, it can be saved to the location where your Project Files are stored. Manager Memo appears in the Word program window in Print Layout view.

3. **Replace Alice Wegman's name in the From line with your name**

4. **Scroll down until you can see the table and the body of the memo, then click the right scroll arrow on the horizontal scroll bar so you can see the entire table, as shown in Figure A-7**
   The Word document is the source file, and the blank Excel workbook is the destination file.

5. **Position the pointer in the selection bar next to the top row of the table until the pointer changes to ⇗, press and hold the mouse button to select the top row of the table, drag the pointer down until all of the rows are selected, then release the mouse button**

   > **QuickTip**
   > You also can select the Word table, click the Copy button on the Word Standard toolbar, click the top, left destination cell in Excel, then click the Paste button on the Excel Standard toolbar.

6. **Press and hold [Ctrl], click in the table so the pointer looks like ⇖, drag the pointer to the Excel worksheet, position the outline of the table in the range A1:D6 as shown in Figure A-8, then release the mouse button and [Ctrl]**
   The information in the Word table is copied into the Excel worksheet, as shown in Figure A-9. Using drag and drop is the easiest way to copy information from a source file to a target file. You can now work with the data in the Excel workbook.

7. **Click the Save button on the Excel Standard toolbar, then save the workbook as Manager Sales in the location where your Project Files are stored**

8. **Close the Manager Sales workbook and exit Excel**

9. **Close the Manager Memo document and exit Word without saving changes**

FIGURE A-7: Manager Memo open

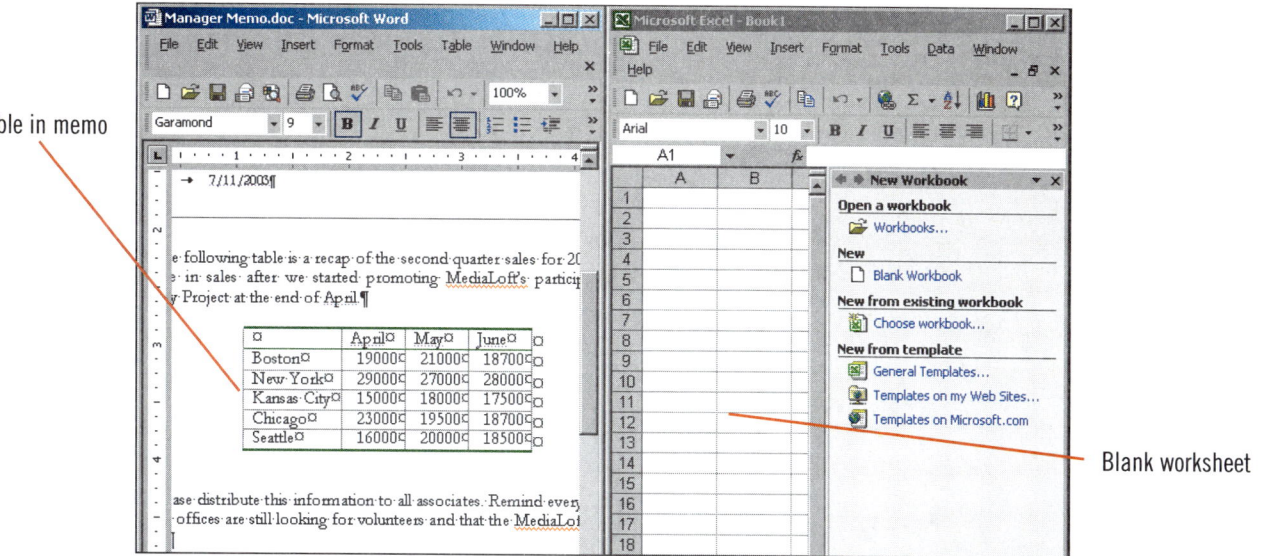

FIGURE A-8: Word text dragged and dropped into an Excel worksheet

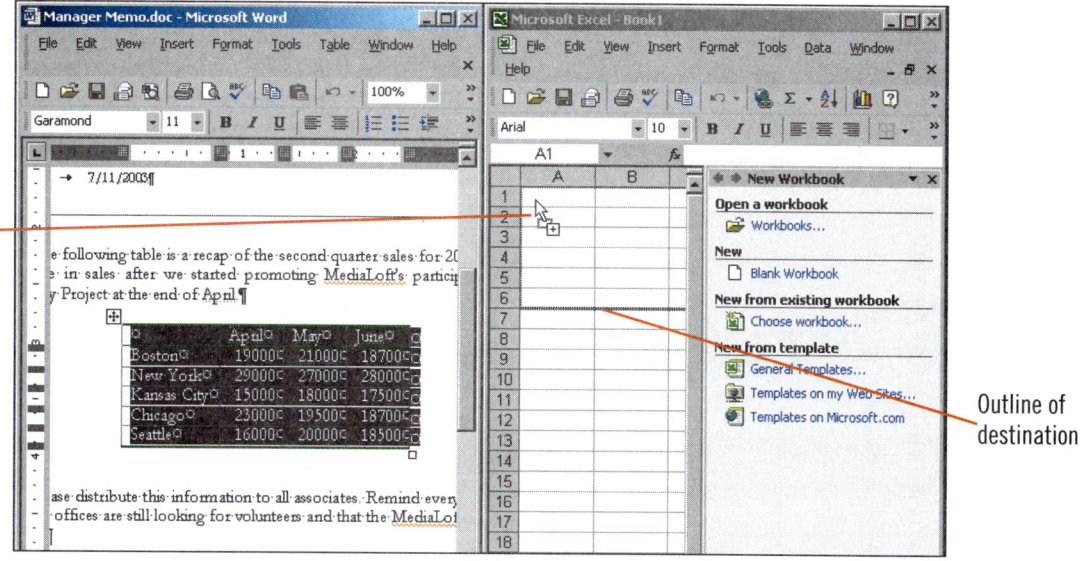

FIGURE A-9: Word table data copied into an Excel workbook

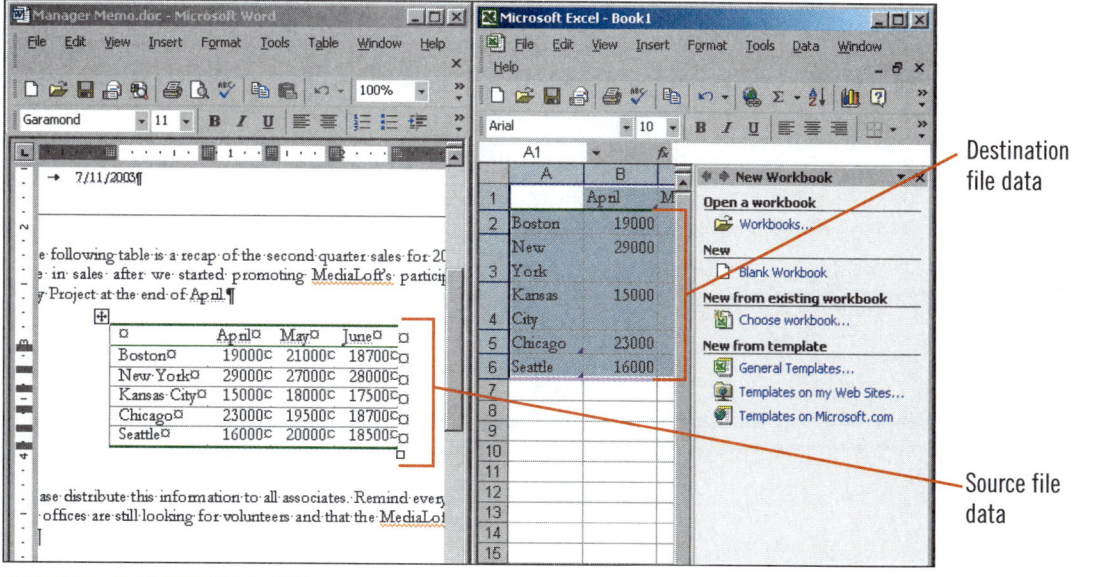

INTEGRATING WORD AND EXCEL

Integration | **Practice**

▶ Independent Challenge 1

The Hispanic Chamber of Commerce realizes that to improve their advertising coverage, they need to hire an outside consultant. A list of promising consultants is being assembled by other Chamber members. Your job is to create a memo that gives them an overview of the Chamber's advertising efforts.

   a. Start Excel, open the Excel file INT A-2 from the location where your Project Files are stored, then save it as **Chamber Statistics**. Start Word, open the Word file INT A-3 from the location where your Project Files are stored, then save it as **Chamber Consultants**.
   b. Examine the Chamber Consultants document and determine what additions you need to make to best inform the prospective consultant.
   c. Examine the chart in the Chamber Statistics workbook. Do you think you can use this chart within the memo, or do you need to create another type of chart to better convey the information? Can you add any enhancements to the chart to make it clearer?
   d. The memo to the board should contain three charts. Create the additional charts you need in Excel; for example, you can create a column chart that shows how much money is spent on each type of advertising, or a bar chart showing the different types of advertisements and the money spent on each one. Add any enhancements, such as text annotations and arrows, that will call attention to the charts in the memo.
   e. Create the document text to accompany each chart, then copy the charts into the document.
   f. Update the date in the Chamber Consultants document to reflect the current date and replace the text after FROM with your name, then preview the document and print a copy.
   g. Save and close the document and the workbook, and exit both programs.

 Independent Challenge 2

MediaLoft is considering expanding its stores in the United Kingdom. Before Alice Wegman hires a marketing firm to target this area, she wants to learn about this country's demographics. She has asked you to use the Web to find census data for the United Kingdom, and then prepare a synopsis of the information.

   a. Connect to the Internet and use a search engine to locate Web sites that have information on the United Kingdom census data. If your search does not produce any results, you might try the following sites:
      www.cia.gov/cia/publications/factbook/index.html
      www.felixent.force9.co.uk/europe/uk/07.html
   b. Locate and print data that details age distribution by gender—that is, the percentage of men and women in different age brackets—then disconnect from the Internet.
   c. Start Excel, then create a workbook named **Population Projections**.
   d. Enter data for the information on age distribution by gender, adjusting column widths as necessary.
   e. Format the statistical data using the comma format showing no decimals.
   f. Create a 3-D column chart that graphically describes this data.
   g. Start Word, then create a document named **Population Analysis**.
   h. Create original text that explains the data and the chart you created in Excel.
   i. Copy and paste the Excel data and chart into the Word document.
   j. Include any links that you used to get your data.
   k. Copy and paste the Excel chart into the Word document.
   l. Add your name as the last line in the document, then save and print your work.
   m. Close the document and the workbook, and exit both programs.

Integration

Unit B

Integrating
Word, Excel, and Access

Objectives

- ▶ Merge data between Access and Word
- ▶ Use Mail Merge to create a form letter
- ▶ Export an Access table to Excel

You have learned how to use Word, Excel, and Access individually to accomplish specific tasks more efficiently. Now you will learn how to integrate files created with these programs so that you can use the best features of each one. Maria Abbott, the general sales manager for MediaLoft, wants to establish a profile of MediaLoft's corporate customers so that she can incorporate this information into the annual report. To do this, she creates a survey and mails it to these customers. She also wants to export the Access database of corporate customer names and addresses to an Excel worksheet so that she can create an Excel chart showing corporate sales by state and include this chart in the report.

Merging Data Between Access and Word

Companies often keep a database of customer names and addresses, which they use to send form letters to their customers. With Office, you can combine, or **merge**, data from an existing Access table with a Word document to automatically create personalized form letters. Maria wants to survey MediaLoft's corporate customers. She has written a form letter using Word, and she wants to merge her form letter with the customer names and addresses that already exist in an Access table.

Steps

QuickTip
If you plan to do the steps in this unit again, be sure to make and use a copy of the Access file MediaLoft-IB.

1. **Start Access, open the file MediaLoft-IB.mdb from the location where your Project Files are stored, click the Tables button on the Objects bar if necessary, make sure Customers is selected, then click the Open button on the Database window toolbar**
   The datasheet for the Customers table opens. The Customers table is the **data source** for the mail merge.

2. **Click Tools on the menu bar, point to Office Links, then click Merge It with Microsoft Word**
   The Microsoft Word Mail Merge Wizard dialog box opens, as shown in Figure B-1. The Mail Merge Wizard links your data to a Microsoft Word document. The customer survey form letter already exists as a Word document, so the default option, Link your data to an existing Microsoft Word document, is correct.

3. **Click OK**
   The Select Microsoft Word Document dialog box opens.

Trouble?
If the Access window remains on top as the active window, click the Word program button on the taskbar.

4. **Select the file INT B-1.doc from the location where your Project Files are stored, then click Open**
   Word opens and the document INT B-1 appears in the document window.

5. **If the Word program window does not fill the screen, click the Word program window Maximize button, then if necessary, click the Show/Hide ¶ button on the Standard toolbar to display formatting marks**
   Compare your screen to Figure B-2. The Mail Merge task pane is open. The Mail Merge task pane contains hyperlinks to commands that you use to perform a mail merge. The Mail Merge task pane is organized like a wizard, so there are actually six different Mail Merge task panes. This one is Step 3 of 6. The Mail Merge toolbar appears below the Formatting toolbar. The buttons on the Mail Merge toolbar are used to perform many of the same commands as the hyperlinks in the Mail Merge task pane. The document you just opened is the **main document** for the mail merge.

6. **Replace Maria Abbott's name with Your Name**

7. **Save the document as Survey Form Letter to the drive and location where your Project Files are stored**

INTEGRATION B-2 INTEGRATING WORD, EXCEL, AND ACCESS

FIGURE B-1: Microsoft Word Mail Merge Wizard dialog box

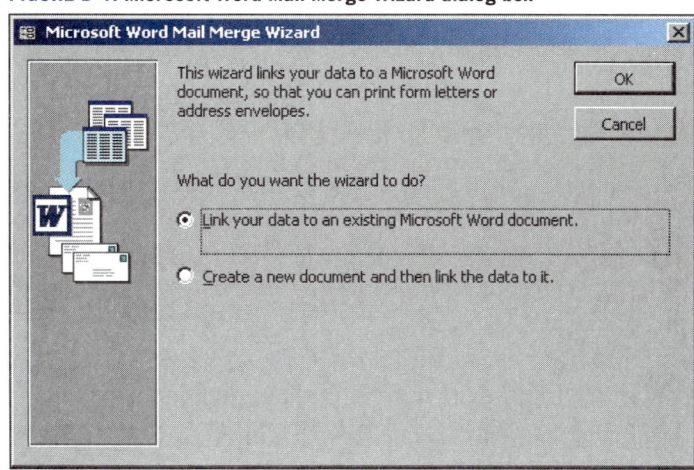

FIGURE B-2: Main document

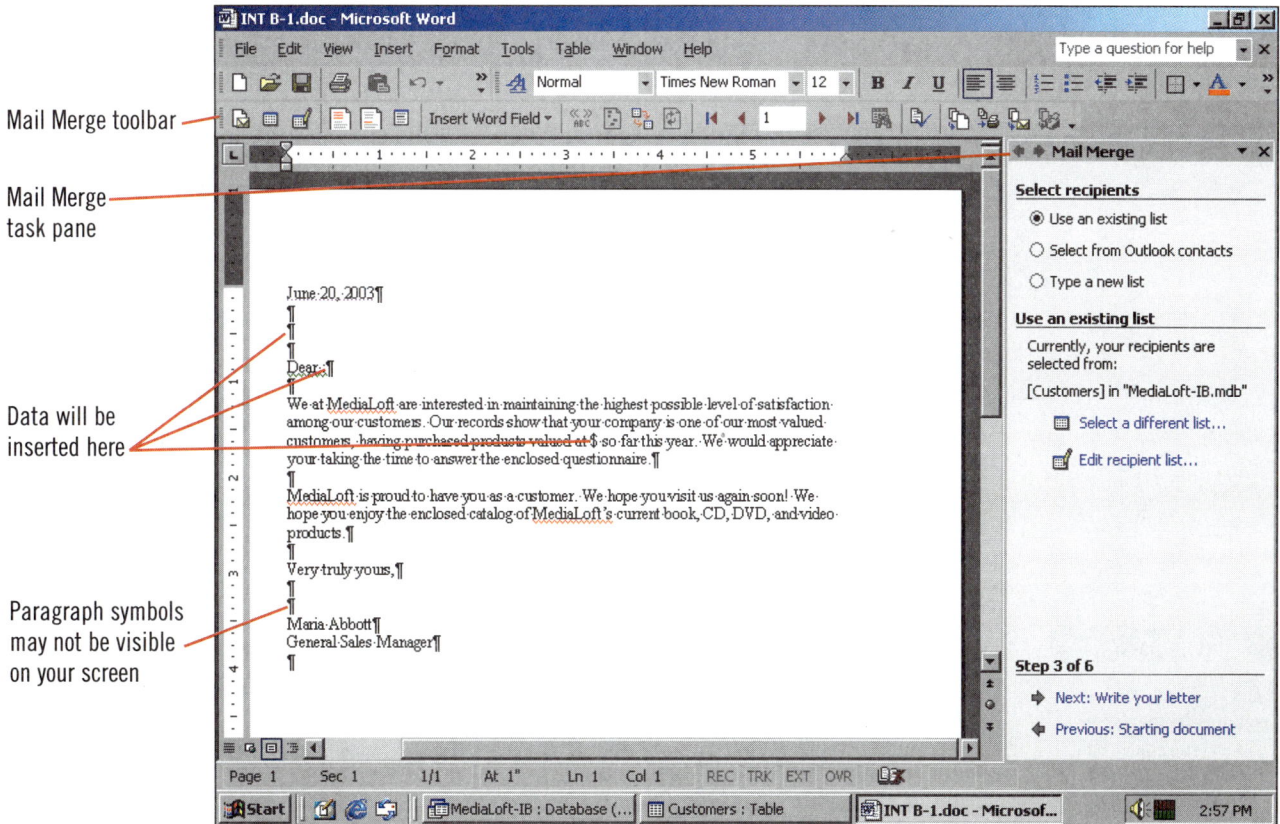

TABLE B-1: Mail Merge buttons

name	button	name	button	name	button
	Insert Address Block		Highlight Merge Fields		Find Entry
	Insert Greeting Line		Match Fields		Check for Errors
	Insert Merge Fields		First Record		Merge to New Document
	View Merged Data		Last Record		Merge to Printer

INTEGRATING WORD, EXCEL, AND ACCESS

Using Mail Merge to Create a Form Letter

Once you have opened and linked the form letter and the Access table, you are ready to insert **merge fields**, placeholders for the merged data, into the letter. When you perform the mail merge, Access looks for the merge fields in the main document and replaces them with the appropriate fields from the data source. After opening the data source and selecting the main document, Maria needs to insert merge fields into the main document.

Steps

1. Click the **Next: Write your letter hyperlink** in the task pane, click to the **left of the colon** in the greeting, then click the **More items hyperlink** in the Mail Merge task pane
   The Insert Merge Field dialog box opens. This dialog box contains a list of fields in the Access database. You need to insert the field representing each customer's first name.

2. Click **First**, click **Insert**, click **Close**, position the pointer to the right of the $ (dollar sign) in the first paragraph, click the **More items hyperlink** in the Mail Merge task pane, click **YTDSales**, click **Insert**, then click **Close**
   The First and the YTDSales fields are inserted between angled brackets in the form letter.

   > **QuickTip**
   > Click the Highlight Merge Fields button on the Mail Merge toolbar to highlight the merge fields.

3. Position the insertion pointer in the **second empty paragraph** below the date, then click the **Address block hyperlink** in the Mail Merge task pane
   The Insert Address Block dialog box opens. You use this dialog box to determine the appearance of information in the address block.

4. Click **Joshua Randall Jr.** in the recipient's name format list, then click **Match Fields**
   The Match Fields dialog box opens, similar to Figure B-3. If the field names in the data source you are using approximately match the field names in the Match Fields list on the left, the corresponding field name from your data source will be listed in the drop-down lists on the right side of the dialog box. The Mail Merge field name "Address 1" wasn't matched with anything in the MediaLoft-IB database.

5. Click the **Address 1 list arrow**, click **Street**, compare your settings to Figure B-3, click **OK**, then click **OK** to close the Insert Address Block dialog box
   The Address Block field appears in the document, as shown in Figure B-4.

   > **QuickTip**
   > Click the Edit recipient list hyperlink to open Access and edit the database. Click Exclude this recipient to exclude the current record from the final mail merge.

6. Click the **Next: Preview your letters hyperlink** in the Mail Merge task pane
   The data from the first record (David Friedrichsen at Sprint) appears correctly in the main document.

7. Click the **Next Record button** in the task pane
   The data from the second record (Liz Douglas at KGSM) appears in the document. Maria decides to merge the letters into one file so she can examine the final product before printing.

   > **QuickTip**
   > To merge the files directly to the printer, click the Print hyperlink in the task pane.

8. Click the **Next: Complete the merge hyperlink** in the task pane, click the **Edit individual letters hyperlink** in the task pane, then click **OK** in the Merge to New Document dialog box

9. Click the **Save button** on the Standard toolbar, save the document as **Survey Letters** to the location where your Project Files are stored, click **File** on the menu bar, click **Print**, click the **Current page option button** to print only the first form letter, then click **OK**
   The first form letter prints.

10. Click **File** on the menu bar, click **Exit**, then click **No** to save changes to Survey Form Letter
    Word closes and returns you to Access.

FIGURE B-3: Match Fields dialog box

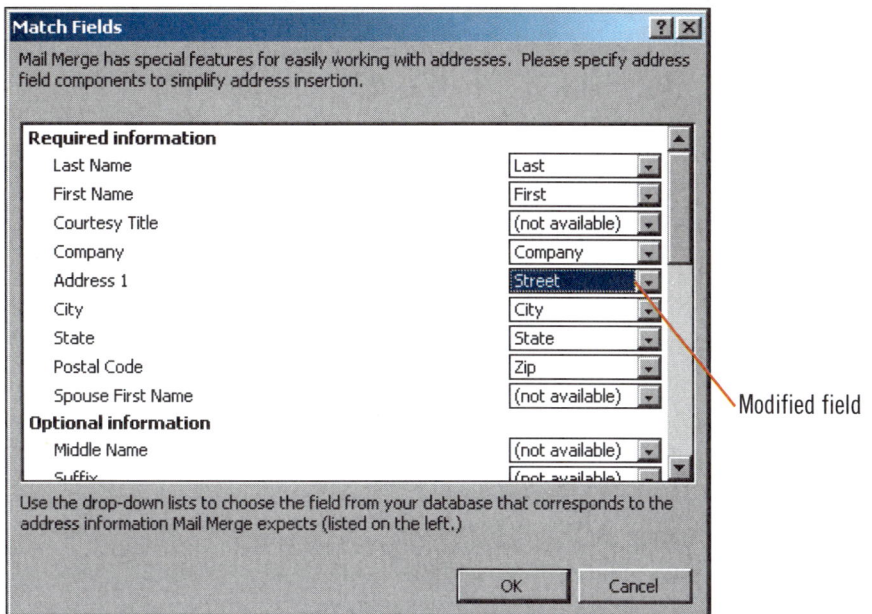

FIGURE B-4: Main document with merge fields inserted

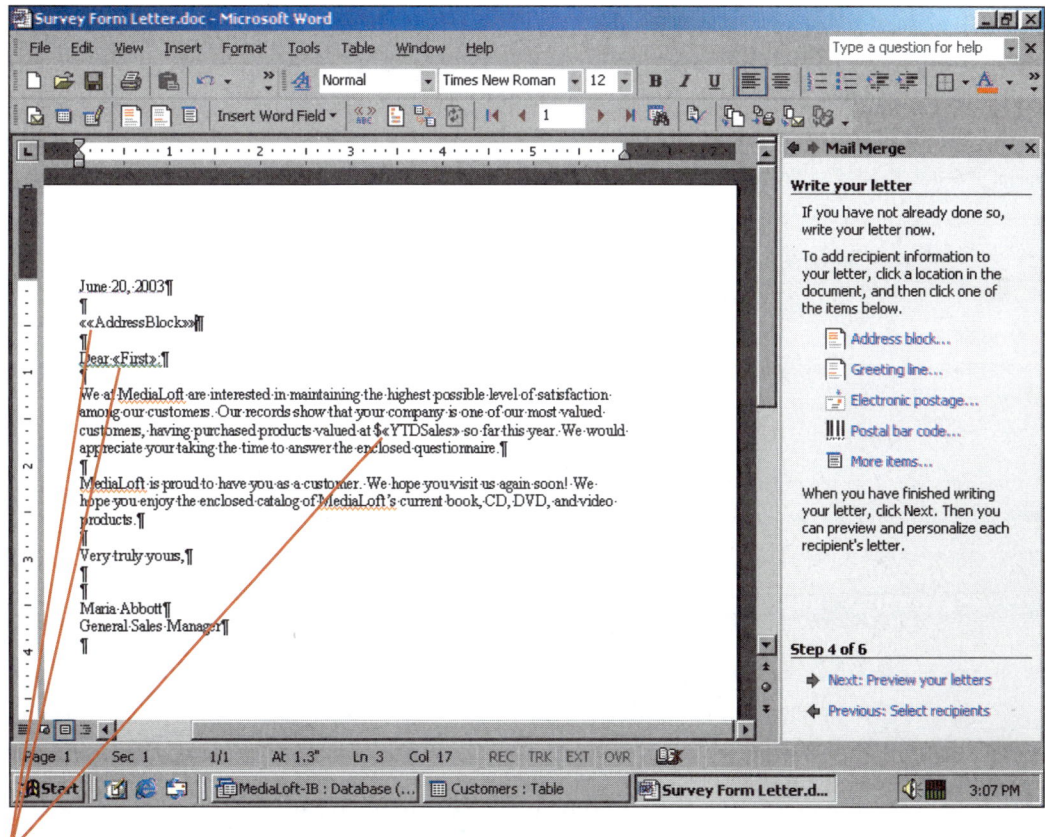

Exporting an Access Table to Excel

You can export data in an Access table to Excel and several other Office programs. When you export a table, a copy of the data is created in a format acceptable to the other program, and the original data remains intact. ✐ Maria wants to export the Customers table in the MediaLoft-IB database into Excel so that she can analyze the data. At some point, she will create a chart that shows the distribution of MediaLoft's corporate customer sales.

Steps

1. Make sure that the Customers table datasheet is still open, click **Tools** on the menu bar, point to **Office Links**, then click **Analyze It with Microsoft Excel**

    The exported data appears in an Excel workbook named Customers that contains only one worksheet, also named Customers. When you import data into Excel, only one worksheet is supplied, although you can add more.

2. If necessary, click the Excel program window **Maximize button** 🗖

    Maria does not need the Phone, Fax, Birthdate, or E-mail columns.

    > **QuickTip**
    > The green triangle in the upper-left corner of the cells in column H is an error indicator. In this case, it appears because the Zip code appears to be a number, but it is formatted as text. You can ignore it.

3. Scroll to the right, select the **I through L column selector buttons**, click **Edit** on the menu bar, click **Delete**, then press **[Ctrl][Home]** to return to cell A1

    All the remaining columns are now visible on the screen.

4. Click **Data** on the menu bar, then click **Sort**

    The Sort dialog box opens, similar to Figure B-5. Notice that the Header row option button at the bottom of the dialog box is selected. This means that the first row in the worksheet will not be sorted.

5. Click the **Sort by list arrow**, scroll down and click **State**, click the first **Then by list arrow**, scroll down and click **YTDSales**

    Compare your dialog box to Figure B-5.

6. Click **OK**

    The data is now sorted in ascending order by state, and within each state, by year-to-date sales. Compare your screen to Figure B-6.

7. Click **File** on the menu bar, click **Page Setup**, click the **Page tab** if necessary, click the **Landscape option button**, click **Print**, then click **OK**

    The worksheet prints on one page.

8. Scroll down and enter **Your Name** in **cell A30**, press **[Ctrl][Home]**, click **File** on the menu bar, click **Save As**, switch to the drive and folder where you are saving your Project Files, then click **Save**

    Your changes are saved to the file Customers in the location where your Project Files are stored.

9. Click **File** on the menu bar, click **Exit** to exit Excel, in the Access program window, click **File** on the menu bar, then click **Exit** to exit Access

FIGURE B-5: Sort dialog box

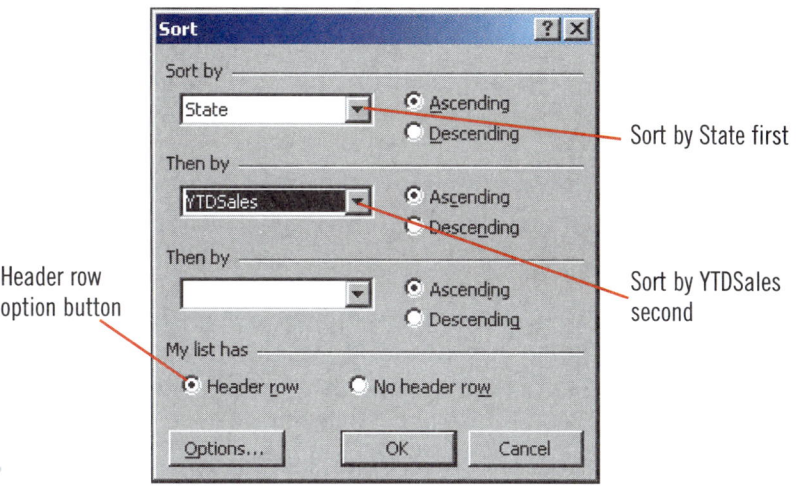

FIGURE B-6: Excel worksheet with sorted data

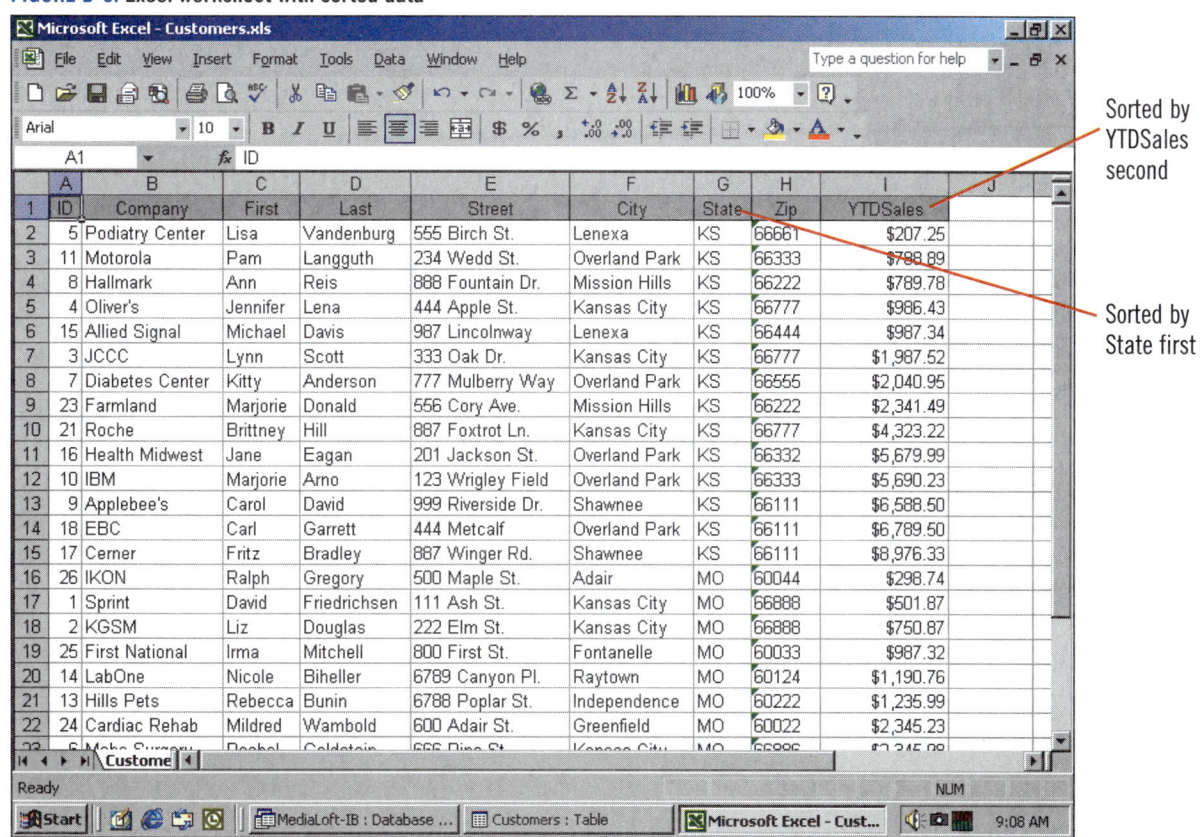

Exporting an Access table to Word

You can export an Access table to Microsoft Word by using the Publish It with MS Word feature. To export a table, open the Access database with the table you want to export, select the table name or open the table datasheet, click Tools on the menu bar, point to Office Links, then click Publish It with Microsoft Word. The table is exported to a Word table in a new Word document, and the document file is automatically saved in rich text format with the same name as the Access table.

Integration | **Practice**

▶ Independent Challenge 1

As the administrator for Monroe High School, you want to keep track of student records and generate reports for the principal and school district. You need to create a database containing information about the students currently enrolled in the high school. Once the database table is complete, export the table information to Excel and Word to create reports.

a. Start Access and create a new database called **Student Records**.
b. Create a table called **Student Info**. Decide what fields should be included in the database, but make sure you include fields for each student's first name, last name, address, phone number, gender, birth date, grade level, and cumulative grade point average (GPA).
c. Create a form to facilitate the entry of your student records, then print one record to show a sample of the form.
d. Add 20 records to your table, then sort the students by last name and then by first name.
e. Export the Student Info table to an Excel worksheet, then resize the columns to fit the table.
f. Scroll down to row C23 and enter **Your Name** in cell 23.
g. Print out your results, then save your worksheet as **Student Info** to the location where your Project Files are stored. Close the worksheet and exit Excel.
h. In Access, use the Publish It with MSWord command to export the Student Info table to a Word table, resize columns to fit the table, then format the table to make the document more attractive.
i. Change the page orientation to Landscape, sort the table by grade level and then by last name, then format the table to make the document more attractive.
j. Press [Enter] twice at the bottom of the document, then type your name.
k. Save the **Student Info** document in the location where your Project Files are stored, print it, close the document, then exit Word.
l. Close the Student Records database and exit Access.

Independent Challenge 2

MediaLoft sponsors the Pleasantown Players, a regional theater group that is supported by ticket revenues and private donations. You have been asked to help the theater group by writing a fundraising letter and merging it with a database of selected MediaLoft corporate customers. To maximize your results, you decide to send out the initial mailing to customers who have spent more than $2,000 at MediaLoft so far this year. You need to modify the current Customers table and create a query to find the appropriate customers. Then you need to create a form letter, which you will merge with the data stored in the query.

a. Open the Project File MediaLoft-IB.mdb from the location where your Project Files are stored, create a query called **Highest Revenue Listing** to find corporate customers who have spent more than $2,000 at MediaLoft so far this year. You are going to merge this query with a form letter, so make sure you include all the fields you will merge into the letter in the query.
b. Create a main document (form letter) in Word called **Funding Letter** in the location where your Project Files are stored. Use all the fields you feel are necessary. In the letter, you want to tell customers how important it is to support local, nonprofessional theater. For the letter content, tell the customers about the Pleasantown Players. Invent any information that adds informative, persuasive facts to your funding request.
c. Type your name in the signature block in the letter.
d. Merge the document Funding Letter and the query you created into a new document named **Pleasantown Letters**.
e. Print the current page of the Pleasantown Letters file.
f. Save your changes to the document, close the document, exit Word, then close the databse and exit Access.

Integration

Integrating
Word, Excel, Access, and PowerPoint

Objectives

- Understand embedding and linking
- Insert a Word outline into a PowerPoint presentation
- Embed an Excel chart into a PowerPoint slide
- Link an Excel worksheet to a PowerPoint slide
- Update a linked Excel worksheet in PowerPoint
- Export a PowerPoint presentation to Word

PowerPoint can be easily integrated with the other Office programs. For example, to help you develop a PowerPoint presentation, you can insert a document from Word, or objects, such as an Excel worksheet, directly into the slides of your presentation. In this unit Maria Abbott, MediaLoft's general sales manager, creates a company status presentation that will be used at this year's executive meeting. To complete the presentation, Maria gathers some data herself and collects more from other employees at MediaLoft. Because everyone at MediaLoft uses Microsoft Office, Maria knows that all the files are compatible.

Understanding Embedding and Linking

Sometimes the easiest way to add information to a PowerPoint presentation is to insert information or an object created in another Office program. For example, you might have an existing Excel chart that you can insert to complete a presentation. There are two ways to add objects to the slides of your presentation; you can embed them or you can link them. The **source file** is the original file that contains the data or object that you want to paste, such as a chart in an Excel workbook or a table in a Word document. The **source program** is the program used to create the source file. The **destination file** is the file that the data or object is pasted into, and the **destination program** is the program used to create the destination file. Maria wants to learn more about embedding and linking.

Details

▶ Embedding objects

When you **embed** an object, you are actually copying an object from its source file and pasting it into a destination file. Once embedded, an object becomes a part of the destination file, and the object is stored in the destination file. You can open the source program and manipulate an embedded object as long as you have access to the source program (either installed on your computer or over a network). Because an embedded object's data is stored in the destination file, the destination file's size increases relative to the file size of the embedded object. To embed an object in most Office programs, you use the Object command on the Insert menu, or you can use the Copy command in the source file and the Paste or Paste Special command in the destination file.

▶ Linking objects

When you **link** an object to a PowerPoint slide, a representation, or picture, of the object is placed on the slide instead of the actual object; this representation of the object is connected, or linked, to the original file. The object is still stored in the source file, unlike an embedded object that is stored directly in a slide. Any changes you make to a linked object's source file are reflected in the linked object. You can open the source file and make changes to the linked object as long as you have access to the source program (either installed on your computer or over a network), and to the source file. To link an object to most Office programs, you use the Object command on the Insert menu, and then click the Link check box in the Insert Object dialog box. You can also copy the object in its source program, click the Paste Special command on the Edit menu in the destination file, and then click the Paste Link option button. The differences between embedding and linking are summarized in Table C-1.

▶ Editing embedded and linked objects

To edit an embedded object, double-click the object. The source program starts, and the menu and toolbars of the source program appear. Changes made to an embedded object in its source program are reflected in the destination file, but these modifications do not affect the original object in the source file because embedded objects have no link to their source files. See Figure C-1.

To edit a linked object, double-click the object to open its source file in its source program, and then make your changes. Close the linked object's source program window when you are finished making changes. The changes made to a linked file are reflected in both the source file and in the linked object in the destination file. See Figure C-2.

FIGURE C-1: Embedding an object

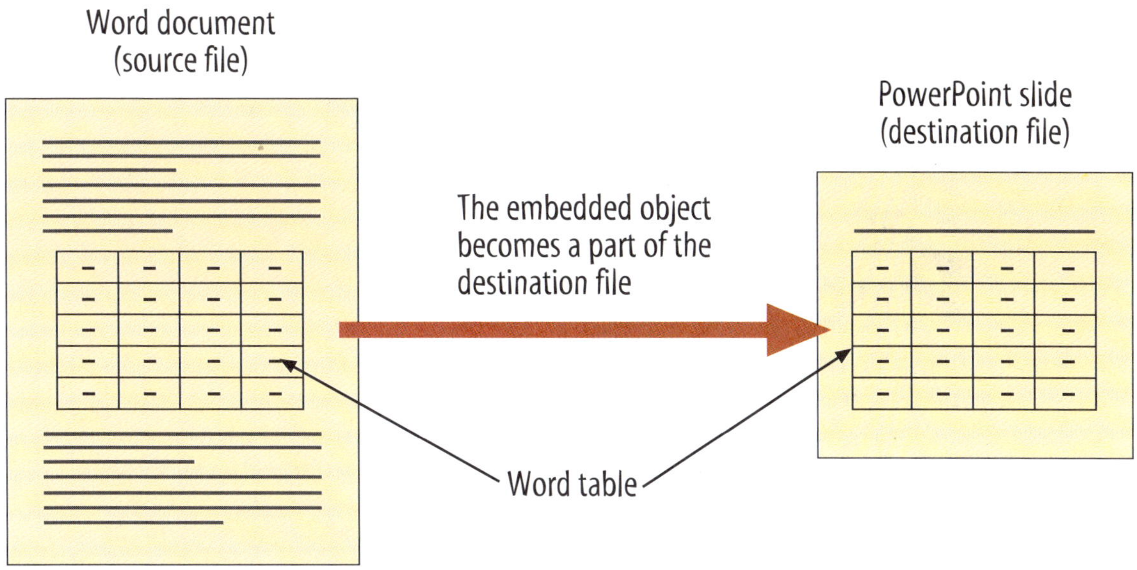

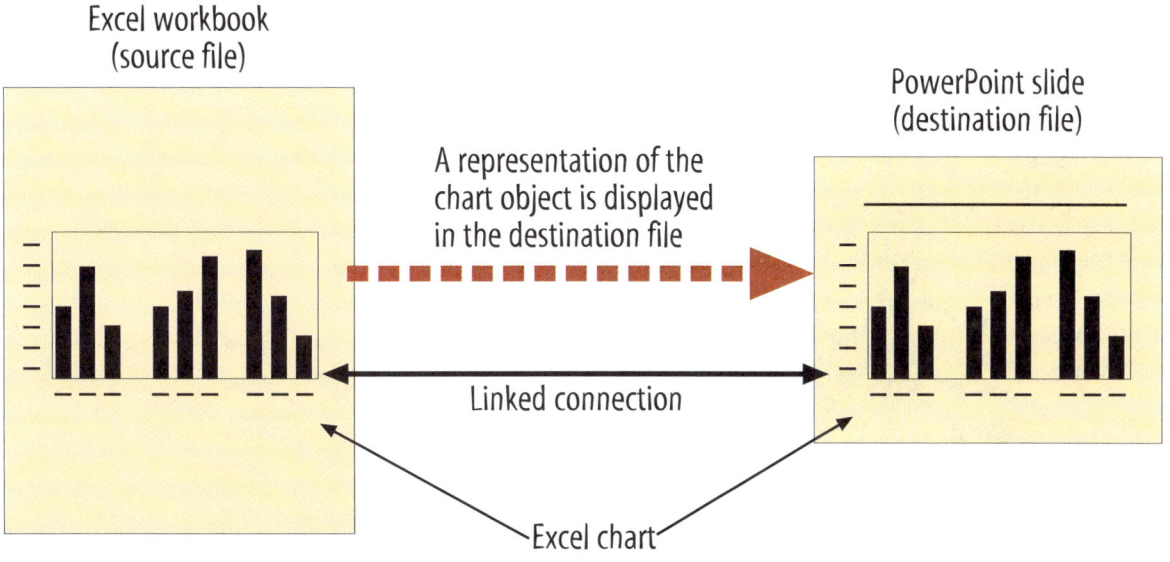

FIGURE C-2: Linking an object

TABLE C-1: Embedding vs. Linking

action	situation
Embed	You are the only user of an object, and you want the object to be a part of your presentation.
Embed	You want to access the object in its source program, even if the source file is not available.
Embed	You want to update the object manually while working in PowerPoint.
Link	You always want your object to have the latest information.
Link	The object's source file is shared on a network or where other users have access to the file and can change it.
Link	You want to keep your presentation file size small.

Inserting a Word Outline into a PowerPoint Presentation

Although it is very easy to create an outline in PowerPoint, it is unnecessary if the outline already exists in a Word document. You can easily insert a Word document into PowerPoint to create a presentation outline. The Word document can be formatted with heading styles. A **style** is a named collection of font attributes and paragraph formats; for example, a style named Heading 1 might be a paragraph formatted as 16-point, bold Arial font with extra space above and below the paragraph. When you insert a Word outline formatted with heading styles, the headings in the outline are converted to text levels in PowerPoint. For example, every Word paragraph with the style Heading 1 is converted to a new slide, and every Word paragraph with the style Heading 2 is converted to a subpoint under a slide title. If the Word outline you are inserting doesn't use styles, the outline is converted into slides based on the structure of the document; that is, each new paragraph indicates a new slide, and each new paragraph followed by a tab indicates a subpoint. Maria inserts a Word outline created by Alice Wegman, MediaLoft's marketing manager, into her presentation.

1. **Start PowerPoint**
   A new blank presentation opens.

2. **Click the Choose presentation hyperlink under New from existing presentation in the task pane**
   The New from Existing Presentation dialog box opens.

3. **Open the file INT C-1.ppt from the location where your Project Files are stored, then save it as Company Status**

> **Trouble?**
> Close any other open presentations, then repeat Step 5.

4. **Click View on the menu bar, click Task Pane, click Window on the menu bar, then click Arrange All**
   Now your screen matches the figures in this unit. Compare your screen to Figure C-3. The presentation currently contains two slides.

5. **Click anywhere in the text of Slide 2 in the Outline tab**
   When you insert the Word document, it begins with a new slide after the current slide.

6. **Click Insert on the menu bar, then click Slides from Outline**
   The Insert Outline dialog box opens.

> **Trouble?**
> If you see a message saying that PowerPoint needs to install this feature, insert your Office CD in the appropriate drive and click Yes. Ask your instructor or technical support person for assistance.

7. **Select the file INT C-2.doc from the location where your Project Files are stored, click Insert, then scroll in the Outline tab to see the new slides**
   The Word document is inserted as five new slides. See Figure C-4. You can insert a Word document in the Slide or Outline tab in Normal view. Once an outline is inserted into a presentation, you can edit it as if it had been created in PowerPoint.

8. **Make sure Slide 3 is selected in the Outline tab, click the Slides tab, then click the thumbnails for Slides 4-7 to view each new slide**

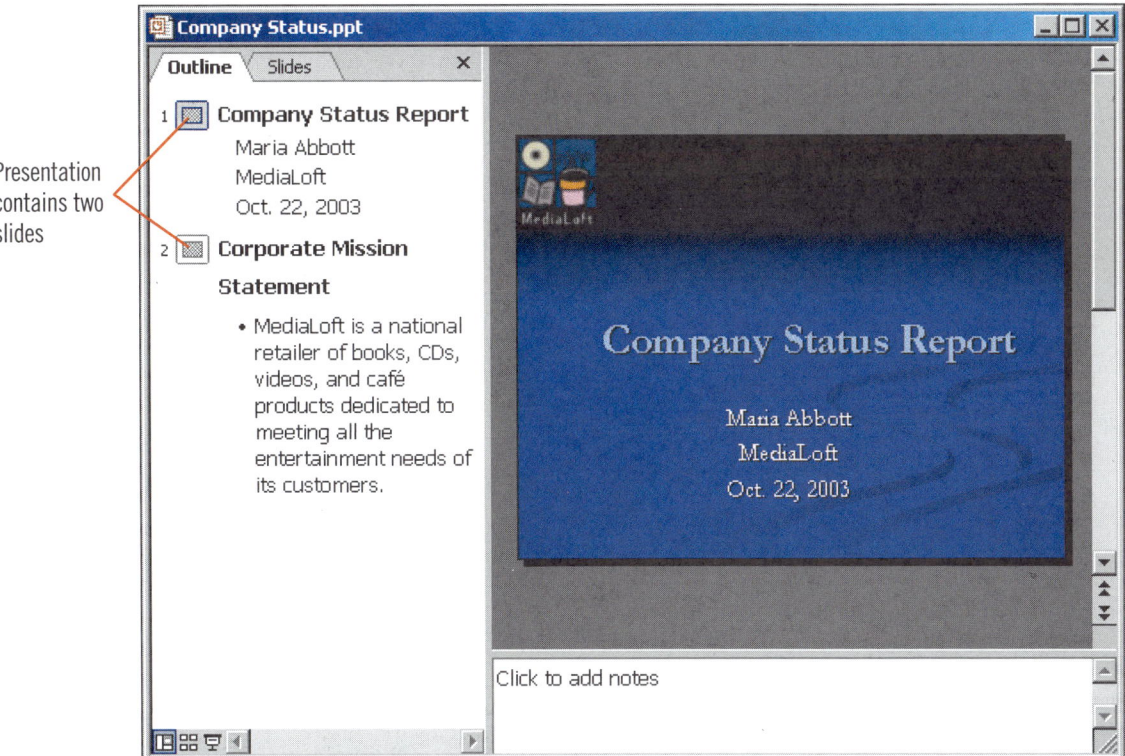

FIGURE C-3: Maria's slide presentation

Presentation contains two slides

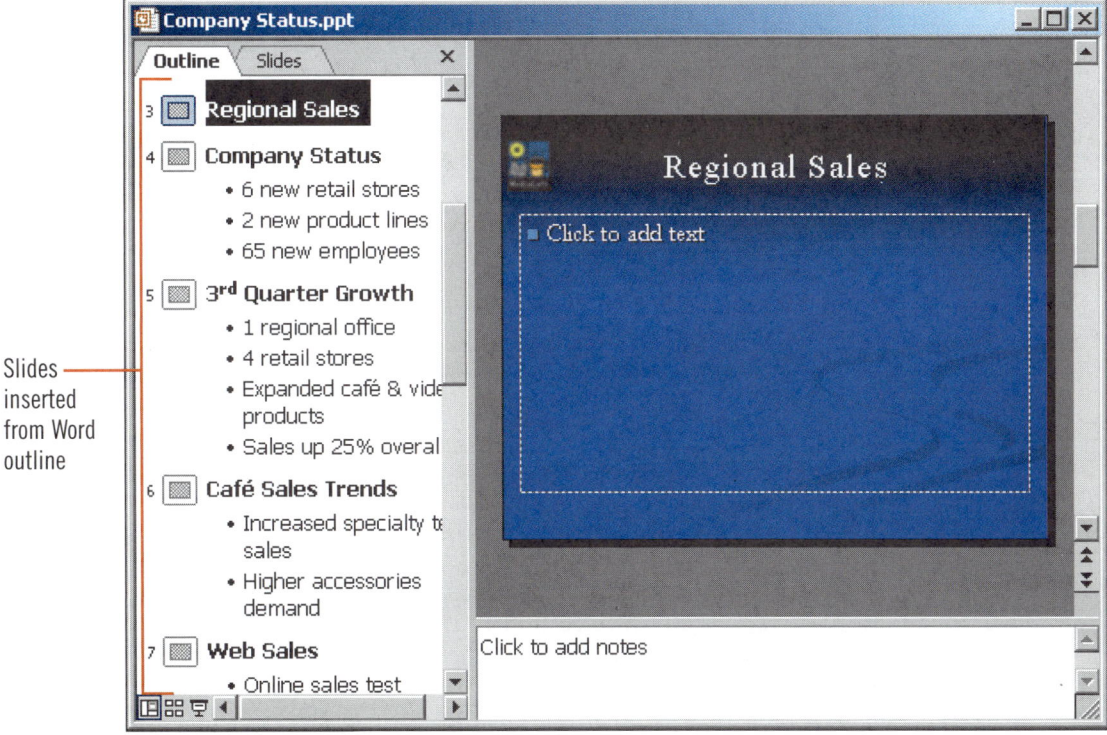

FIGURE C-4: New slides inserted in the Outline tab

Slides inserted from Word outline

Embedding an Excel Chart into a PowerPoint Slide

You can easily embed an Excel chart into a PowerPoint presentation. Because it is embedded, you can double-click a chart to edit it using Excel tools. The original Excel chart object remains unchanged. ✐ Maria decides to include in her presentation an Excel chart that she received from the Accounting Department. She wants to format the chart after she adds it to her presentation, so she embeds it.

Steps

1. Click the **Slide 3 thumbnail** on the Slides tab, click the **Other Task Panes list arrow** on the task pane title bar, click **Slide Layout**, then click the **Title Only layout** under Text Layouts

2. Click **Insert** on the menu bar, then click **Object**
   The Insert Object dialog box opens.

   > **QuickTip**
   > You can reposition the chart on the slide by dragging it.

3. Click the **Create from file option button**, click **Browse**, select the file **INT C-3.xls** from the location where your Project Files are stored, click **OK**, then click **OK** in the Insert Object dialog box
   The Excel chart appears on the slide. Compare your screen to Figure C-5.

4. Click the **Fill Color list arrow** on the Drawing toolbar, then click the **light purple** square (labeled Follow Title Text Scheme Color)
   The chart text would be more readable if it were larger.

   > **Trouble?**
   > If the Chart toolbar does not appear, click View on the menu bar, point to Toolbars, then click Chart.

5. Double-click the **chart object**
   The PowerPoint menu bar and toolbars are replaced with the Excel menu bar and toolbars, and the Excel Chart toolbar appears.

6. Click the **Chart Objects list arrow** on the Chart toolbar, click **Chart Title**, click the **Format Chart Title button** on the Chart toolbar, click the **Font tab**, click **28** in the Size list, then click **OK**
   The change in the Excel chart is reflected in the embedded object in PowerPoint. Because this is an embedded object, editing the object does not alter the original Excel file.

7. Double-click the **vertical axis** to open the Format Axis dialog box, click the **Font tab**, click **16** in the Size list, click **OK**, then repeat this for the **horizontal axis**

8. Repeat Step 7 to make the **legend** larger, then resize the legend to display all the text, if necessary

9. Drag the corner selection handles and reposition the worksheet object until it is approximately the same size and in the same position as in Figure C-6

10. Click outside the chart object to exit Excel, then click outside the chart object again to deselect it
    Compare your slide to Figure C-6.

FIGURE C-5: Embedded chart object

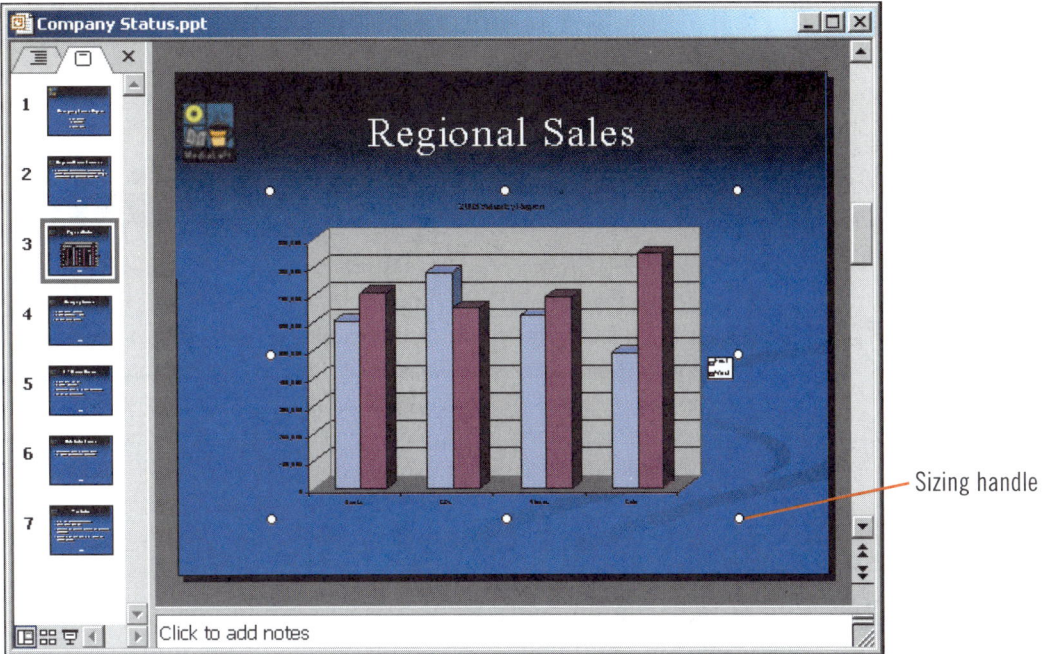

Sizing handle

FIGURE C-6: Formatted Excel chart embedded in a slide

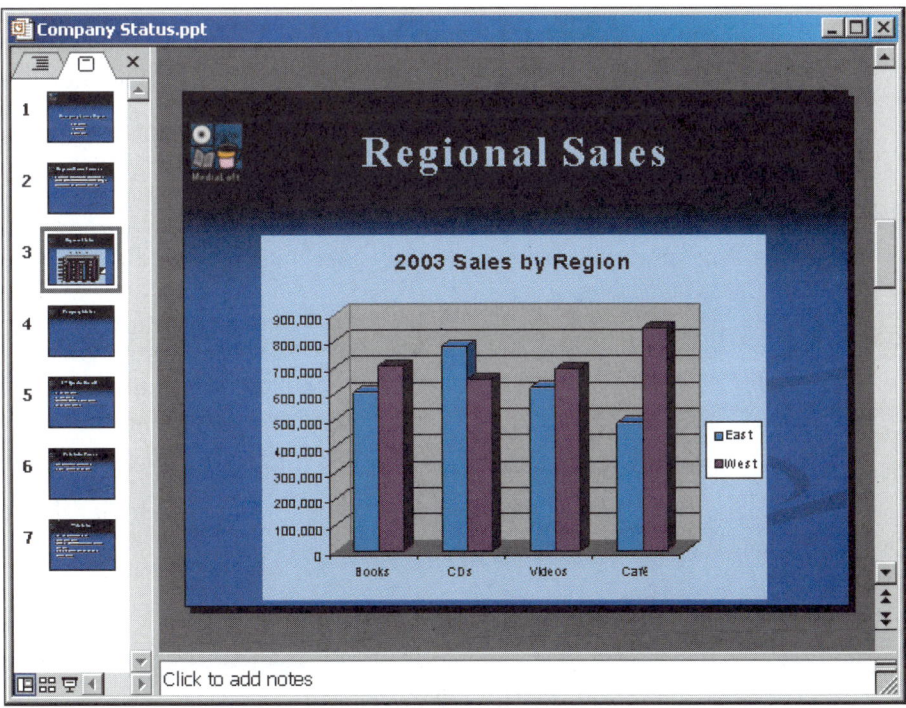

Embedding objects using Paste Special

You can also embed an object or selected information from another Office program into PowerPoint by copying and pasting the information. For example, assume that you want to embed a worksheet from an Excel file. Open the Excel file that contains the worksheet, select the worksheet, and copy it to the Clipboard. Open your PowerPoint presentation, click Edit on the menu bar, click Paste Special, then click OK in the Paste Special dialog box.

INTEGRATING WORD, EXCEL, ACCESS, AND POWERPOINT

Linking an Excel Worksheet to a PowerPoint Slide

You can connect objects to your presentation by establishing a link between the file that created the object and the PowerPoint presentation that contains the object. When you modify a linked object, either in its source file or in the destination file, the object changes in both files when you update the link. ✏️ Maria needs to insert an Excel worksheet from Jeff Shimada, the director of café operations, into her presentation. Jeff saved the worksheet to MediaLoft's company network of computers. Maria decides to link the worksheet because she knows Jeff will have to update the worksheet before the presentation.

Steps

QuickTip
If you plan to do the steps in this unit again, be sure to make a copy of the Excel file Cafe Profit before you proceed.

1. Click the **Slide 6 thumbnail** on the Slides tab, then change the layout to **Title and Text over Content** under Text and Content layouts in the task pane

2. Click **Insert** on the menu bar, then click **Object**
   The Insert Object dialog box opens. You want to create a linked object from an existing file.

3. Click the **Create from file option button**, click **Browse**, select the file **Cafe Profit.xls** from the location where your Project Files are stored, then click **OK**

4. Click the **Link check box** in the Insert Object dialog box to select it
   Compare your screen to Figure C-7.

5. Click **OK**
   The Excel worksheet is linked to the PowerPoint slide. The worksheet would be easier to read if it were larger.

Trouble?
If Excel opens while you are trying to resize or move the worksheet, click the Close button in the Excel program window.

6. Drag the corner selection handles and reposition the worksheet object until it is approximately the same size and in the same position as in Figure C-8
   The chart text is difficult to read against the dark background.

7. Click the **Fill Color list arrow** on the Drawing toolbar, click the **white color cell** (second from left), then click a blank area of the slide to deselect the object
   Compare your screen to Figure C-8.

8. Save your work

FIGURE C-7: Insert Object dialog box

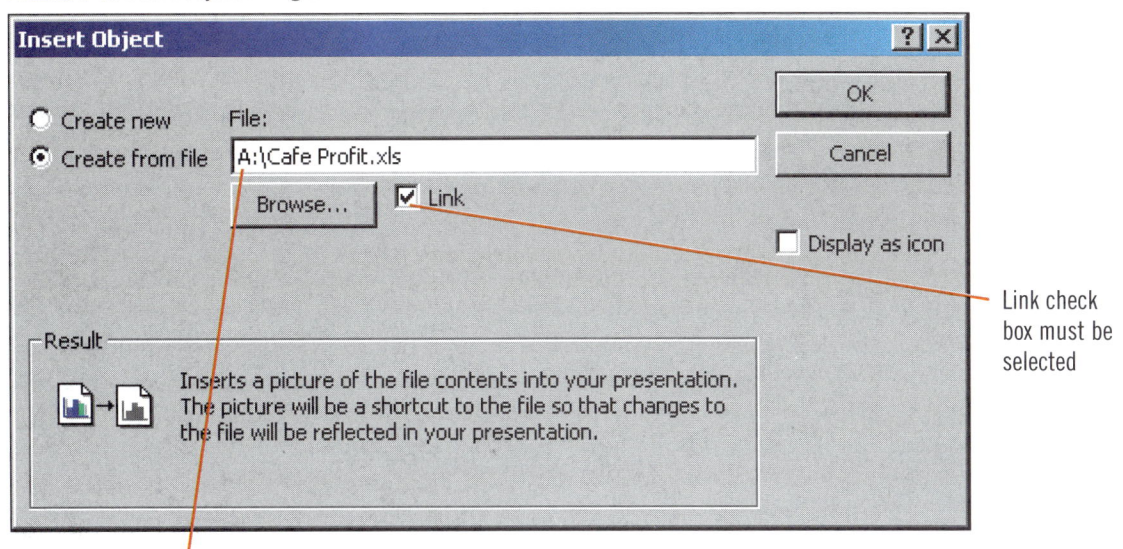

Link check box must be selected

Excel worksheet filename appears here

FIGURE C-8: Formatted Excel worksheet linked to a slide

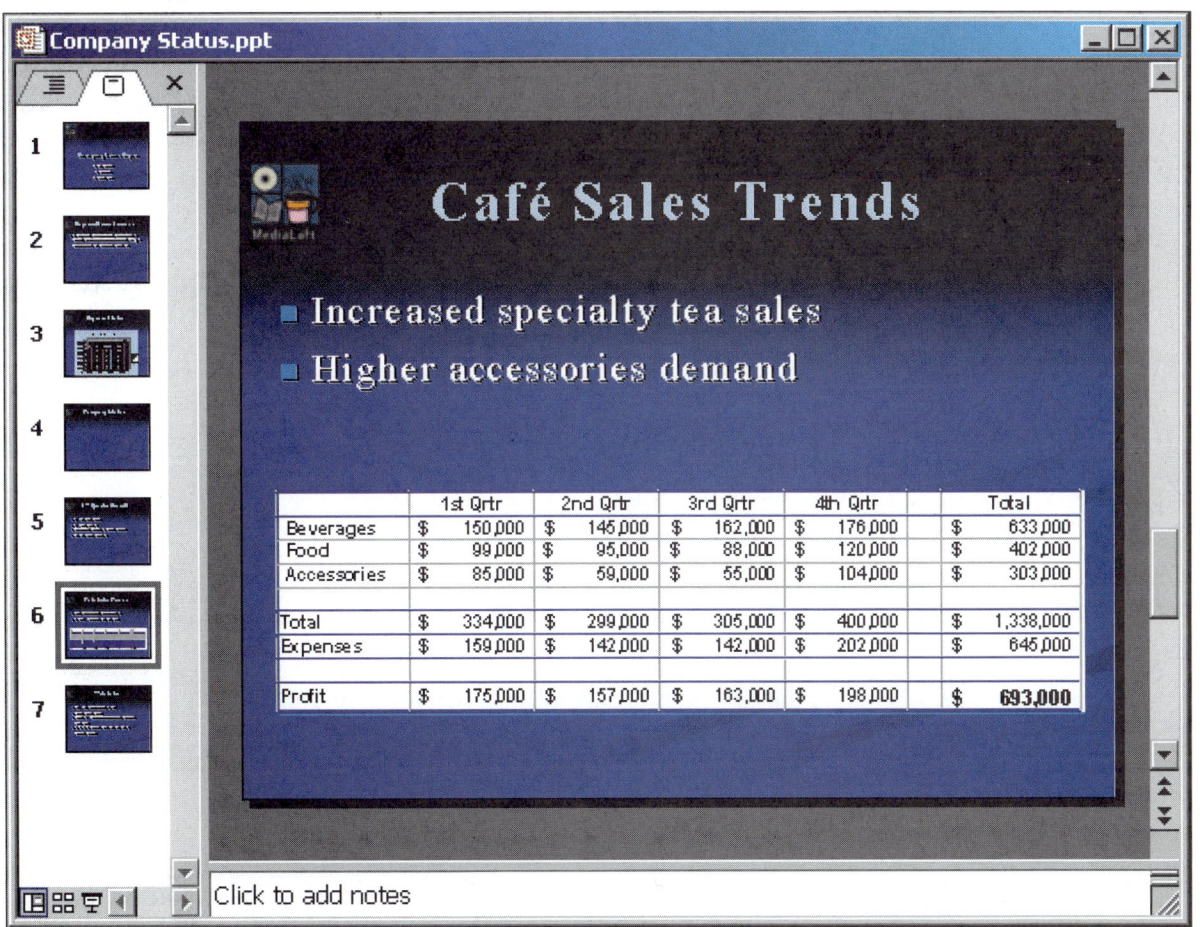

INTEGRATING WORD, EXCEL, ACCESS, AND POWERPOINT

Updating a Linked Excel Worksheet in PowerPoint

To edit or change the information in a linked object, you must open the object's source file. You can open the object's source file and the program it was created in by double-clicking the linked object in the destination file. If you modify a linked object's source file in the source file program, PowerPoint asks you if you want to automatically update the file in the linked presentation the next time you open the PowerPoint file. Maria needs to update the linked worksheet because the wrong number was reported for accessory sales for the third quarter.

Trouble?
To edit or open a linked object in your presentation, the object's source program and source file must be available on your computer or network.

1. Double-click the **worksheet object** on slide 6
   Excel opens in a small window, showing the linked worksheet, and the Excel program button appears on the taskbar.

2. Click the **Maximize button** in the Excel program window if necessary

3. Click cell **D4**, type **74,000**, then press **[Enter]**
   The number you typed appears in cell D4. Notice that the numbers in cells D6, D9, G4, and G9 all change to reflect the new number in cell D4.

4. Click the **Close button** in the Excel program window, then click **Yes** to save the changes
   Microsoft Excel closes, and the linked Excel worksheet shows the change you made in Excel. If you opened the file named Cafe Profit.xls in Excel, you would see this same change in the worksheet. Compare your screen to Figure C-9.

5. Click the **Spelling button** on the Standard toolbar and correct any spelling errors in the presentation

6. Click the **Save button** on the Standard toolbar to save the changes you made

7. Click the **Slide Sorter View button** below the Slide tab, click in the **Zoom box** on the Standard toolbar, type **50**, then press **[Enter]**
   Compare your screen to Figure C-10. You changed the zoom percentage so you can see all of the slides in the window.

8. Double-click **Slide 1**, then click the **Slide Show button** and view the final presentation

9. Add your name as a footer to all slides and handouts

10. Click **File** on the menu bar, click **Print**, select **Pure Black and White** in the Color/grayscale list, select **Handouts** in the Print what list, select **3 Slides per page**, then click **OK** to print the slides

FIGURE C-9: Data change reflected in linked worksheet

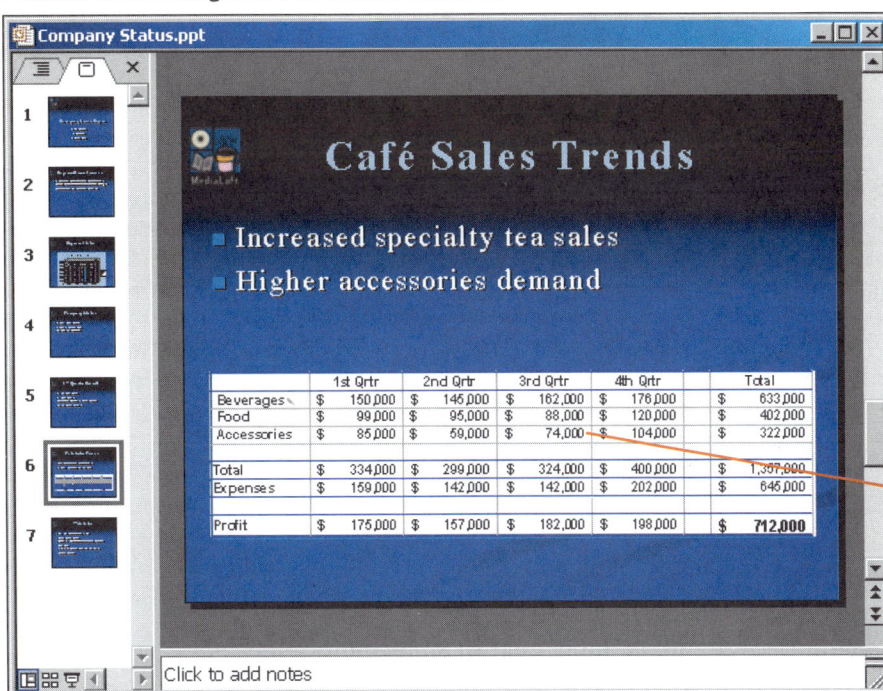

Modified data in Excel worksheet

FIGURE C-10: The final presentation in Slide Sorter view

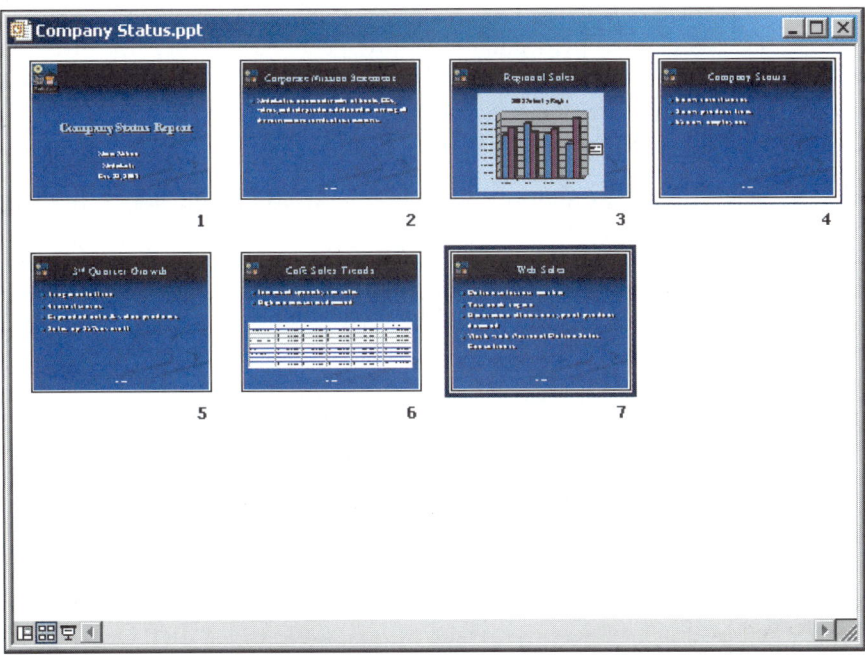

Updating links

If the PowerPoint file is closed when you change the source file, the linked object will still be able to reflect the changes you made in the source file. When you open the file containing the linked object, a dialog box opens reminding you that the file contains links and asking if you want to update the links now. Click OK to update the links, or click Cancel to leave the linked object unchanged. If you choose Cancel, you can still update the link later. Click Edit on the menu bar, then click Links to open the Links dialog box. Click the filename of the link you want to update, then click Update Now.

Exporting a PowerPoint Presentation to Word

You can export a PowerPoint presentation to Word. When you choose the Send To Microsoft Word command on the File menu, Word starts and the outline of the current PowerPoint presentation is exported to a Word document. You can choose one of five layouts for the Word document. Once the PowerPoint outline is in Word, you can save and edit the document. ✒ Maria wants to create handouts with blank lines so the audience can take notes during the presentation.

Steps

1. **Click File on the menu bar, point to Send To, then click Microsoft Word**
   The Send to Microsoft Word dialog box opens, similar to Figure C-11.

2. **Click the Blank lines next to slides option button**
   You want your handouts to automatically reflect any changes you make to the presentation.

3. **Click the Paste link option button at the bottom of the dialog box**

4. **Click OK**
   Microsoft Word opens, and the slides appear in a table in a new document. This process may take a little while to complete. See Figure C-12. The slide numbers are in the first column, the slides are in the second column, and blank lines appear next to the slides in the third column. There are three slides per page.

5. **Select the first column, then click the Bold button B on the Formatting toolbar**

6. **Press [Ctrl][End], then type your name**

7. **Save the Word file as Handouts for Status Meeting to the drive and location where your Project Files are stored**

8. **Click the Print button on the Standard toolbar**
   The handouts print.

9. **Click the Close button on the Word program window, then click the Close button on the PowerPoint program window, saving changes if prompted**
   The programs close.

> **QuickTip**
> To print speaker notes with your slides, choose either the Notes next to slides option or the Notes below slides option. To print fewer pages, choose the Notes next to slides option or the Blank lines next to slide option; the slides will print three per page.

FIGURE C-11: Send to Microsoft Word dialog box

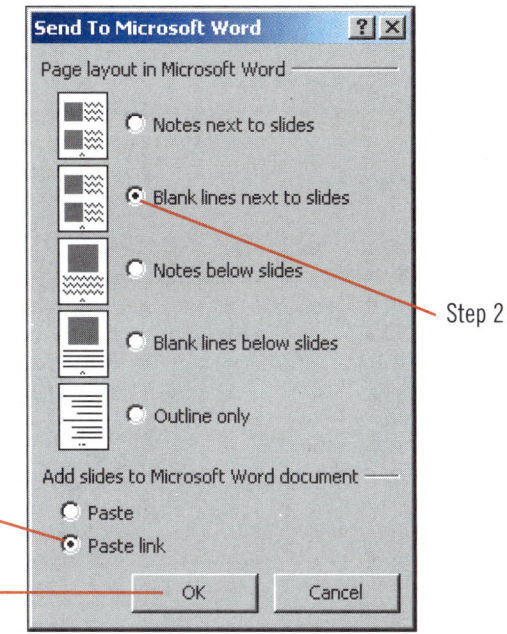

FIGURE C-12: Exported PowerPoint presentation in Word

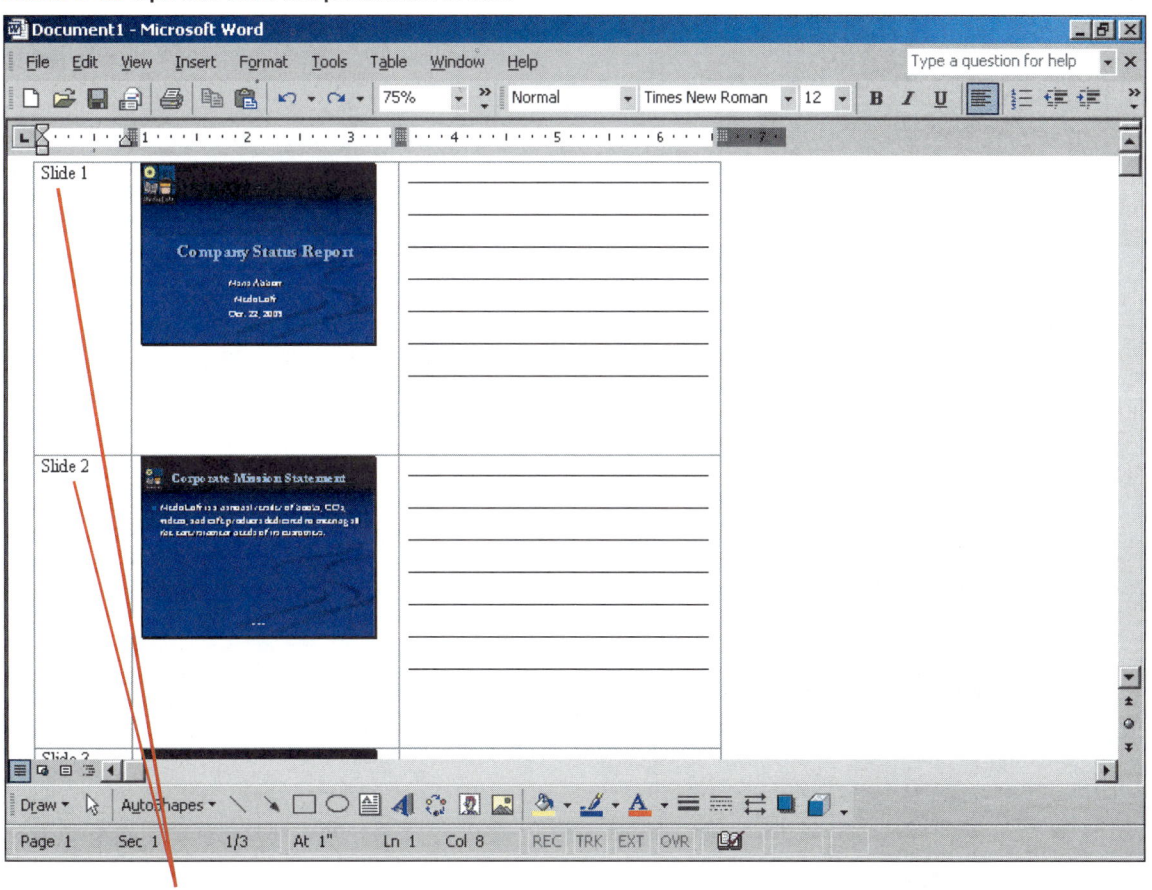

INTEGRATING WORD, EXCEL, ACCESS, AND POWERPOINT

Integration | **Practice**

Independent Challenge 1

You are responsible for recommending which software packages your company should purchase. You have decided to recommend Microsoft Office. Create a PowerPoint presentation illustrating the advantages of each program in the Microsoft Office suite. Your presentation should also contain slides that show how first-time computer users feel about computers and why Microsoft Office is a good choice for them. Information about first-time computer users is provided in the Word file INT C-4.doc in the location where your Project Files are stored. Think about what you want the presentation to say and what graphics you want to use.

a. Plan your presentation, determining its purpose and the look that will help communicate your message.
b. Start PowerPoint, create a presentation, insert your name as the footer on all slides and handouts, then save the presentation as **Office Review** to the location where your Project Files are stored.
c. Insert the Word document INT C-4.doc into your presentation outline. This file contains information about how first-time computer users feel about computers.
d. Add slides explaining why Office is a good choice for your company and explaining the advantages of each of the Office suite programs. Your final presentation should contain at least 10 slides.
e. Create the title slide for your presentation, then save your work.
f. Add an appropriate design template, graphics, and slide show special effects to the presentation. Check each of the slides created from the outline and make sure they convey the information clearly.
g. Check the spelling in your presentation.
h. Run the slide show and evaluate your presentation. Is your message clear? Are the slides visually appealing? Make any changes necessary and save the presentation.
i. Print the slides and outline of your presentation, then close all open files and programs.

Independent Challenge 2

To augment the Census Bureau's data on marriage and birthrate statistics, you have been asked to prepare a PowerPoint presentation that will run continuously in the lobby at the local census office. Charts on the data need to be linked to PowerPoint slides because data is occasionally updated. Use the data found in the two worksheets in the Excel file INT C-5.xls in the location where your Project Files are stored. Create a presentation that explains this data.

a. Start Excel, open the file INT C-5.xls from the location where your Project Files are stored, then save it as **Statistics**.
b. Create at least four charts using the data in the Marriages worksheet, and create one chart using the data in the Birthrates worksheet.
c. Examine the data and the charts you created, then create a new Word document containing an outline for your presentation. Summarize the data and explain what the charts show.
d. Type your name at the top of the document, save it as **Stat Outline** to the location where your Project Files are stored, then print this outline.
e. Start PowerPoint and open a new presentation. Apply a template of your choice. Insert your name as a footer on all slides and handouts, then save it as **Bureau** to the location where your Project Files are stored.
f. Create a title slide for the presentation, then insert the file Stat Outline.doc into the presentation.
g. Link the four charts in the Marriages worksheet to slides in the presentation. Update one of the numbers in the worksheet from within PowerPoint and verify that the number in the presentation is also updated.
h. Add the chart in the Birthrates worksheet to a slide in the presentation.
i. Create handouts in Word so the audience can take notes. Link the presentation in case you make changes. Type your name as the last line in the file, then save this file as **Bureau Handouts** to the location where your Project Files are stored.

j. Switch back to the presentation, then add slide show special effects, such as transitions and animation effects, to the slides.
k. Check the spelling in your presentation, then run the final slide show and evaluate your presentation.
l. Save and print the slides of your presentation.
m. Switch back to the Bureau Handouts file in Word, update the link, then save and print the document. (*Hint*: To update the link, use the Links command on the Edit menu.)
n. Close all open files and programs, saving any changes.

▶ Independent Challenge 3

You have been hired as an associate in the Marketing department at Nomad Ltd, an outdoor sporting gear and adventure travel company. Nomad recently completed a big marketing campaign promoting its bicycle tour packages. Nomad now needs to focus in its other tour packages. Sales of some tour packages, such as bungee jumping, have decreased lately. Concerned about the falling sales, the Nomad board of directors has suggested adding rock climbing and jeep tours to the Nomad tour line to broaden Nomad's customer base. Your job is to develop a marketing presentation that addresses these concerns.

You decide to send a questionnaire to customers who have taken tour packages to ask how they can be improved. You need several charts to show tour trends and the potential sales for the new tours.

a. Start Word and open the file INT C-6.doc from the drive and location where your Project Files are stored. Add your name to the bottom of the letter, then save it as **Cover Letter**. This is the cover letter for the questionnaire.
b. Use the Insert Picture command to add the Nomad logo to the top of the letter. The logo, named Nomad.tif, is in the location where your Project Files are stored. Save your changes, then close the document.
c. Start Access and open the file Customer Data from the location where your Project Files are stored. Create a query that lists all of the information about customers who have taken the bungee tour. Save the query as **Bungee Customers**.
d. Use Mail Merge to merge the cover letter and the Access query you have created. Insert the date and appropriate merge fields in the cover letter. Save the merged file, print the first letter, then close the merged file.
e. Start Excel and open the INT C-7.xls file from the location where your Project Files are stored. Save it as **Tour Type**. This worksheet contains data for road bike, mountain bike, and bungee tour sales. Create two charts on this worksheet: one that compares the sales numbers of the tours and the other that shows the tours as a percentage of all tours. Use drawing tools and color, if appropriate, to point out weak sales. Name this worksheet **Current**.
f. Copy the data from the Current worksheet to a new worksheet. In the new worksheet, add a formula that calculates an increase in the bungee tour sales numbers by 20%, then show this increase in your charts. Use drawing tools and color, if appropriate, to indicate which figures are speculative. Name this worksheet **Bungee Increase**.
g. Copy the increased bungee tour sales data to another new worksheet, then add two more rows for the rock climbing and jeep tours. Assume that their sales equal the sales of the increased bungee tour sales. Create two more charts to show the new tours. Name this worksheet **New Tours**.
h. Add titles to all three charts to identify them. Use drop shadows and other formatting effects to make them more attractive.
i. Start PowerPoint and create a new presentation. Save it as **Tour Evaluation** to the location where your Project Files are stored. This presentation illustrates your marketing ideas to increase sales.
j. Create a title slide, then insert the Word outline INT C-8.doc from the location where your Project Files are stored. Add to the outline your own ideas on how to strengthen bungee tour sales and generate new sales for the new tours. You can suggest additional tours, too.
k. Include any relevant Excel charts on your slides by using the method you feel is best: linking or embedding. Use drawing tools and color, if appropriate, to point out the new tours.
l. Use templates, clip art, animation effects, and any other PowerPoint features you want to create an effective and professional-looking presentation.

Integration | Practice

m. Insert your name as a footer on all sides and handouts, then print the presentation as handouts (six slides per page).
n. Save and close all files, then close all open programs.

Independent Challenge 4

You work for Royal Canadian Tours, a travel agency in Calgary, Alberta, Canada. Your agency specializes in railroad tour packages throughout Canada. To prepare for a large convention you need to develop a PowerPoint presentation that illustrates the primary rail tours your company offers. You need to develop a 10-slide presentation that briefly describes your company and at least two rail tour packages your company offers. To find data for your presentation, you need to use the Web to locate certain information.

You'll need to find the following information on the Web:
- General data for a table that compares at least two rail tour packages
- Schedule and destination locations
- Information about services provided on the train, as well as information about attractions along the route

a. Connect to the Internet, then use a search engine to locate Web sites that have information on Canadian rail tours. If your search does not produce any results, you might try the following sites:
   www.cprtours.com
   www.rkymtnrail.com
   www.viarail.ca
   Review at least two Web sites that contain information about rail tour packages. Print the Home pages of the Web sites you use to gather data for your presentation.
b. Start Word, add your name to the bottom of the document, then save it as **Rail Tours** to the location where your Project Files are stored. This is the outline for your presentation.
c. Create an outline with the information you've gathered on the Internet. Remember to include enough information for at least 10 slides.
d. Insert the outline into a new PowerPoint presentation and save it as **Royal Tours** to the location where your Project Files are stored.
e. Two slides should include information on schedules and destination cities.
f. Create a new slide, title it **Royal Tours Comparison**, then create a table that compares the features of at least two tour packages.
g. Create a new Excel worksheet and save it as **Royal Tours Data** to the drive and folder where your Project Files are stored. Create a worksheet that identifies the number of people that have toured using the Royal Canadian Tours rail packages over the last three years. Name this worksheet **RCT Tours**. Create your own data, but assume that the number of people have ranged between 10,000 and 50,000, depending on the cost of the tour package. Give a total number of people at the bottom of the worksheet for each year. Link this worksheet to a slide in the presentation.
h. Use templates, clip art, transitions, and any other PowerPoint features you want to create an effective and professional-looking presentation.
i. Insert your name as a footer on all slides and handouts in the presentation, then save and print the presentation as handouts, two slides per page.
j. Save and close all files, then close all open programs.

Integration

Integrating
Office Applications with Internet Explorer

Objectives

- Plan a Web publication
- Create a Web page
- Format a Web page
- Create a Web page from a Word document
- Create a Web page from an Access table
- Create a Web page from an Excel workbook
- Create Web pages from a PowerPoint presentation
- Add hyperlinks

The Web page features of Office XP give you the tools to easily create professional Web pages from scratch or to convert existing Office documents into Web pages. A **Web page** is a file that can be stored on a special computer called a **Web server** so it can be viewed on the World Wide Web or an intranet using a browser. Web pages use **Hypertext Markup Language (HTML)** formatting. HTML is the programming language used to describe how each element of a Web page should appear when viewed with a browser. Karen Rosen is the director of human resources at MediaLoft. Karen wants to create a set of Web pages that she will eventually post, or **publish**, on the MediaLoft intranet to help new employees learn more about employee benefits and programs. Karen uses Office XP to create the Web pages.

Planning a Web Publication

A **Web publication** is a group of associated Web pages focused on a particular theme or topic. It is important to plan your Web pages carefully before creating them. Planning a Web publication involves thinking about the content to include, determining the design to use, sketching the organization of the Web pages, and including the links between them. Karen plans the content and organization of her Web pages and outlines the steps involved in creating the Web publication and posting it to the MediaLoft intranet.

In planning her Web pages, Karen is careful to:

▶ **Sketch each Web page**
Draw a sketch of how you want each page to look and diagram the links between pages. Karen identifies the content that will be useful to employees. She then determines the documents she wants to include on the intranet, sketches the layout, and adds notes, as shown in Figure D-1.

▶ **Create each Web page**
You can save an existing Office file as a Web page, or you can start with a blank document and create a new Web page. Word includes Web page templates that make it easy to create many standard types of Web pages from scratch. If you want to create a Web page from an existing file, you can use the features in each Office program to convert the file to HTML. Karen will create a new Web page in Word and then convert several existing Office files to HTML files.

▶ **Format each Web page**
You can use Word to edit most Web page documents—even those not created in Word—and to add images and apply visual themes and backgrounds to Web pages. Karen will use the tools available in Word to enhance the appearance of the Web pages in her Web publication. She will apply a common visual theme to each Web page and insert the MediaLoft company logo on the Welcome page.

▶ **View each Web page using a browser**
Before finalizing the content and design of each Web page, view the Web page in your browser to make sure it is readable and formatted properly. If necessary, you can use Word to make editing and formatting corrections. Karen will view the Web pages in Internet Explorer to make sure they look as expected.

▶ **Format hyperlinks**
Once you have finalized the text and graphics of your Web pages, you can add hyperlinks to connect them. Before publishing your Web publication, view it again in your browser to test each hyperlink and make sure it works as you intended. Karen's sketch indicates that she will create links between the home page, which is the Welcome page, and each Web page in the publication. Also, she will eventually create links to the MediaLoft Training page and to the MediaLoft Human Resources page after publishing the Web publication on the MediaLoft intranet.

FIGURE D-1: Karen's Web publication sketch

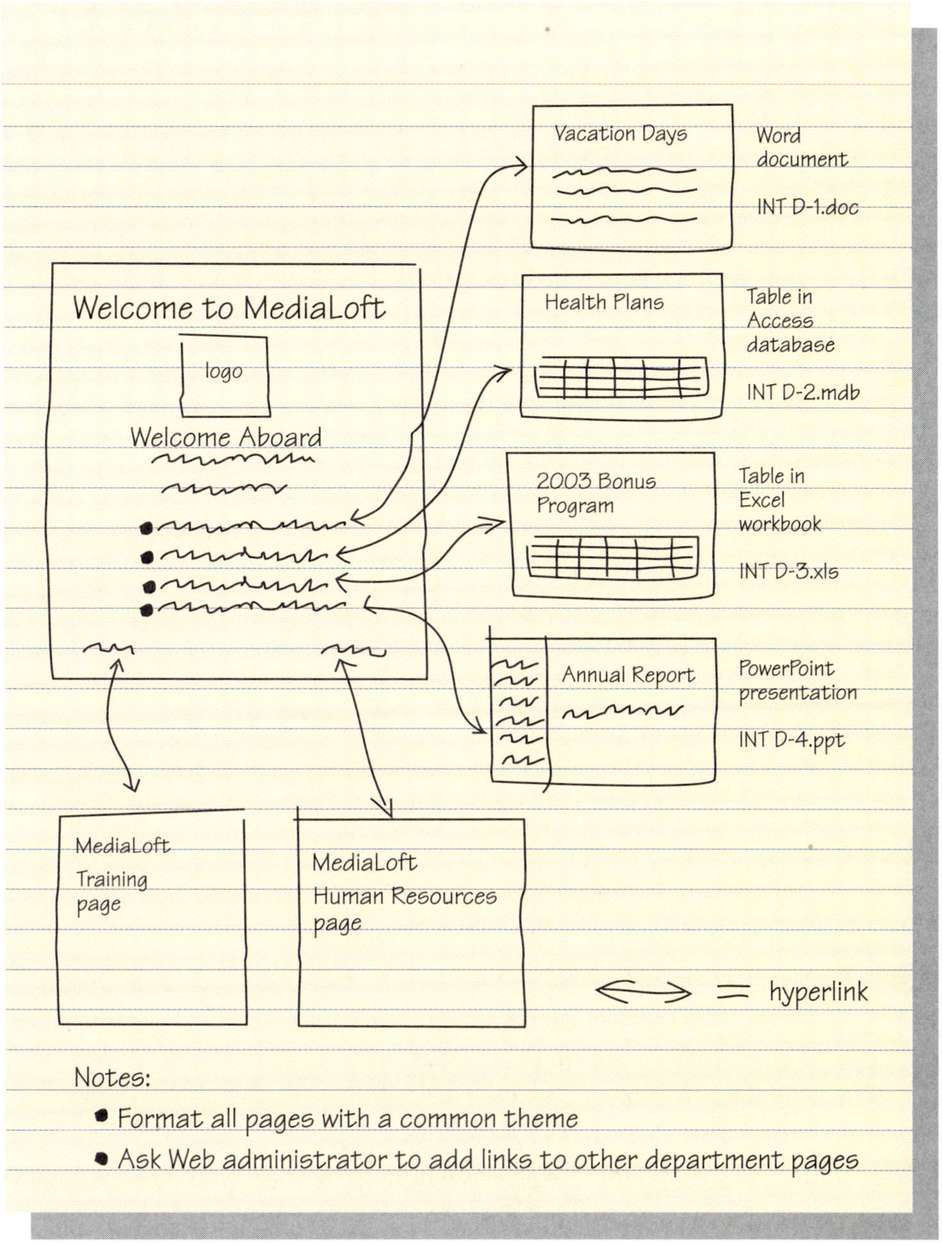

Naming Web Pages

Determining the filenaming conventions and the folder structure you will use for your Web pages is an important aspect of planning a Web publication. Different operating systems place different restrictions on filenames, so it's important to find out what operating system your Web server uses and name your files accordingly. It's safest to name Web pages using the standard eight-dot-three naming convention, which specifies that a filename have a maximum of eight letters followed by a period and three-letter file extension – mypage.htm or chap_1.htm, for example. Therefore, if you intend to publish to the Web, filenames should use all lowercase letters and include no special characters or blank spaces. Valid characters include letters, numbers, and the underscore character. It's also advisable to create a system for naming the Web pages in a large Web publication so that you can easily locate and organize the files.

INTEGRATING OFFICE APPLICATIONS WITH INTERNET EXPLORER

Creating a Web Page

To create a Web page, you must create a document that uses HTML formatting. HTML places codes, called **tags**, around the elements of a Web page to describe how each element should appear when viewed using a browser. When you create an HTML document in Word, Word automatically inserts the HTML tags for you. A quick way to create a Web page in Word is to start with a Web page template. Word includes templates for many standard types of Web pages, such as a table of contents page or a frequently asked questions (FAQ) page. ✒ Karen uses a Web page template in Word to create the basic structure of the home page, the MediaLoft Welcome page. When completed, the Welcome page will include links to the other Web pages.

Trouble?
If the New Document task pane is not open, click File on the menu bar, then click New.

1. **Start Word**, click the **General Templates hyperlink** in the New Document task pane, then click the **Web Pages tab** in the Templates dialog box
   The Web Pages tab of the Templates dialog box, shown in Figure D-2, includes templates for creating different types and styles of Web pages. It also includes the Web Page Wizard.

2. Click the **Simple Layout icon**, verify that the **Create New Document option button** is selected, then click **OK**
   A new Web page document based on the Simple Layout template opens in the document window in Web Layout view. Web Layout view displays a document as it would look when viewed in a Web browser. The text is placeholder text that you will replace with your own information.

3. Click **Format** on the menu bar, then click **Theme**
   The Theme dialog box opens and displays a list of themes. A **theme** is a predesigned set of formats that you can apply to Web pages to give them a consistent look.

Trouble?
Choose a different theme if Willow is not available to you.

4. Scroll to the bottom of the Choose a Theme list box, click **Willow,** examine the preview that appears in the Sample of theme Willow box, then click **OK**
   The Willow theme is applied to the Web page.

QuickTip
If you want your name on the printed solution, add it to the page title when you save the Web pages.

5. Click the **Save button** 🖫 on the Standard toolbar, click **Change Title** in the Save As dialog box, type **Welcome to MediaLoft** in the Set Page Title dialog box, then click **OK**
   The page title appears in the title bar when the Web page is viewed with a browser, so it's important to assign a page title that not only describes the Web page but that you would want visitors to see.

Trouble?
The file extension might not appear in your title bar; Windows can be set to display or not display file extensions.

6. Drag to select **Simple Web Page.htm** in the File name text box, type **Welcome**, make sure the drive and folder where your Project Files are stored is displayed in the Save in list box, then click **Save**
   The document file is saved as a Web page in HTML format. The filename Welcome.htm appears in the title bar when the document is viewed in Word. Word automatically created a folder named Welcome_files in the same location as the HTML file to contain all the files used in the Web page, such as the files for the graphics, background, bullets, and other Web page elements.

7. Select **Main Heading Goes Here**, type **Welcome to MediaLoft**, select **Section 1 Heading Goes Here,** type **Welcome Aboard**, replace the next paragraph with the paragraph shown in Figure D-3, press **[Enter]** twice, then type the four-line list shown in Figure D-3
   Later you will format each item in the list as a hyperlink to another Web page.

8. Press **[Enter]** twice, type **MediaLoft Training page**, press **[Enter]**, then type **MediaLoft Human Resources page**
   Later you will format these items to create hyperlinks to the Training page and to the Human Resources page.

9. Use the pointer to select the remaining placeholder text, press **[Delete]**, then click

▶ INTEGRATION D-4   **INTEGRATING OFFICE APPLICATIONS WITH INTERNET EXPLORER**

FIGURE D-2: Web Pages tab in Templates dialog box

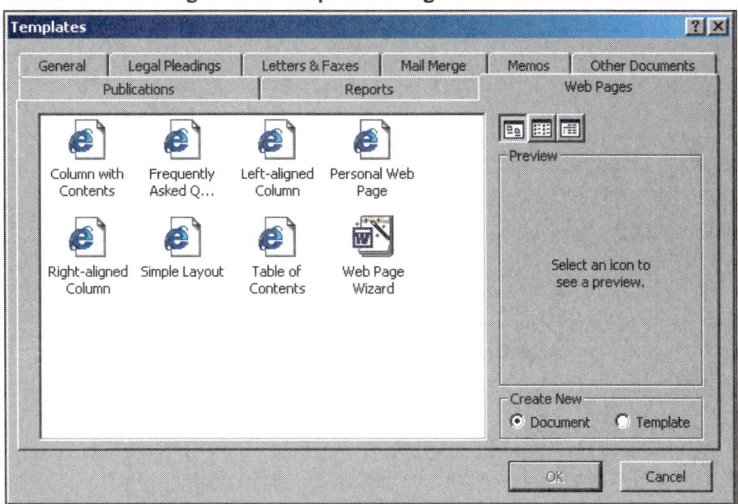

FIGURE D-3: Text entered for the Welcome page

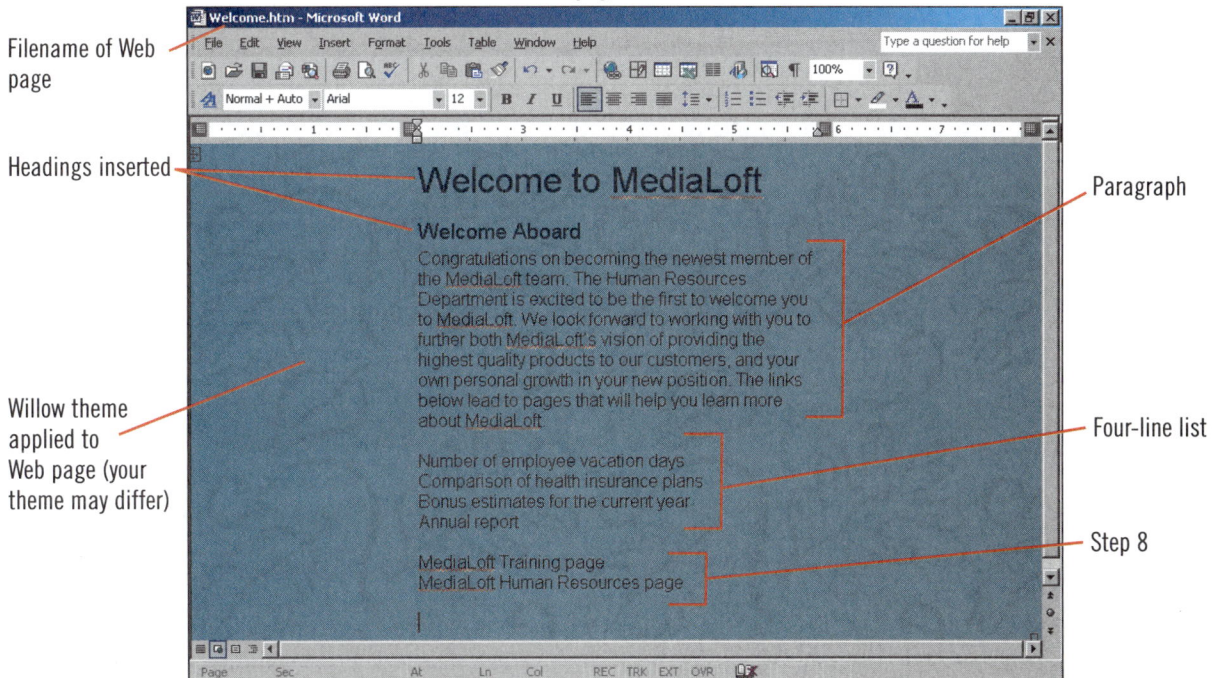

- Filename of Web page
- Headings inserted
- Willow theme applied to Web page (your theme may differ)
- Paragraph
- Four-line list
- Step 8

Clues to Use

Choosing Web page content and style

Examining the style, layout, and content of other Web pages can inspire new ideas about how to present information in your own Web publications. A well-designed Web page is not only readable and eye-catching, but communicates a visual message that complements the purpose of the Web publication. By viewing a wide variety of Web pages, you will develop a sense of what kinds of styles, formats, and elements help to communicate messages effectively. When creating a Web publication, keep in mind that the design and tone of your Web pages express your personality or the character of your company to the world.

INTEGRATING OFFICE APPLICATIONS WITH INTERNET EXPLORER

Formatting a Web Page

When you format an HTML document in Word, you use the same tools you use to format print documents. For example, when you apply bold to text by using the Bold button on the Formatting toolbar, Word automatically inserts the HTML tags necessary for the Web browser to interpret and then display the text as bold. Karen uses Word's formatting tools to enhance the appearance of her Web page. She also inserts the MediaLoft logo in the Web page.

Steps

1. Select the heading **Welcome to MediaLoft**, click the **Bold button** on the Formatting toolbar, then click the **Center button** on the Formatting toolbar

    The heading text becomes darker and thicker and is centered between the left and right margins of the page. Although you cannot see the HTML tags for bolding and centering the text, Word added them automatically to the file.

2. Select the heading **Welcome Aboard**, click the **Style list arrow** on the Formatting toolbar, then click **Heading 2**

    The heading is formatted in the Heading 2 style. A **style** is a set of formats, such as font, font size, and paragraph alignment, that are named and stored together. Each theme includes styles that you can apply to text to format it quickly and easily.

    > **QuickTip**
    > The styles shown on the Style list are the HTML-compatible styles included in the theme.

3. Select the four-line list that begins with Number of employee, click the **Bullets button** on the Formatting toolbar, then deselect the text

    The four lines change to a bulleted list using the bullet style included in the theme. See Figure D-4.

4. Place the insertion point at the beginning of the heading **Welcome Aboard**, press **[Enter]**, then place the insertion point in the blank line between the headings

    The new blank line will be the location for the MediaLoft logo.

5. Click **Insert** on the menu bar, point to **Picture**, then click **From File**

    The Insert Picture dialog box opens.

6. Navigate to the location where your Project Files are stored, select **MLoft.jpg**, then click **Insert**

    The MediaLoft logo is inserted between the two headings.

7. Select the logo, click, then deselect the logo

    The logo is centered. Web Layout view displays a document as it will look when viewed in a browser, but you can confirm the appearance of a Web page by opening it in Internet Explorer.

    > **Trouble?**
    > If the Picture toolbar opens when you select the graphic, close the toolbar.

8. Click **File** on the menu bar, click **Web Page Preview**, then maximize the Internet Explorer window if necessary

    The Welcome to MediaLoft Web page opens in the Internet Explorer window, as shown in Figure D-5.

9. Close Internet Explorer, save the changes to the document, then close the document

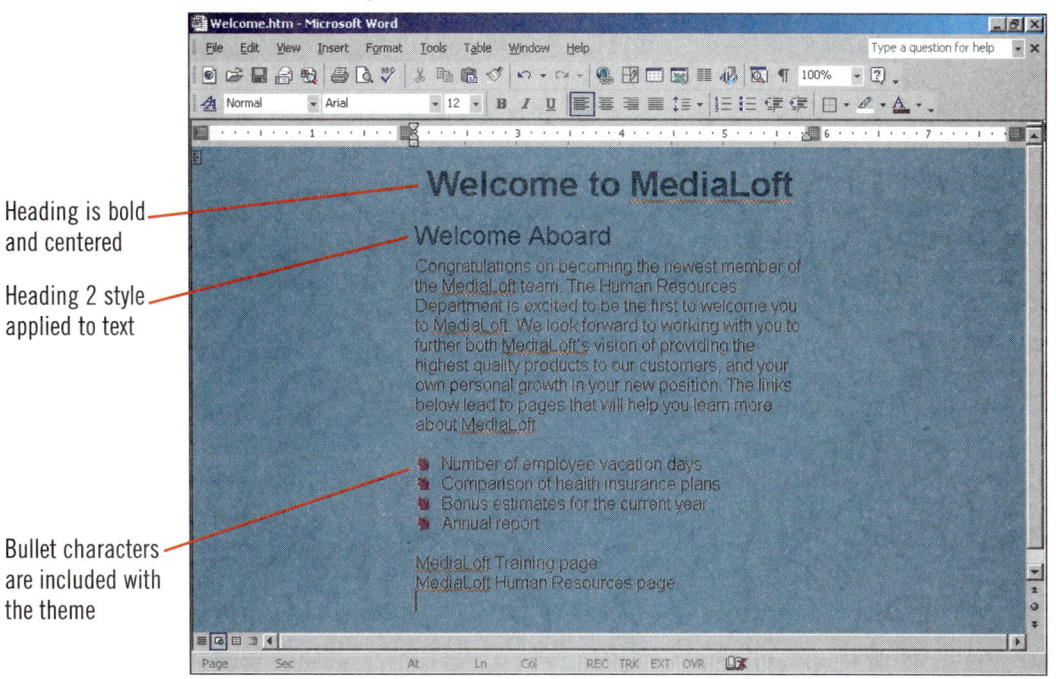

FIGURE D-4: Headings and list formatted

Heading is bold and centered

Heading 2 style applied to text

Bullet characters are included with the theme

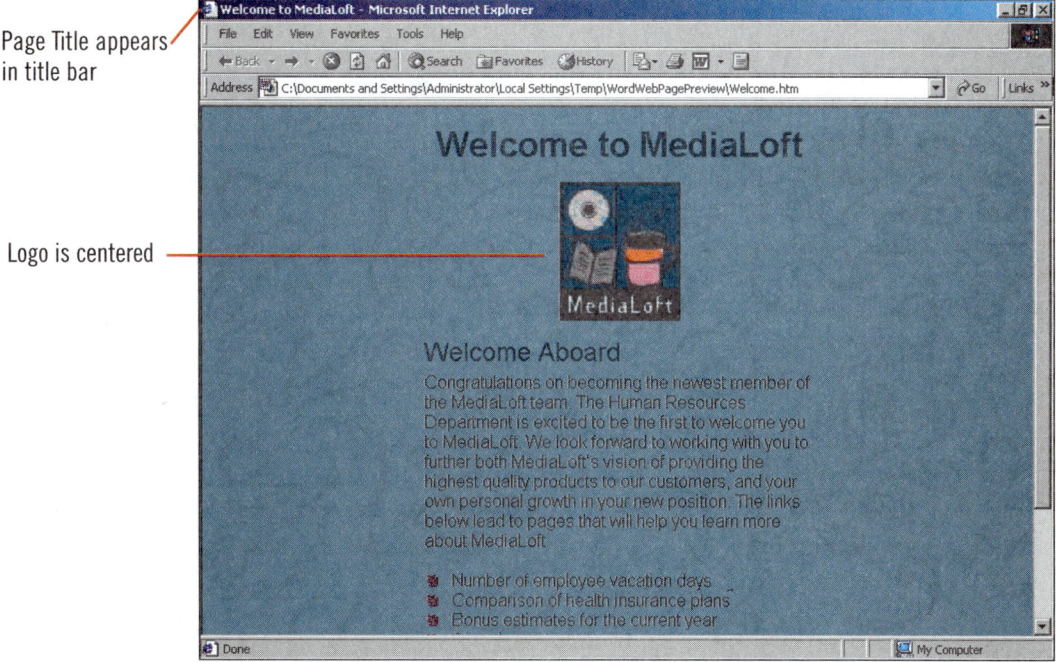

FIGURE D-5: Completed Welcome page in Internet Explorer

Page Title appears in title bar

Logo is centered

Creating a Web Page from a Word Document

By saving a file in HTML format, you can easily create Web pages from existing Office files. Saving a file as HTML converts the file from the Office format to HTML to make it available on the Web or an intranet. After you convert an Office file to HTML, you can format it using Word. As noted in her original sketch, Karen plans to create Web pages using several existing Office documents. She starts by creating a Web page about company vacation days from a Word document file.

Steps

Trouble?
If the file INT D-1.doc does not appear your list of Project Files in the Open dialog box, change the Files of type list box to display "All Files" or "All Word Documents".

1. In Word, open **INT D-1.doc** from the drive and folder where your Project Files are stored
   The document, which contains a description of MediaLoft's policy on vacation days for employees, opens in Normal view.

2. Click **File** on the menu bar, then click **Save as Web Page**
   The Save As dialog box opens. Notice that the Save as type is Web page (*.htm;*.html). In order to save a file as a Web page, you need to specify a page title and filename.

3. Click **Change Title**, type **Vacation Days** in the Set Page Title dialog box, click **OK**, type **Vacation** in the File name text box, make sure the drive or folder where your Project Files are located is displayed in the Save in list box, then click **Save**
   Word saves a copy of the document in HTML format and switches to Web Layout view. The filename in the titlebar is Vacation.htm.

4. Select the heading **Vacation Days**, click the **Style list arrow** on the Formatting toolbar, click **Heading 1**, then click the **Center button** on the Formatting toolbar

5. Press **[Ctrl][End]** to move the insertion point to the end of the document, press **[Enter]**, then type **Return to Welcome page**
   You will later format "Return to Welcome page" as a hyperlink.

6. Select the five-line list that begins with After completing, click the **Bullets button** on the Formatting toolbar, then deselect the text
   The list is formatted as a bulleted list. Your Vacation Days Web page should match Figure D-6.

7. Click **Format** on the menu bar, click **Theme**, click **Willow** (or the theme you selected in the previous lesson) in the Choose a Theme list box, then click **OK**
   The Willow theme is applied to the Web page, as shown in Figure D-7. The completed Vacation Days Web page now matches the appearance of the Welcome page you created.

8. Save the changes to the document, click **File** on the menu bar, click **Web Page Preview**, then examine the Web page in Internet Explorer

9. Close Internet Explorer, then close the document

FIGURE D-6: Vacation Days Web page

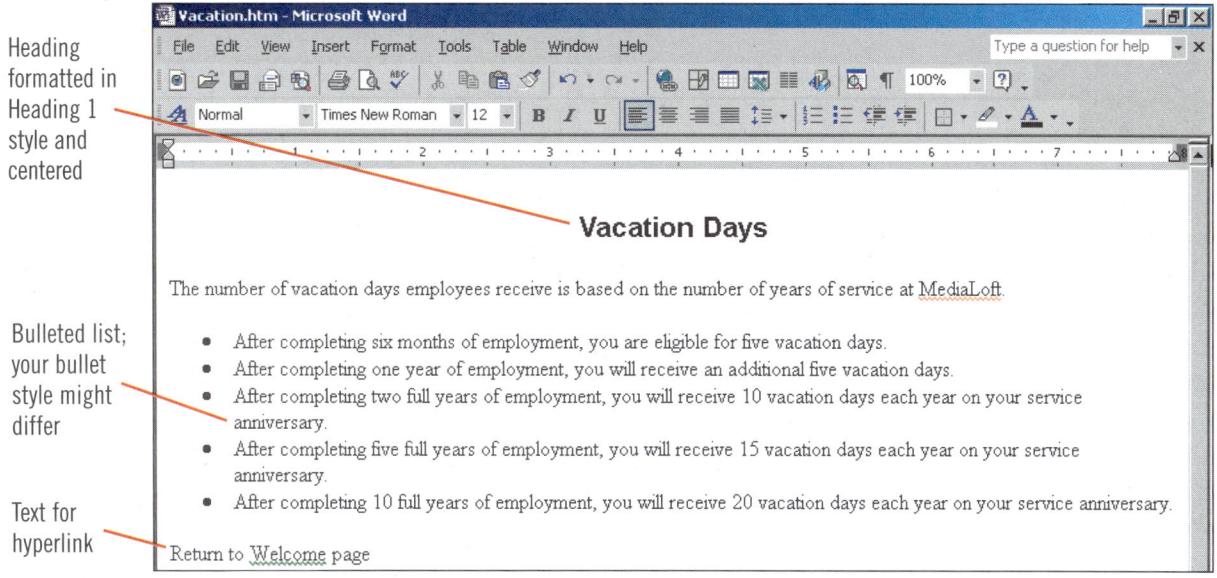

FIGURE D-7: Completed Vacation Days Web page

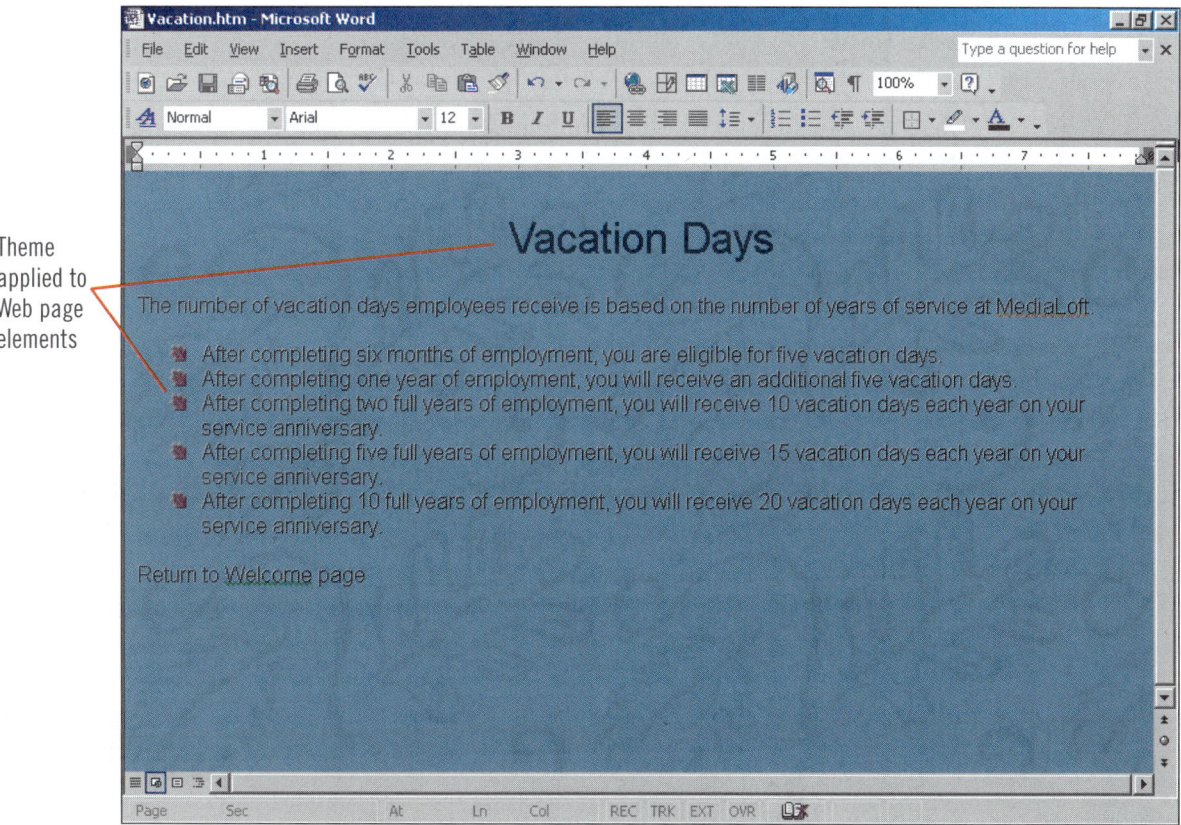

Creating a Web Page from an Access Table

Like Word, Access allows you to save data as Web pages. You can create static HTML documents from table, form, and query datasheets, as well as from reports. When you save data as a static HTML document, the resulting Web page reflects the data at the time the document was saved; subsequent updates to the data are not reflected in the HTML document. Once you save data in HTML format, you can format the file using Word. Karen wants to create a Web page that contains a table comparing the health insurance plans available to MediaLoft employees. This information is stored in an Access database table. She exports the table to HTML and then formats it using Word.

1. Start Access, click the **More files** link in the New File task pane, open **INT D-2.mdb** from the drive and folder where your Project Files are stored, click **Tables** on the Objects bar in the INT D-2 database window, click the **Open button** on the Database Window toolbar, review the datasheet, then close the datasheet
   The Health Plans table is selected automatically in the INT D-2 database window.

2. Click **File** on the menu bar, then click **Export**
   The Export Table 'Health Plans' To dialog box opens, as shown in Figure D-8. You have the option of exporting the data only, or you can export the data and the table format to HTML.

3. Click the **Save as type list arrow**, click **HTML Documents (*.html;*.htm)**, click the **Save formatted check box**, then click **Export**
   The HTML Output Options dialog box opens.

4. Remove the check mark from the **Select a HTML Template check box** if necessary, then click **OK**
   After a few moments, although there are no apparent changes on the screen, the table is exported.

Trouble?
If a message box opens asking if you want to make Word your default Web page editor, click No.

5. Exit Access, then open the file **Health Plans.html** in Word
   The table opens in Word in Web Layout view.

6. Click **Format** on the menu bar, click **Theme**, click **Willow** (or the theme you selected in the previous lessons) in the Choose a Theme list box, then click **OK**
   The theme is applied to the Health Plans Web page.

7. Press **[Ctrl][End]** to move the insertion point to the bottom of the table, press **[Enter]**, then type **Return to Welcome page**
   Later you will format this text as a hyperlink.

8. Select the table heading **Health Plans**, click the **Style list arrow** on the Formatting toolbar, scroll down, click **Table Theme**, click the **Style list arrow**, click **Heading 1**, click the **Center button** on the Formatting toolbar, then deselect the text
   The table is formatted with the table format settings included with the theme. Also, the table heading is formatted in the Heading 1 style and centered in the table. The Web page appears as shown in Figure D-9.

9. Save your changes to the document, click **File** on the menu bar, then click **Web Page Preview**
   The Web page opens in Internet Explorer, as shown in Figure D-10.

10. Close Internet Explorer, then close the document

INTEGRATING OFFICE APPLICATIONS WITH INTERNET EXPLORER

FIGURE D-8: Export Table 'Health Plans' to dialog box

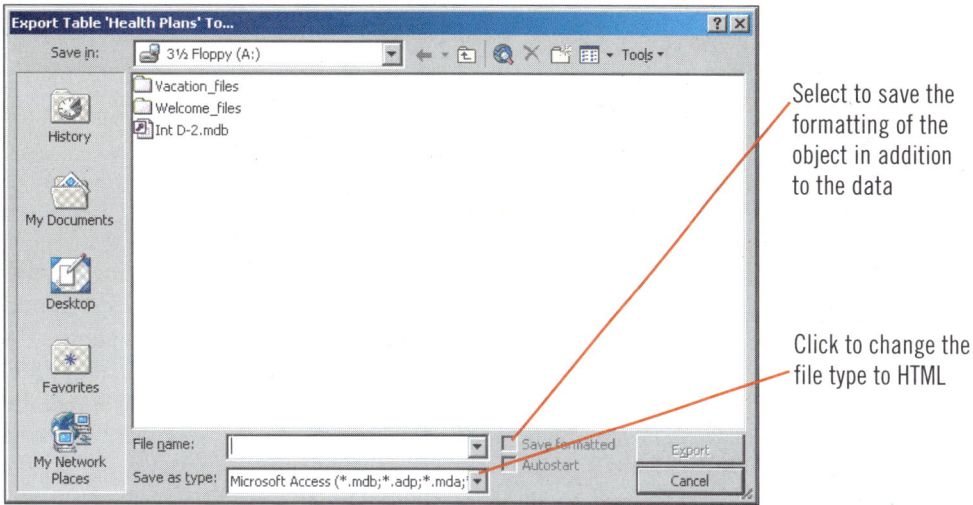

Select to save the formatting of the object in addition to the data

Click to change the file type to HTML

FIGURE D-9: Completed Health Plans Web page in Word

Table from Access database formatted in the Willow theme

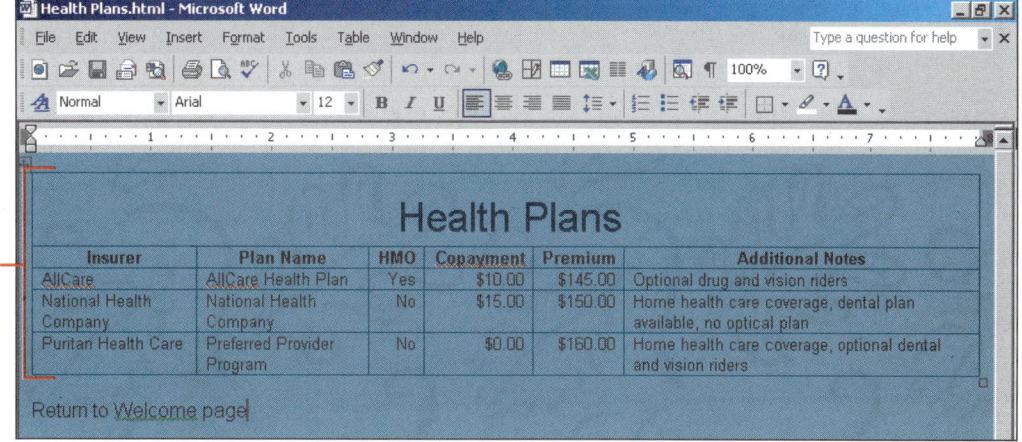

FIGURE D-10: Health Plans Web page in Internet Explorer

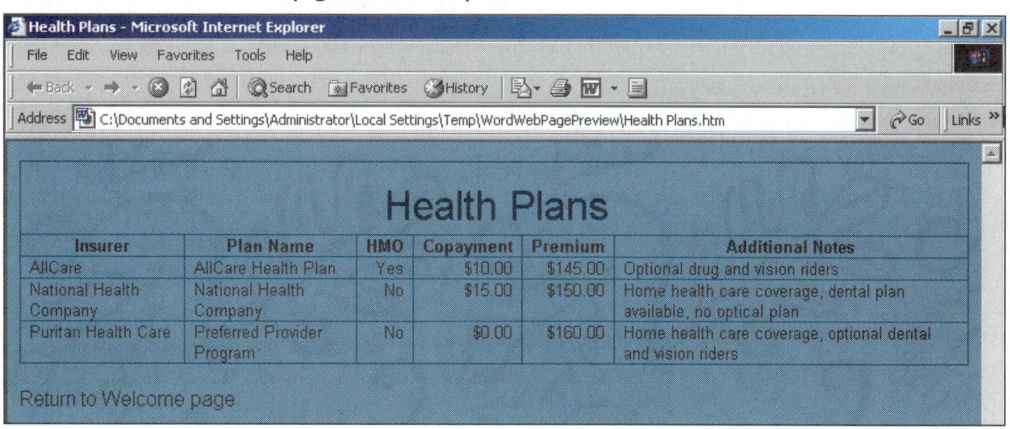

Using Access to create static and dynamic Web pages

You can convert Access objects to static or dynamic Web pages. A static HTML page contains only the information contained in the database at the time you converted the object to a Web page. A Data Access page, on the other hand, is dynamically linked to the database file so that changes to the data are reflected in the Web page and changes made to the data through the Web page are reflected in the underlying table.

INTEGRATING OFFICE APPLICATIONS WITH INTERNET EXPLORER

Creating a Web Page from an Excel Workbook

Like Word and Access, you can create Web pages using existing Excel files. Excel lets you specify worksheet ranges to use as sources for Web pages, instead of having to include all of the worksheets or cells in a workbook. Karen wants to add another Web page to the Welcome publication. Titled "2003 Bonus Program", this page will highlight MediaLoft's bonus program and show the estimated bonus percentages for employees by quarter and by department. Karen creates this page from an existing Excel workbook.

Steps

QuickTip
If you want users to be able to enter and calculate data on the Web page, you can click the Add Interactivity check box.

1. Start Excel, open the Project File **INT D-3.xls**, click and drag to select the range **A1:G7**, click **File** on the menu bar, then click **Save as Web Page**
   The Save As dialog box opens. You use this dialog box in Excel to specify the page title and filename for the Web page.

2. Select the **Selection: $A$1:$G$7 option button**, click **Change Title**, type **2003 Bonus Program Estimates** in the Set Page Title dialog box, then click **OK**
   The title will appear as the page title in the browser title bar and as a heading centered over the table in the Web page.

3. Type **Bonus** in the File name text box, click **Save**, then exit Excel without saving changes to the file INT D-3.xls

Trouble?
If you do not see the Bonus.htm file in the folder with your Project Files, click the Files of type list arrow, then click All Files. If the file opens in Excel, exit Excel, then repeat Step 4. Make sure you use the Open in Microsoft Word option to open the file correctly.

4. In Word, click the **Open button** on the Standard toolbar, click **Bonus.htm** in the Open dialog box, click the **Open button list arrow**, then click **Open in Microsoft Word**
   The 2003 Bonus Program Web page opens in Word, as shown in Figure D-11. The page title you created is added as a heading centered above the table.

5. Press **[Ctrl][End]**, press **[Enter]**, type **Return to Welcome page**, click **Format** on the menu bar, click **Theme**, click **Willow** (or the theme you chose in the previous lessons) in the Choose a Theme list box, then click **OK**
   The theme is applied to the document.

6. Place the insertion point in the first row of the table, which contains the heading 2003 Bonus Program, click **Table** on the menu bar, point to **Delete**, then click **Rows**
   The first row of the table is deleted.

7. Place the insertion point in the table, click **Table** on the menu bar, point to **AutoFit**, then click **AutoFit to Window**
   The width of the table columns is adjusted so that the table fills the document window.

8. Select the heading **2003 Bonus Program Estimates**, click the **Style list arrow** on the Formatting toolbar, click **Heading 1**, click the **Center button** on the Formatting toolbar, then deselect the text
   Now the table and the Web page are formatted with the same theme and font styles as the other Web pages you are creating for the MediaLoft intranet, as shown in Figure D-12.

9. Save your changes to the document, click **Yes** to overwrite the file, click **File** on the menu bar, then click **Web Page Preview**
   The Web page opens in Internet Explorer, as shown in Figure D-13.

10. Close Internet Explorer, then close the document

FIGURE D-11: 2003 Bonus Program Estimates Web page in Word

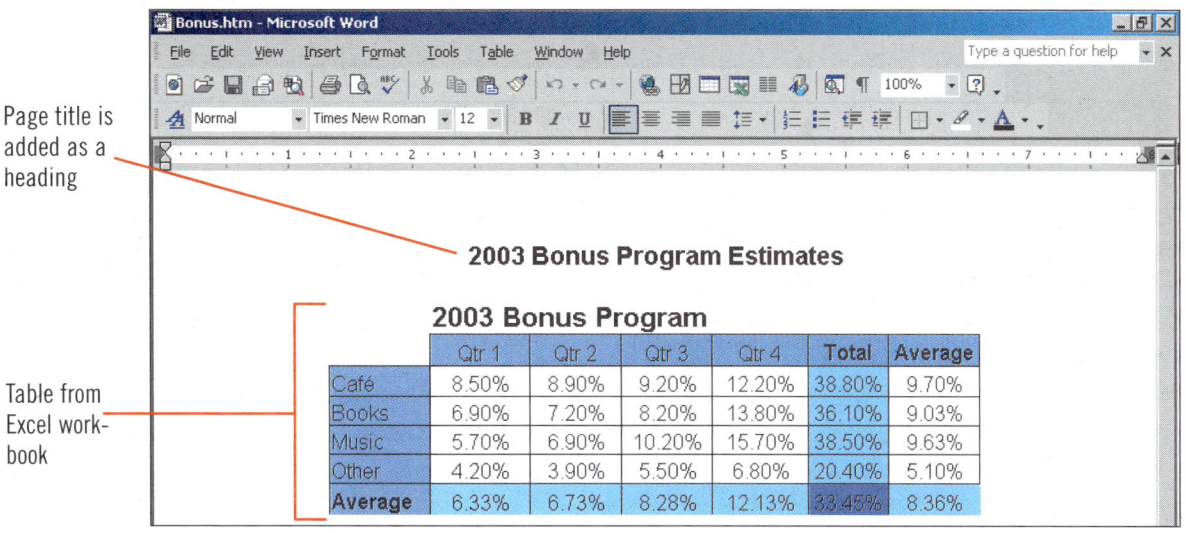

Page title is added as a heading

Table from Excel workbook

FIGURE D-12: Completed 2003 Bonus Program Estimates Web page

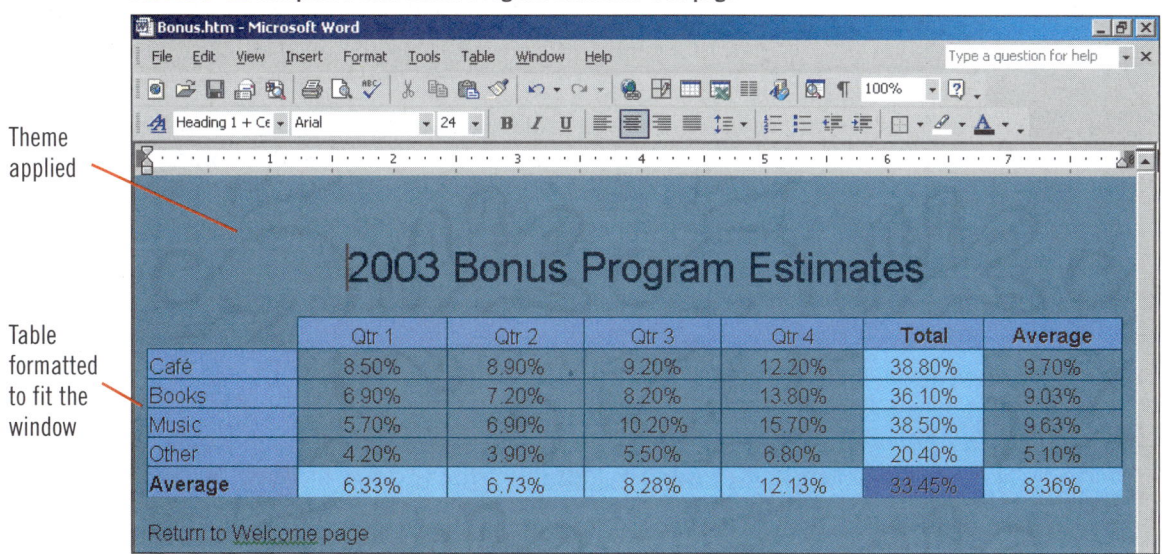

Theme applied

Table formatted to fit the window

FIGURE D-13: 2003 Bonus Programs Web page in Internet Explorer

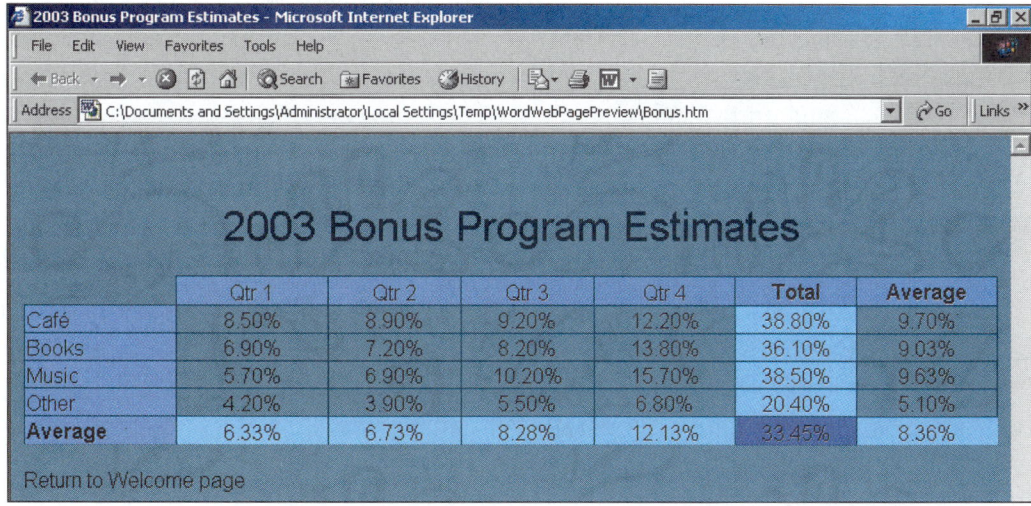

INTEGRATING OFFICE APPLICATIONS WITH INTERNET EXPLORER

Creating Web Pages from a PowerPoint Presentation

PowerPoint presentations contain multiple screens of information, called slides. When you convert a PowerPoint presentation to HTML format, PowerPoint creates a separate Web page for each slide and groups the pages in a folder. This differs from the other Office files where only one HTML file is created for each file or Access object converted. When viewing your presentation with a browser, the audience can navigate through the Web pages much as they would navigate through the slides in PowerPoint. Karen converts a PowerPoint presentation from the company's annual report to HTML format. She then formats a hyperlink back to the home page.

Trouble?
Click or press any key to view the next slide.

1. Start PowerPoint, open the Project File **INT D-4.ppt**, click **Slide Show** on the menu bar, click **View Show**, then view the entire presentation
   The presentation's six slides outline the company's accomplishments and goals.

QuickTip
If you want your name on the printed solution, add it to the page title.

2. Click **File** on the menu bar, click **Save as Web Page**, click **Change Title** in the Save As dialog box, type **Annual Report** in the Set Page Title dialog box, click **OK**, type **AR Presentation** in the File name text box, then click **Save**
   PowerPoint exports the presentation to HTML format. It may take several minutes to save the file. Because PowerPoint creates a group of associated Web pages when you save a presentation as HTML, you could consider the Web pages based on this presentation as a publication within your publication.

3. Click **File** on the menu bar, then click **Web Page Preview**
   The presentation opens in Internet Explorer, as shown in Figure D-14. The title of each slide in the presentation appears in the left frame of the browser window. When you point to a title, the pointer changes to the hyperlink pointer and the title is highlighted. You can click a title in the left frame to open that Web page, or you can click the Previous Slide and Next Slide buttons at the bottom of the browser window to view the slides.

4. Click the **PowerPoint program button** on the taskbar to switch to PowerPoint, display **slide 1**, place the insertion point after **2002** on the title slide, press **[Enter]** twice, click the **Decrease Font Size button** on the Formatting toolbar three times, then type **Return to Welcome page**
   You want this text to be a hyperlink to the Welcome page. Because the PowerPoint Web publication is a group of pages instead of a single page, you must use PowerPoint to create the actual link, whereas in other Office files you can create all your links in Word.

5. Select **Return to Welcome page**, then click the **Insert Hyperlink button** on the Standard toolbar
   The Insert Hyperlink dialog box opens. You use the Insert Hyperlink dialog box to select the Web page, document, or e-mail address to which you want to link the selected text.

6. Select the **Welcome.htm** file, then click **OK**
   The hyperlink to the Welcome file is created. You will test the link in the next lesson.

7. Save your changes to the presentation, click **File** on the menu bar, then click **Web Page Preview**
   Internet Explorer displays the first slide from the presentation, as shown in Figure D-15.

8. View the entire presentation in Internet Explorer, close Internet Explorer, then exit PowerPoint

FIGURE D-14: Annual Report presentation in Internet Explorer

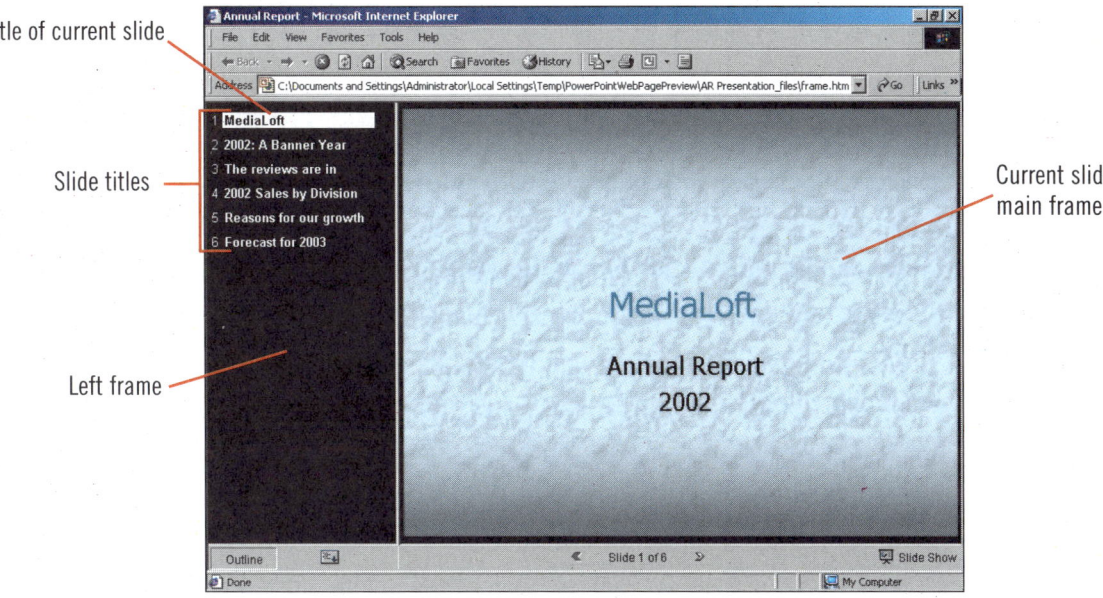

- Title of current slide
- Slide titles
- Left frame
- Current slide in main frame

FIGURE D-15: Title slide with hyperlink added

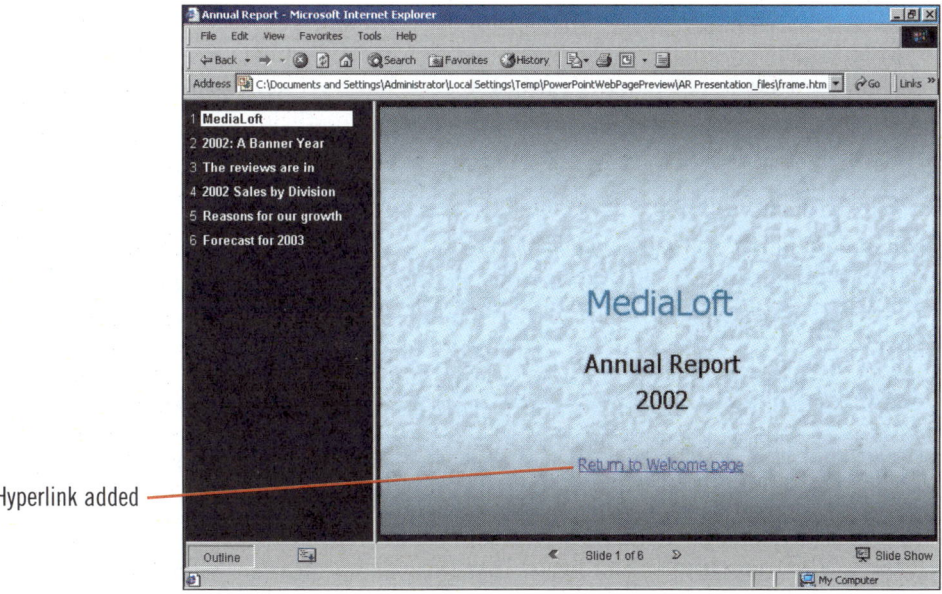

- Hyperlink added

Using frames

Frames help users to navigate a group of associated Web pages. It is most useful to organize a Web page using frames when you want common navigation elements for all the Web pages in a publication. Although frames are convenient, you have to consider that some older Web browsers may not support them. A popular way to address this problem is to create two versions of a publication—one with frames and one without—and to offer a choice between the two on the publication's home page. If time or resources limit you to one version, then base your decision on your audience's capabilities. For example, if you create a page for a company intranet and know that every computer has the latest version of a browser installed, adding frames to your publication makes sense. However, if you create a page for a Web publication and want the largest possible audience, using frames excludes some users from viewing your publication.

Adding Hyperlinks

After you create the Web pages for your publication, you need to add hyperlinks both between pages of the publication and from the publication to other Web pages so that your audience can easily navigate the Web site. Karen's sketch shows links from the Welcome page to each of the other Web pages in the publication. It also shows a link back to the Welcome page from each associated page. She begins by adding hyperlinks to the Welcome page.

1. In Word, open the Project File **Welcome.htm**, then scroll down until the bulleted list is visible in the document window

2. Select **Number of employee vacation days**, but not the bullet character, then click the **Insert Hyperlink button** on the Standard toolbar
   The Insert Hyperlink dialog box opens, as shown in Figure D-16.

3. Select **Vacation.htm**, then click **OK**
   The text for the first bullet is formatted as a hyperlink—underlined and formatted in the hyperlink font style used by the theme. The hyperlink you created is a **relative link**, or a link that gives another page's address in relation to the current page. Creating relative links allows you to publish the pages to the Web or an intranet in their current directory structure and have the links remain accurate.

   > **QuickTip**
   > Use **absolute links**, which contain a fixed address, when you don't want the addresses of your links to change at all.

4. Move the mouse pointer over the **Number of employee vacation days** hyperlink
   A ScreenTip appears above the hyperlink, as shown in Figure D-17. By default the ScreenTip shows the path and filename of the linked page, but you can customize the ScreenTip text by clicking the ScreenTip button in the Insert Hyperlink dialog box or in the Edit Hyperlink dialog box.

   > **QuickTip**
   > To edit a hyperlink, right-click it, then click Edit Hyperlink on the shortcut menu. To remove a hyperlink, right-click it, then click Remove Hyperlink.

5. Repeat Steps 2 through 4 to create and verify the relative links for the three remaining lines of bulleted text—link the second bullet to the **Health Plans.html** file, link the third bullet to the **Bonus.htm** file, link the fourth bullet to the **AR Presentation.htm** file—then save the **Welcome.htm** file

6. Press **[Ctrl]**, then click the **Number of employee vacation days** hyperlink
   You can follow a hyperlink in Word by pressing [Ctrl] and clicking the hyperlink. The Vacation Days Web page opens in Internet Explorer.

7. Click the **Edit with Microsoft Word button** on the Internet Explorer toolbar, select **Return to Welcome page** in the Vacation.htm document that opens in Word, click, select **Welcome.htm** in the Insert Hyperlink dialog box, click **OK**, save, then close the document
   The text is formatted as a hyperlink to the Welcome page.

   > **QuickTip**
   > If you want your name on the printed solution, add it to the bottom of the Web page below the hyperlink.

8. Repeat Steps 6 through 7 to add a hyperlink back to the Welcome page on the Health Plans and Bonus Web pages, then close all open files except for the Welcome file in Word
   You already created the hyperlink to the Welcome page in the Annual Report presentation.

9. Save the **Welcome** file in Word, click **File** on the menu bar, click **Web Page Preview**, then use the hyperlinks in the Web publication to view each Web page in Internet Explorer and return to the Welcome page

10. Click the **Print button** in Internet Explorer to print each Web page, exit Internet Explorer, then exit Word
    You have successfully created and tested the links between the files in your Web publication. Eventually, Karen will add links on the Welcome page to take users to the Training page and the Human Resources page on the MediaLoft intranet site.

INTEGRATING OFFICE APPLICATIONS WITH INTERNET EXPLORER

FIGURE D-16: Insert Hyperlink dialog box

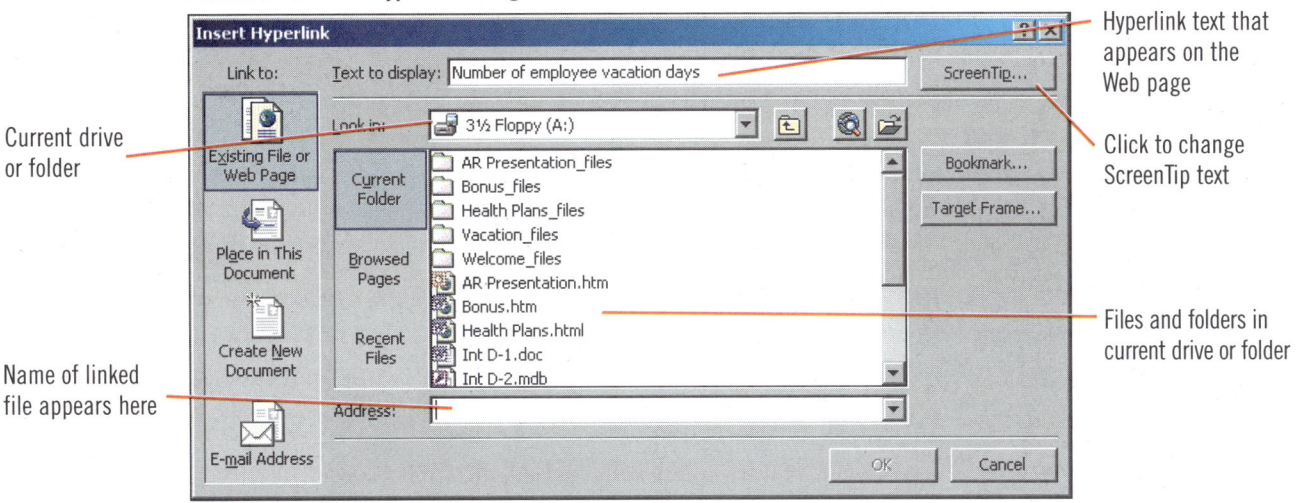

FIGURE D-17: Welcome page with hyperlink added

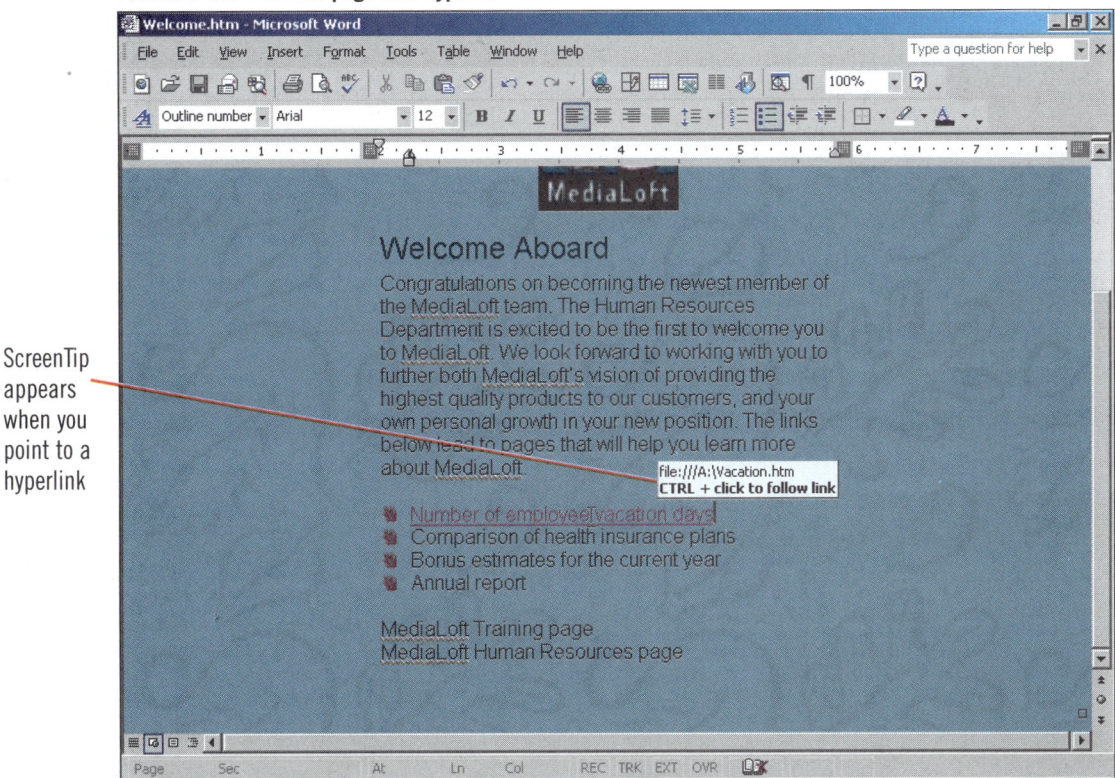

Publishing your Web pages

Your Web publication is not available to anyone outside your local computer network or workgroup until you publish it by placing a copy either on the Web or an on intranet server. Remember, the links you create on your home page are one-way: they help users viewing your page to find other interesting pages, but do not help others locate your page in the first place. Try the following to advertise your Web publication: ask friends and colleagues to create links to your home page on their pages; ask the administrator of your server to add your home page to the index of the site's Web pages; or e-mail information about your publication to groups, organizations, or people with Web sites. To publish effectively on an intranet, send a memo to employees who you think might be interested in your page or ask the network administrator and the owners of other relevant pages to add links to your publication on their pages.

INTEGRATING OFFICE APPLICATIONS WITH INTERNET EXPLORER INTEGRATION D-17

Integration | Practice

▶ Skills Review

1. **Plan a Web publication.**
   a. Using a pencil and a sheet of paper, sketch an outline of a Web publication for the MediaLoft Sales department, including a Sales News home page, a report on the results of a recent customer survey, a table of contact information for sales representatives, a table of recent sales figures, and a presentation from the eastern division. The Web publication will be posted to the MediaLoft intranet site.
   b. Draw arrows on your sketch to indicate the hyperlinks between the pages in the publication.

2. **Create a Web page.**
   a. Start Word, then create a new document using the Table of Contents Web page template.
   b. Save the document as a Web page to the drive and folder where your Project Files are stored. Use the filename **TOC** and the Web page title **Sales News home page**.
   c. Apply the Blends theme to the Web page. If Blends is not available to you, select a different theme.
   d. Replace the template text with the text shown in Figure D-18, then delete the remaining placeholder text.
   e. Save the changes.

FIGURE D-18

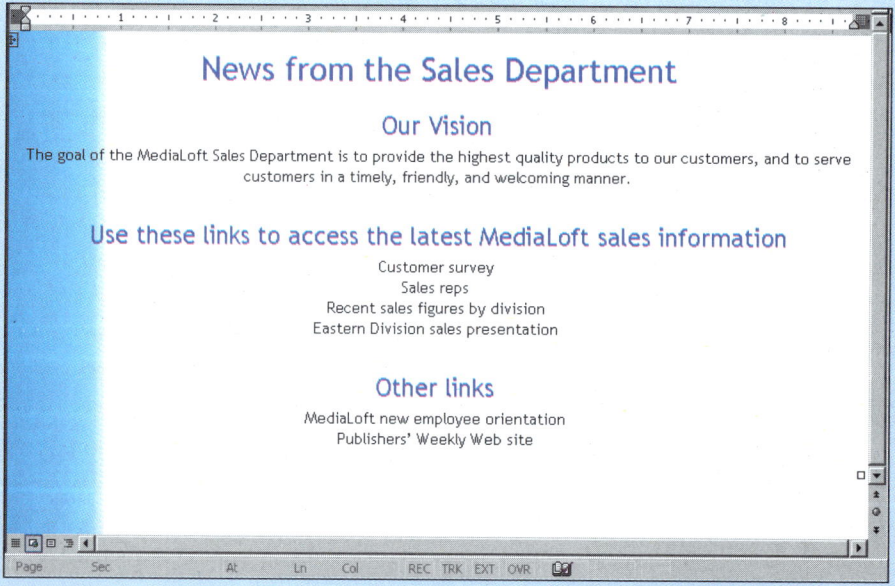

3. **Format a Web page.**
   a. Apply the Heading 3 style to the Our Vision, Use these links…, and Other links headings.
   b. Apply the Normal style to the vision statement.
   c. Apply the Normal style to the links listed under the Use these links…, and Other links headings.
   d. Format the links as a bulleted list.
   e. Insert a blank line above the Our Vision heading.
   f. Insert the Project File MLoft.jpg on the blank line you created. The file is a graphic file of the MediaLoft logo.
   g. Center the logo.
   h. Save the changes, preview the Web page in Internet Explorer, close Internet Explorer, then close the TOC file.

Practice

4. **Create a Web page from a Word document.**
   a. Open the Project File INT D-5.doc in Word.
   b. Save the file as a Web page with the page title **Customer Survey** and the filename **Survey**.
   c. Apply the Blends theme to the page.
   d. Apply the Heading 1 style to the heading **MediaLoft 2003 Customer Survey**, then center the heading.
   e. Apply the Heading 3 style to the heading **Customer Profile**.
   f. Format the five-line list that begins with percentages under the Customer Profile paragraph as a bulleted list.
   g. Apply the Heading 3 style to the headings Purchasing Habits, Preferred Genres, and Customer Satisfaction.
   h. Select the chart and center it.
   i. Press [Ctrl][End], press [Enter] twice, then type **Return to Sales News home page** at the bottom of the Web page.
   j. Save the changes, preview the Web page in Internet Explorer, close Internet Explorer, then close the Survey file.

5. **Create a Web page from an Access table.**
   a. Start Access, then open the Project File INT D-6.mdb in Access.
   b. Open the Sales Reps Table datasheet, review the records, then close the datasheet.
   c. Export the Sales Rep table as a formatted HTML document. Use the filename **Sales Reps**.
   d. Exit Access, then open the Sales Reps file in Word.
   e. Apply the Blends theme to the page.
   f. Use the Style list arrow to apply the Table Theme style to the table.
   g. AutoFit the table to fit the window. (*Hint*: Click in the table, click Table on the menu bar, point to AutoFit, then click AutoFit to Window.)
   h. Apply the Heading 1 style to the table heading Sales Reps, then center the heading.
   i. Press [Ctrl][End], press [Enter], then type **Return to Sales News home page** at the bottom of the Web page.
   j. Save the changes, preview the Web page in Internet Explorer, close Internet Explorer, then close the Survey file.

6. **Create a Web page from an Excel workbook.**
   a. Start Excel, then open the Project File INT D-7.xls in Excel.
   b. Select the range A1:H6, then save the selected range as a Web page with the filename **Division Sales** and the title **MediaLoft 2003 Monthly Sales by Division**.
   c. Exit Excel without saving changes, then open the Division Sales file in Word.
   d. Delete the first two rows of the table. (*Hint*: Select the rows, right-click, then click Delete Rows.)
   e. Press [Ctrl][End], press [Enter], then type **Return to Sales News home page** at the bottom of the Web page.
   f. Apply the Blends theme to the page.
   g. Apply the Heading 1 style to the heading MediaLoft 2003…, then center the heading.
   h. Save the changes, click Yes to overwrite the file, then preview the Web page in Internet Explorer.
   i. Close Internet Explorer, then close the Division Sales file.

7. **Create Web pages from a PowerPoint presentation.**
   a. Start PowerPoint, open the Project File INT D-8.ppt, then view the presentation.
   b. Place the insertion point after 2003 Fiscal Year on the title slide, press [Enter] twice, use the Decrease Font Size button to reduce the font size to 18 points, then type **Return to Sales News home page**.
   c. Format the text as a hyperlink to the file TOC.htm.
   d. Save the presentation as a Web page with the page title **Eastern Division Report** and the filename **Eastern Presentation**.
   e. Preview the entire presentation in Internet Explorer.
   f. Close Internet Explorer, close the file, then exit PowerPoint.

Integration Practice

8. Add hyperlinks.
   a. In Word, open the file TOC.htm, then scroll to the bottom of the Web page.
   b. Format each item in the bulleted list of links under the Use these links... heading as a hyperlink to the appropriate Web page. Use the Web pages you created in the previous steps. (*Hint*: If you make a mistake and link the wrong file to a hyperlink, right-click the hyperlink, click Remove Hyperlink, then create the hyperlink again.)
   c. Format the text MediaLoft new employee orientation as a hyperlink to the Project File Employee.htm.
   d. Format the text Publishers' Weekly Web site as a hyperlink. To do this, type the URL www.publishersweekly.com in the Address text box in the Insert Hyperlink dialog box.
   e. If you want your name on the printed solution, press [Enter] twice at the bottom of the Web page, then type your name.
   f. Save the changes to the TOC.htm file.
   g. In Word, open each additional Web page you created and format the text Return to Sales News home page as a hyperlink to the file TOC.htm. If you want your name on the printed solution, add it to the bottom of each Web page below the hyperlink. Save your changes, then close each file when you finish.
   h. Return to the TOC.htm file in Word, then preview it in Internet Explorer.
   i. Test each hyperlink in your Web publication in Internet Explorer. Use the Return to Sales News home page hyperlink when appropriate. Click the Back button on the Internet Explorer toolbar to return to the Sales News home page from the New employee orientation page and the Publishers' Weekly Web site. You must be connected to the Internet to view the Publishers' Weekly Web site.
   j. Print each of the Web pages you created using the Print button in Internet Explorer. Print only the first slide of the presentation.
   k. Close all open files then exit all programs.

Independent Challenge 1

You are a volunteer at The Grapevine, an emergency shelter for families in crisis. The Grapevine would like to advertise its programs and services, including requests for donations, on the Internet. At a recent meeting you volunteered to create a Web site for The Grapevine. You'll use existing files for printed material as the basis for most of your Web pages.

   a. Sketch the The Grapevine Web publication. The home page for the publication should include a mission statement, links to other Web pages in the publication, and links to three Internet Web sites devoted to the problem of homelessness. You will create the other Web pages in the publication from existing files: a Word document with information on items sought for donation, an Access table detailing the shelter's programs, an Excel table showing 2003 income and expenses, and a PowerPoint presentation summarizing the shelter's recent activities and immediate goals. Be sure to include the links between the pages in your sketch.
   b. Use your favorite search engine to search the Internet for information on homelessness and programs for the homeless. Use the keyword **homeless** to conduct your search. Write down the page titles and URLs of at least three Web pages you find. You will create hyperlinks from your home page to these Web pages later in this exercise. If your search does not result in links to information on homelessness, try looking at the following Web sites:
   www.hud.gov
   http://nch.ari.net
   www.speakeasy.org/nasna
   c. Start Word and create a home page for The Grapevine using the Simple Layout template and the Sumi Painting theme. (Select a different theme if Sumi Painting is not available to you). Include the text and formatting shown in Figure D-19 on your home page. (*Hint*: Format the main heading in bold and center it.) For the links listed under the For more information... heading, substitute the page titles of the Internet Web pages you found in Step b.

FIGURE D-19

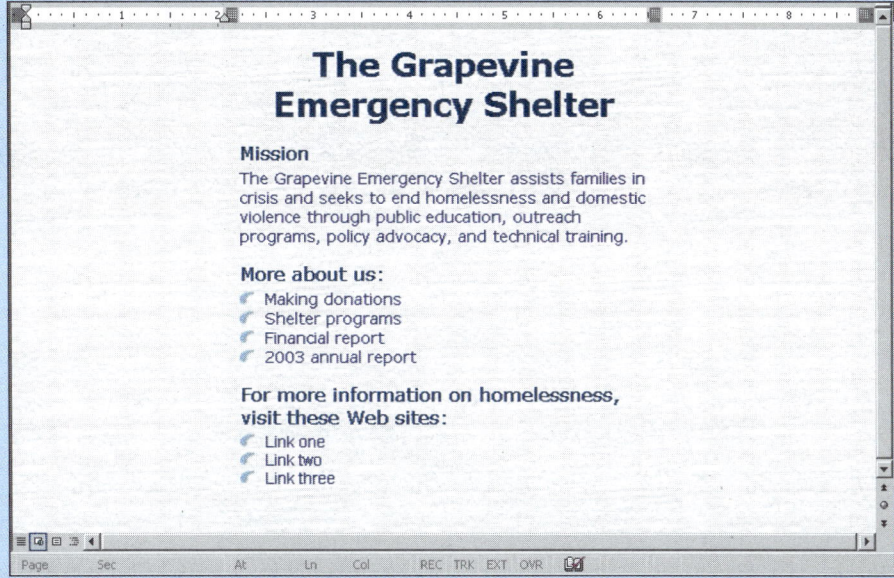

d. Save the Web page with the filename **Grapevine Home** and the page title **The Grapevine Home Page**. (*Hint*: If you want your name on the printed solution, add it to the page title.) Close the Grapevine Home file.

e. Create a Web page from the Project File INT D-9.doc. Save the Web page with the filename **Donations** and the page title **Donations to The Grapevine**. Apply the Sumi Painting theme and format the Web page with styles and bullets.

f. At the bottom of the Web page, insert a hyperlink to the home page file Grapevine Home. Save your changes, preview the Web page in Internet Explorer, make any necessary adjustments to the file in Word, then save and close the file.

g. Start Access and create a formatted HTML document from the Programs table in the Project File INT D-10.mdb. Name the HTML file **Programs**.

h. Exit Access, then open the Programs.html file in Word. Apply the Sumi Painting theme, apply the Table theme style to the table, then autofit the table contents to fit the window. Change the table heading to **Grapevine Programs**, then apply a heading style to the table heading.

i. At the bottom of the Web page, insert a hyperlink back to the home page. Save your changes, preview the Web page in Internet Explorer, make any necessary adjustments to the file in Word, then save and close the file.

j. Start Excel and create a Web page from the range A1:F20 in the Project File INT D-11.xls. Save the Web page with the filename **Financial Report** and page title **Grapevine Financial Report**, then exit Excel without saving changes.

k. Open the Financial Report.htm file in Word. Delete the heading **Grapevine Financial Report**, then apply the Sumi Painting theme. Format the Web page with styles so its look is consistent with the other Web pages and it is easy to read.

l. At the bottom of the Web page, insert a hyperlink back to the home page. Save your changes, clicking Yes to overwrite the file, preview the Web page in Internet Explorer, make any necessary adjustments to the file in Word, then save then close the file.

m. Start PowerPoint and create a Web publication from the Project File INT D-12.ppt. Use the filename **Grapevine Annual Report** and the page title **Grapevine 2003 Annual Report**.

n. At the bottom of the first slide, insert a hyperlink back to the home page. Save your changes, preview the presentation in Internet Explorer, make any necessary adjustments to the file in PowerPoint, save and close the file, then exit PowerPoint.

o. Open the home page file, **Grapevine Home**, in Word. Format the hyperlinks under the More about us heading to link to the to the appropriate Web pages. Format the hyperlinks under the For more information… heading to link the appropriate URLs.

p. Save your changes, then preview the Web publication in Internet Explorer, making sure to test each hyperlink.

Integration | Practice

q. Use the Print button in Internet Explorer to print each Web page you created and the first page of each Internet Web site you created a hyperlink to.

r. Close Internet Explorer, then exit Word.

 Independent Challenge 2

You work in the public relations office at Meed Oil Corporation. Recognizing public concern following recent oil spills by other companies, Meed Oil wants to publicize the steps it is taking to guard against oil-tanker spills. Your supervisor asks you to adapt documents created for print and television ad campaigns to create a Web publication for Meed's Internet site.

a. Sketch the Web publication for Meed Oil. The home page for the publication should include a heading, a graphic that enhances the environmentally-friendly message, links to other Web pages in the publication, and links to two Web sites devoted to oil spill prevention. You will create the other Web pages in the publication from existing files: a press release saved in Word, an Access table detailing Meed's oil spill prevention programs, an Excel table showing a 30-year history of oil spills by major oil companies, and a PowerPoint presentation highlighting Meed's oil spill record and its efforts to prevent future spills. Be sure to include links between the pages in your sketch.

b. Use your favorite search engine to search the Internet for information on oil spill prevention. Use the keywords **oil spill** to conduct your search. Write down the page titles and URLs of at least two Web pages you find. You will create hyperlinks from the home page to these Web sites later in this exercise. If your search does not result in links to information on oil spills, try looking at the following Web sites:

www.epa.gov
www.state.ak.us

c. Start Word and create a home page for the oil spill prevention publication. Apply the Nature theme, and include the text and formatting shown in Figure D-20. For the links under the Research heading, substitute the page titles of the Internet Web pages you found in Step b. Insert the clip art graphic shown in Figure D-20 or use another appropriate clip art image. (*Hint*: Click Insert on the menu bar, point to Picture, then click Clip Art to open the Insert Clip Art task pane. You can search on the keyword **nature** or **environment**. You may need to resize the clip art graphic after you insert it.)

d. Save the Web page with the filename **Oil Spill Home** and the page title **Meed Oil—Oil Spill Prevention Home Page**. (*Hint*: If you want your name on the printed solution, add it to the page title.) Close the Oil Spill Home file.

e. Create a Web page from the Project File INT D-13.doc. Save the Web page with the filename **Press Release** and the page title **Meed Oil Press Release**. Apply the Nature theme and format the Web page so it is attractive and easy to read.

f. At the bottom of the Web page, insert a hyperlink back to the home page. Save your changes, preview the Web page in Internet Explorer, make any necessary adjustments to the file in Word, then save and close the file.

g. Start Access and create a formatted HTML document from the Prevention Programs table in the Project File INT D-14.mdb. Name the HTML file **Prevention Programs**.

h. Exit Access, then open the Prevention Programs.html file in Word. Apply the Nature theme and format the Web page so it is attractive and easy to read. Change the table heading to **Meed Oil – Oil Spill Prevention Programs**.

i. At the bottom of the Web page, insert a hyperlink back to the home page. Save your changes, preview the Web page in Internet Explorer, make any necessary adjustments to the file in Word, then save and close the file.

FIGURE D-20

j. Start Excel and create a Web page from the range A1:F8 in the Project File INT D-15.xls. Save the Web page with the filename **Oil Spills by Company** and page title **Oil Spills by Major Oil Companies**, then exit Excel without saving changes.

k. Open the Oil Spills by Company.htm file in Word. Delete the text **Oil Spills**, in the first row of the table, then apply the Nature theme. Format the Web page with styles so that its look is consistent with the other Web pages and it is easy to read.

l. At the bottom of the Web page, insert a hyperlink back to the home page. Save the changes, clicking Yes to overwrite the file, preview the Web page in Internet Explorer, make any necessary adjustments to the file in Word, then save and close the file.

m. Start PowerPoint and create a Web publication from the Project File INT D-16.ppt. Use the filename **Oil Spill Presentation** and the page title **Meed Oil's Commitment to Oil Spill Prevention**.

n. At the bottom of the first slide, insert a hyperlink back to the home page. Save your changes, preview the presentation in Internet Explorer, make any necessary adjustments to the file in PowerPoint, save and close the file, then exit PowerPoint.

o. Open the home page file, **Oil Spill Home**, in Word. Format the hyperlinks to link to the Web pages you created. Format the Research hyperlinks to link to the appropriate URLs.

p. Save your changes, then preview the Web publication in Internet Explorer, making sure to test each hyperlink.

q. Use the Print button in Internet Explorer to print the first page of each Web page you created and the first page of each Internet Web site you created a hyperlink to.

r. Close Internet Explorer, then exit Word.

Integration Practice

▶ Visual Workshop

Create the Web publication shown in Figure D-21. Use the Left-aligned Column Web page template in Word to create the Café home page. (*Hint*: The graphic is included in the Web page template.) Create the **Daily Specials** Web pages by creating a presentation in PowerPoint and converting it to HTML. Create the **Contact** Web page by creating a table in Excel and converting it to a Web page. Use the Sandstone theme for the Web pages you format in Word, and use the Maple Design template for the presentation (select a different theme or template if these are not available to you). If you want your name on the printed solution, add it to the page title for each page. Finally, add links between the Web pages. Preview the Web publication in Internet Explorer, then print the first page of each Web page using Internet Explorer.

FIGURE D-21

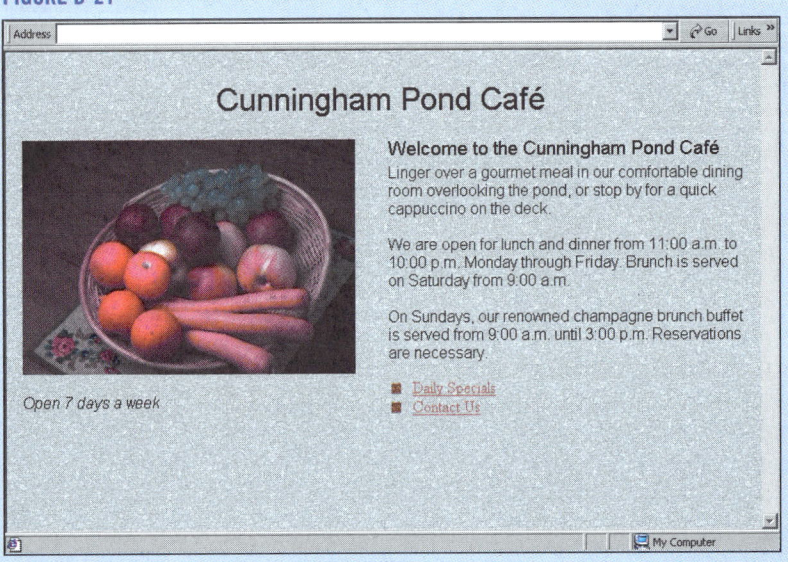

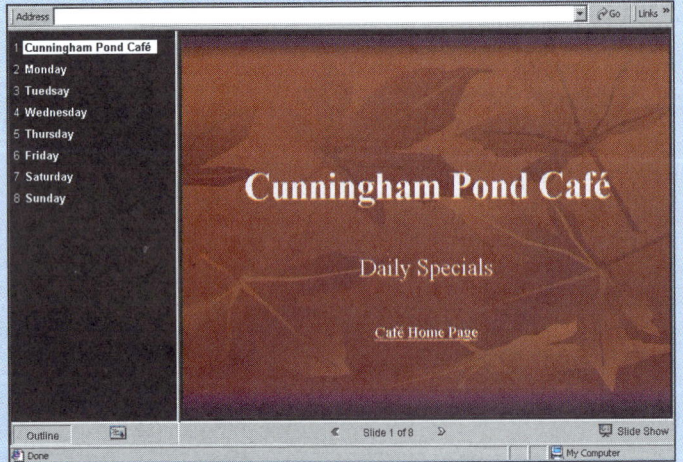

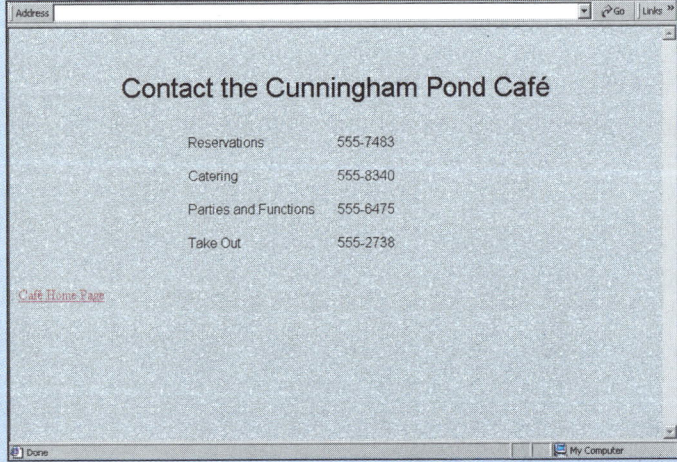

Integration

Integrating
Word and Excel

Objectives

- Link an Excel chart to a Word document
- Embed an Excel worksheet in a Word document
- Insert a hyperlink to an Excel file in a Word document

Sometimes the information you want to include in a Word document is stored in a file that was created in Excel. One way to include Excel data in a Word document is to insert the information into the document as a linked or embedded object. An **object** is an item that can be manipulated and shared among programs, for example, graphics, spreadsheets, charts, or sound and video clips. You can also create a hyperlink from the Word document to the Excel file. Alice Wegman, marketing manager at MediaLoft, is preparing a brief report on MediaLoft San Francisco's quarterly advertising expenditures. She created the report using Word, and she wants to enhance it by adding a worksheet and a chart that she created in Excel. She also wants to insert a hyperlink in the Word document to link it to an Excel file that details all quarterly advertising activity.

Linking an Excel chart to a Word document

When you insert an Excel object in a Word document, you have the option to create a linked object. A **link** is a connection between the source and destination files; changes you make to the source file are automatically updated in the linked object in the destination file. You can link objects using the Object command on the Insert menu or the Paste Special command on the Edit menu. ⮕ Alice uses the Paste Special command to insert an Excel chart into her marketing report as a linked object.

Steps

1. Start Word, open the file **INT E-1.doc** from the drive and location where your Project Files are located, save it as **Advertising Report**, then click the **Show/Hide ¶ button** ¶ on the Standard toolbar to display formatting marks, if necessary
   The report opens in Print Layout view.

2. Start Excel, open the file **INT E-2.xls** from the drive and location where your Project Files are located, then save it as **Q3 Ad Costs**
   The Excel file contains the chart you want to insert in the advertising report.

   QuickTip
   You cannot use the Paste Special command to paste items from the Office Clipboard.

3. Select the **chart**, then click the **Copy button** on the Standard toolbar
   The chart is copied to the Clipboard.

4. Click the **Word program button** on the taskbar, scroll down until the Advertising Expenditures heading is at the top of your screen, then place the insertion point in the **second blank paragraph** under the Advertising Expenditures heading

5. Click **Edit** on the menu bar, then click **Paste Special**
   The Paste Special dialog box opens, as shown in Figure E-1. You use this dialog box to choose between embedding and linking an object, and to select the format you want the pasted object to have.

   QuickTip
   To create an embedded object in the destination file, select the Paste option button in the Paste Special dialog box instead of the Paste link option button.

6. Click the **Paste link option button** to select it, make sure **Microsoft Excel Chart Object** is selected in the As list box, then click **OK**
   The Excel data is inserted in the document as a linked Microsoft Excel chart object, as shown in Figure E-2.

7. Double-click the **chart object**
   The **Q3 Ad Costs** file opens in the Excel program window. You need to update the worksheet.

8. Click cell **B4**, type **45770**, then press **[Enter]**, watching the Print (purple) segment of the pie chart as you do
   The chart is adjusted to reflect the change to the data.

   Trouble?
   If the chart object is not updated, right-click it, then click Update Link on the shortcut menu.

9. Save your changes to the Excel file, then exit Excel
   Excel closes and you return to the Word program window. The change you made to the chart in the Excel source file is reflected in the linked chart in the Word document.

10. With the chart object still selected, click the **Center button** on the Standard toolbar, click outside the object to deselect it, then save your changes
    When an object is selected, you can format it using Word commands. The centered object appears as shown in Figure E-3.

▶ INTEGRATION E-2 **INTEGRATING WORD AND EXCEL**

FIGURE E-1: Paste Special dialog box

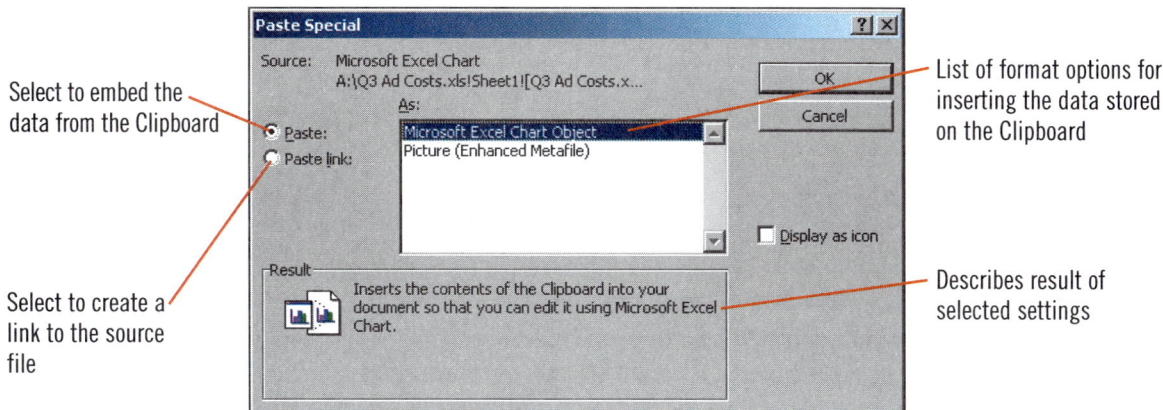

FIGURE E-2: Linked Excel object

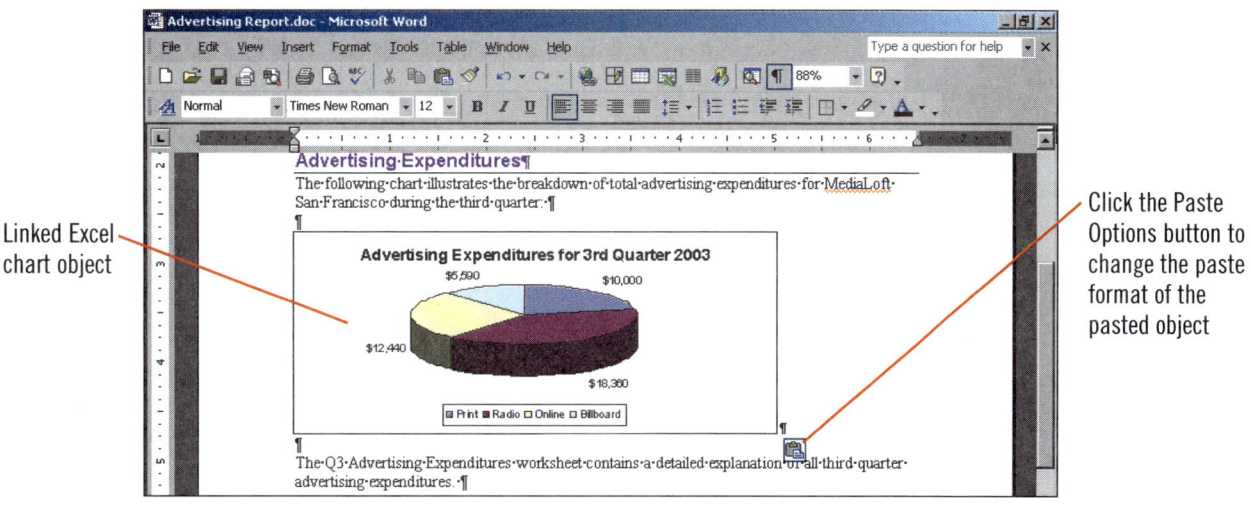

FIGURE E-3: Revised chart in document

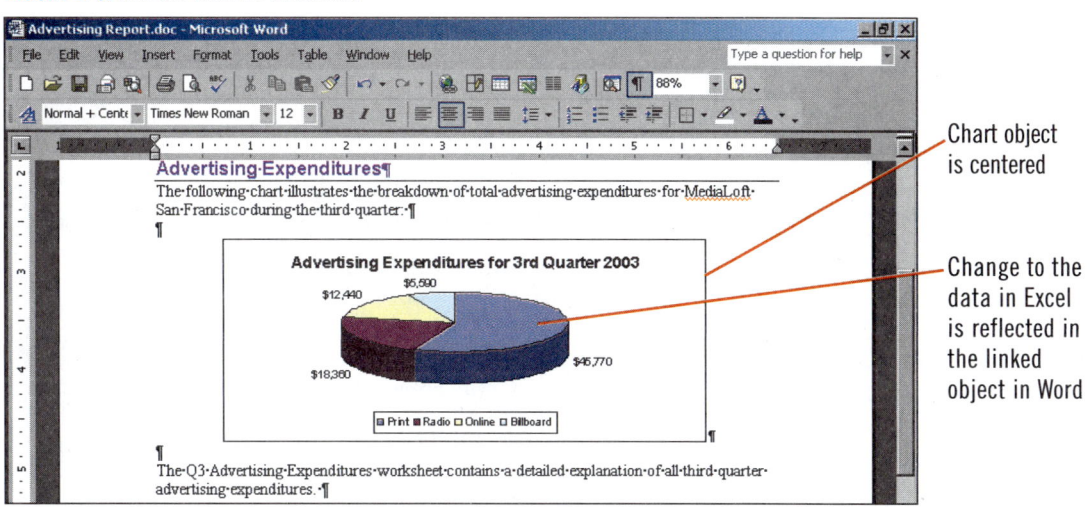

Embedding an Excel worksheet into a Word document

If you do not need to maintain a link between the source and target file, you can embed an object. When you **embed** an object, the object is stored only in the destination file. You can edit the embedded object by double-clicking it to open the source program without ever leaving the destination file. Any change you make to an embedded object is saved only within the destination file. As with linking, you can embed an Excel object in Word by using the Object command on the Insert menu or the Paste Special command on the Edit menu. Alice uses the Object command to embed an Excel worksheet detailing MediaLoft San Francisco's print advertising expenses into her report.

QuickTip
Click the Insert Microsoft Excel Worksheet button on the Standard toolbar to embed a blank worksheet in a document.

1. **Scroll until the Print Advertising heading is near the top of your screen, then place the insertion point in the second blank paragraph under the Print Advertising heading**
   You want to embed the Excel object at the location of the insertion point.

2. **Click Insert on the menu bar, click Object, then click the Create from File tab, if necessary**
   The Object dialog box opens, similar to Figure E-4. You can use the Create New tab in this dialog box to create a new object in your Word document using another program, or you can use the Create from File tab to insert an object from an existing file.

3. **Click Browse**
   The Browse dialog box opens.

QuickTip
To create a linked object in the destination file, select the Link to file check box.

4. **Navigate to the drive and location where your Project Files are located, select the Excel file Int E-3.xls, then click Insert**
   The Excel file Int E-3.xls contains the worksheet you want to embed in the advertising report. Compare your screen to Figure E-4.

5. **Click OK**
   The Excel data is inserted in the document as an embedded Microsoft Excel worksheet object. You want to change the formatting of the embedded object to better match the memo formatting.

6. **Double-click the worksheet object**
   The worksheet opens in an Excel object window, and the menus and toolbars change to Excel menus and toolbars, as shown in Figure E-5.

7. **Select the range A2:F11, click Format on the menu bar, click AutoFormat, select the Classic 2 style in the AutoFormat dialog box, click Options in the dialog box, clear the Font and Alignment check boxes in the Formats to apply area, then click OK**
   The Classic 2 AutoFormat is applied to the embedded worksheet.

8. **Click outside the object to close the Excel object window**
   When you close the object window, the menus and toolbars return to Word menus toolbars.

9. **Click the object once to select it, click the Center button on the Formatting toolbar, deselect the object, then save your changes**
   The centered object appears as shown in Figure E-6. The changes you made to the embedded Excel worksheet object are not made to the source file in Excel.

FIGURE E-4: Object dialog box

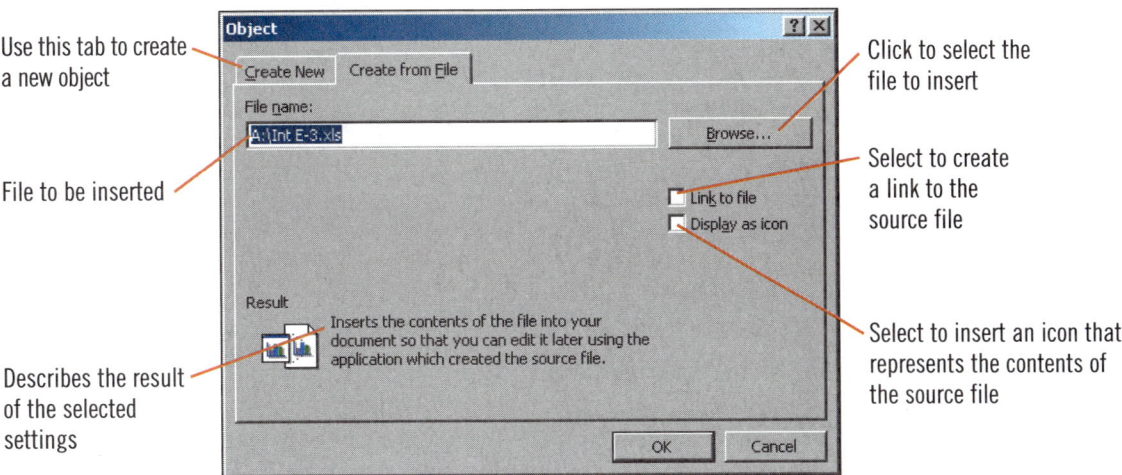

FIGURE E-5: Embedded Excel object

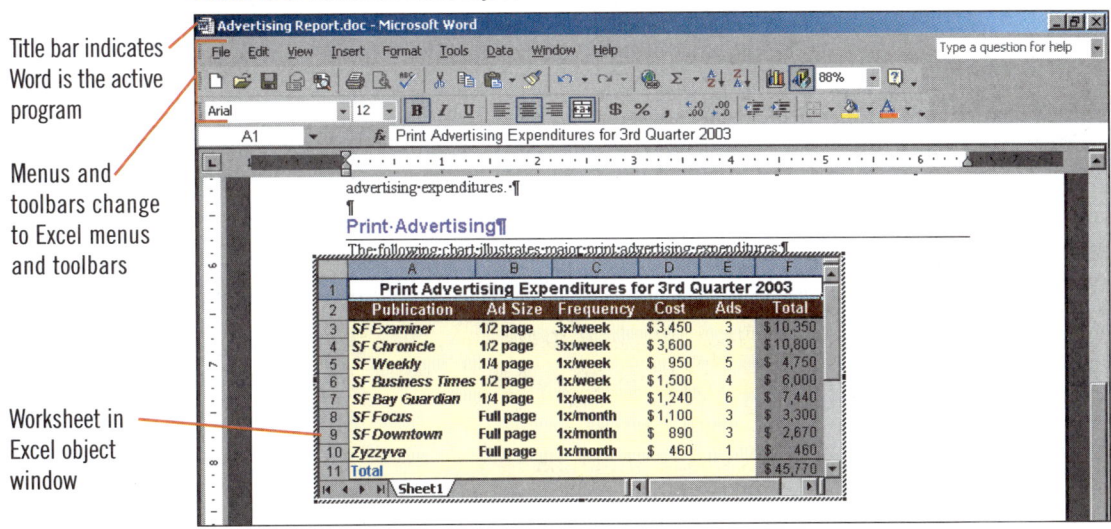

FIGURE E-6: Formatted object in document

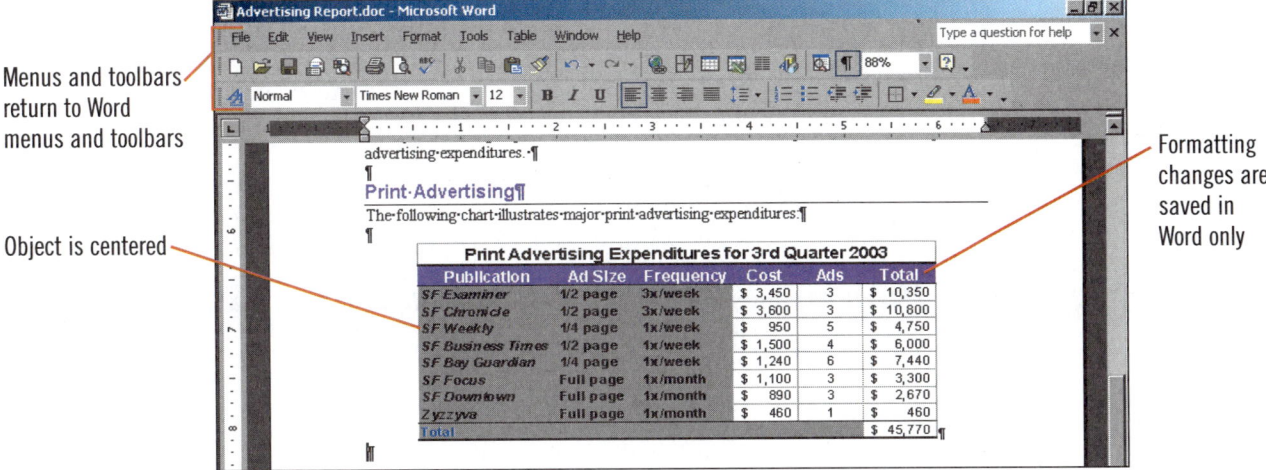

INTEGRATING WORD AND EXCEL

Inserting a hyperlink to an Excel file in a Word document

Another way to include information stored in a different file in a Word document is to insert a hyperlink to the file into the document. A **hyperlink** is text or an object that when clicked opens (or jumps to) another location in the current document, another file, or a Web page. Hyperlinks can also link to an e-mail address. When you create a hyperlink, you specify where you want to jump when the hyperlink is clicked. Alice wants to include the third quarter advertising expenditures in her report. She realizes that not everyone who reads her report will be interested in this level of detail, so instead of inserting this information directly into the report, she creates a hyperlink to an Excel file that contains the detailed information. Anyone who is interested can click the hyperlink to open the worksheet and review the data.

1. Scroll until the Advertising Expenditures heading is at the top of your screen, then select **Q3 Advertising Expenditures worksheet** in the sentence under the chart object
   This text will be the hyperlink to the Q3 Advertising Expenditures worksheet file.

2. Click the **Insert Hyperlink button** on the Standard toolbar
   The Insert Hyperlink dialog box opens, similar to Figure E-7. You use this dialog box to specify the location you want to jump to when the hyperlink is clicked.

   > **QuickTip**
   > Click on the Excel Standard toolbar to insert a hyperlink in a worksheet.

3. Click **Existing File or Web Page** in the Link to area if necessary, use the **Look in list arrow** to navigate to the drive and location where your Project Files are stored, select the file **Q3 Advertising Expenditures.xls**, then click **OK**
   The Insert Hyperlink dialog box closes, and the text in the document is formatted as a hyperlink—colored blue and underlined.

4. Position the pointer over the hyperlink
   When you point to the hyperlink, a ScreenTip showing the path and filename of the linked file appears.

   > **QuickTip**
   > To edit, select, open, copy, or remove a hyperlink, right-click the hyperlink, then click the appropriate command on the shortcut menu.

5. Press and hold **[Ctrl]**
   When you press [Ctrl] while pointing to a link, the pointer changes to .

6. Click the **hyperlink** with the pointer
   The Q3 Advertising Expenditures worksheet opens in the Excel program window. The Web toolbar opens below the Standard and Formatting toolbars. You can use the buttons on the Web toolbar to navigate between hyperlinked files and Web pages.

   > **QuickTip**
   > If you link to another file, the person clicking the link must have access to both files.

7. Click the **Back button** on the Web toolbar
   The Advertising Report document appears in the Word document window. Notice that the hyperlink color has changed to purple, indicating that the hyperlink has been followed.

8. Press **[Ctrl][End]**, press **[Enter]**, click the **Align Right button** on the Formatting toolbar, type **Prepared** by, then type your name
   The completed report is shown in Figure E-8.

9. Save your changes to the Word document, print a copy, close the file, exit Word, then exit Excel

FIGURE E-7: Insert Hyperlink dialog box

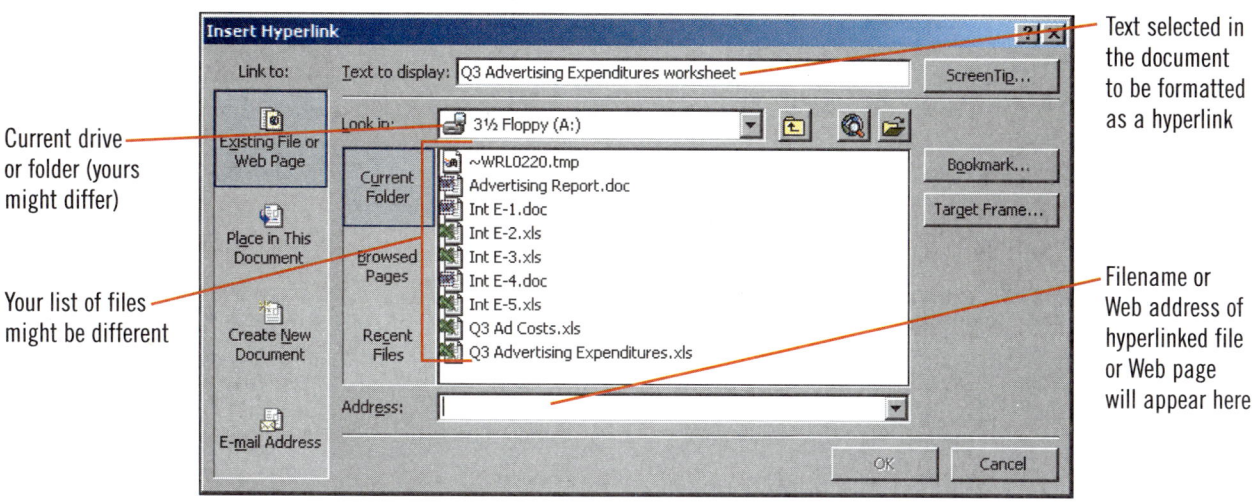

FIGURE E-8: Competed report

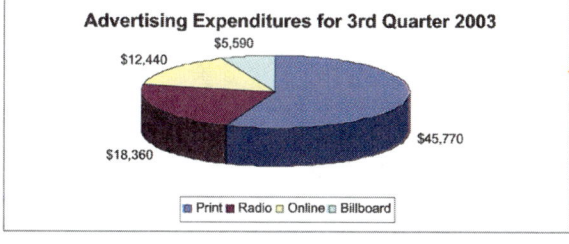

Integration | **Practice**

Independent Challenge 1

As secretary of the Budget Committee for the town of Lysander, it's your job to send the first draft of the budget to the town council. You have prepared a worksheet that summarizes the draft budget for 2004. You'll use the data to create several charts that illustrate the draft budget, and then insert the charts in a memo to the town council.

   a. Start Word, open the file INT E-4.doc from the drive and location where your Project Files are stored, then save it as **Lysander Budget Memo**. Enter your name in the memo header, then read the memo to get a feel for its content.
   b. Start Excel, open the file INT E-5.xls from the drive and location where your Project Files are stored. Enter your name in cell A20, then save it as **Lysander Budget**.
   c. Using the data in the worksheet, create a column chart that compares the budgeted expenditures for 2003 with the actual expenditures. Create the chart on a new chart sheet named **2003**.
   d. Create a pie chart showing the distribution of the 2004 budget among departments. Create the chart on a new chart sheet named **2004**. Format the chart so it is useful, attractive, and readable.
   e. Save your changes to the workbook, then switch to the memo in Word.
   f. Embed the column chart in the memo. Use Excel's formatting features to modify the format of the chart so it is useful, attractive, and readable.
   g. Insert the pie chart in the memo and establish a link to the source file.
   h. Select the text **Lysander Budget.xls** in the second paragraph, and create a hyperlink to the Excel file Lysander Budget.xls (located in the drive and folder where your Project Files are stored.). Test the hyperlink.
   i. In the Excel file Lysander Budget, change the budgeted value for the Water Department to 700,000. Switch back to the Word document and verify that the charts changed to reflect the new data (update the links, if necessary).
   j. Save your changes to the workbook, then close the file and exit Excel.
   k. In the memo, make any necessary formatting changes to the memo.
   l. Save your changes to the memo, print a copy, close the file, then exit Word.

Independent Challenge 2

Your boss has given you a $10,000 budget to buy computer equipment for your department. Before releasing the funds, she would like you to research and prepare a proposal on how you intend to best spend the money. You decide to research computer equipment online.

   a. Determine the type of equipment your department most needs (i.e., computers, printers, scanners, monitors, etc.).
   b. Use your favorite search engine to search the Web for computer price information. Use the keywords **computer equipment**. If your search does not result in links to information on buying computers, try looking at the following Web sites: www.dell.com, www.hp.com, and www.gateway.com.
   c. Start Excel, open a new workbook, then save it as **Computer Budget** to the drive and location where your Project Files are stored.
   d. Create a worksheet that compares prices for similar equipment from at least two different companies. Spend as close to $10,000 as possible. Save your changes.
   e. Start Word, open a new document, then save it as **Computer Memo** to the location where your Project Files are stored.
   f. Type a memo to your boss explaining your recommendations for purchasing computer equipment. Include your name in the memo header.
   g. Embed the worksheet you created in your memo. Format the worksheet so it is attractive and readable.
   h. Insert hyperlinks to the Web pages you consulted into your memo. (*Hint*: Type the URL for the Web page in the document, then press [Spacebar]. Right-click the link, then click Edit Hyperlink to see that the URL appears in the Text to display and Address text boxes in the Insert Hyperlink dialog box.)
   i. Save your changes to the memo, print a copy, close the document, exit Word, then close the workbook and exit Excel.

Integration

Unit F

Integrating
Word, Excel, and Access

Objectives

- ▶ Copy an Access datasheet into a Word document
- ▶ Copying an Access datasheet to Excel
- ▶ Embed an Excel chart into a Word document

Using data from different Office programs to complete a single document is an efficient way to take advantage of existing files. The analytical features of Excel and Access provide valuable ways to integrate information easily and effectively. In this unit, Maria Abbott, the regional sales manager at MediaLoft, is considering reducing the stock of historical books at the Kansas City store, based on the numbers in stock at the end of the fiscal year. She has asked Andrew Fleming, the store manager in Kansas City, to send her information on the stock of history books in his store.

Copying an Access Datasheet into a Word Document

The more files you create using Office programs, the more important it is to be able to merge information together to create documents. Access data can be sent to a new Word document by using the OfficeLinks button on the Standard toolbar or by copying the data from Access and pasting it into Word. The easiest way to merge data from an Access table with an existing Word document is to copy and paste the data from Access to Word. Maria asks Andrew to send her the current History stock list for the Kansas City store, sorted by author.

Steps

1. Start Access, open the **KC StockList-IF.mdb** database from the drive and location where your Project Files are stored, click **Tables** on the Objects bar if necessary, then open **Stock Table** and **Author Table**
   Note that the Stock Table identifies the history books in stock at the Kansas City store. Each book in the table is identified by its ISBN number, title, and an author ID field. The Author Table lists all the history authors' first and last names and each author's Author ID number. The AuthorID field corresponds to the field with the same name in the Stock Table.

2. Create a query named **History Stock** that displays the fields in the following order: **ISBN**, **LastName**, **FirstName**, **BookTitle**, and **Units in Stock**, sorted alphabetically by **LastName**

3. Open the query in Datasheet view
   Compare your query results with those shown in Figure F-1.

4. Start Word, open the file **INT F-1.doc** from the drive and location where your Project Files are stored, then save it as **KC Store Memo.doc**
   You'll copy the Access table into this document.

5. Click the **Zoom button list arrow** on the Standard toolbar, then click **75%**
   Decreasing the zoom setting allows you to see more of the document at one time.

6. Click the **History Stock query Access program button** on the Windows taskbar, select all of the columns in the History Stock query, then click the **Copy button** on the Access Standard toolbar
   The table is copied to the Clipboard.

7. Click the **Word program button** on the Window taskbar, click I to position the insertion point below the heading **History Stock (KC store)**, click the **Paste button** on the Standard toolbar, then scroll the document to view the entire table
   The data from the Access query is pasted into the Word document. The table does not all fit on the first page of the document, so Word creates a second page.

8. Add your name as a footer in the document, save your changes, print and close the document, then minimize the Word program window
   You are returned to the Access program window.

9. Click the **Close button** in the History Stock query datasheet window, then click **No** in the dialog box that asks if you want to save the data stored on the clipboard

10. Close the **Author Table** and **Stock Table** datasheet windows

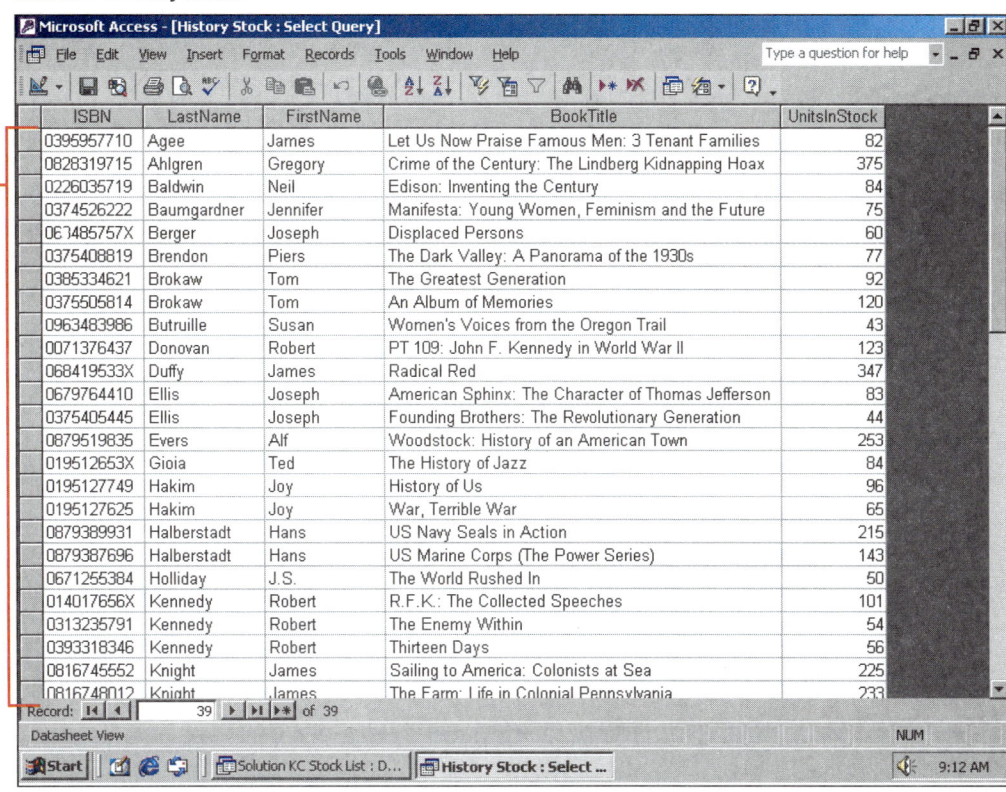

FIGURE F-1: Query results

Modified query showing units in ascending order

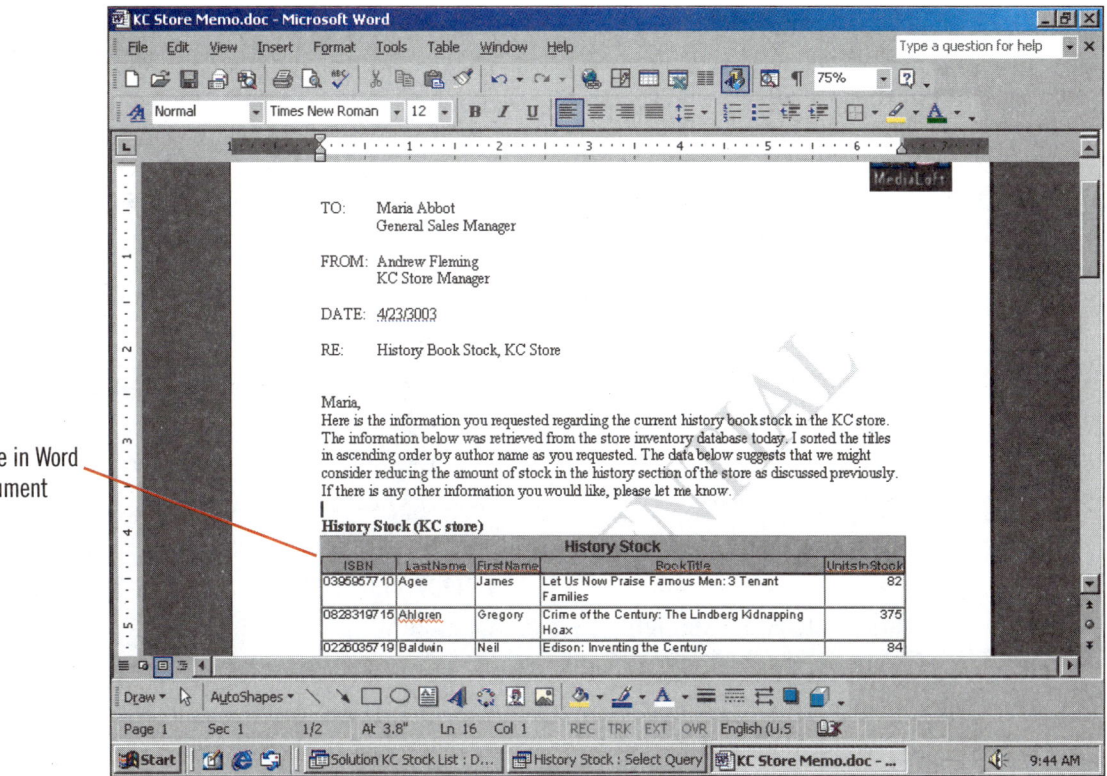

FIGURE F-2: Access table copied into Word document

Table in Word document

INTEGRATING WORD, EXCEL, AND ACCESS INTEGRATION F-3

Copying an Access Datasheet to Excel

As you have learned, each Office program allows you to work with information in a unique way. For example, Access enables you to create and store large amounts of data, such as product inventory information or customer records. Excel, on the other hand, enables you to analyze numerical data by calculating totals, filtering data, and graphing data in ways that the other Office programs do not. Maria has requested that Andrew provide her with more information on the history inventory at his store, including a chart that tracks the numbers of history books in stock at the end of each of the last four years. To do this, Andrew will create a query to retrieve the number of units currently in stock. Next, he'll use Excel to analyze the information, and create a chart that explains the overstock trend for history books in his store.

Steps

1. Create a query named **History Stock Analysis** that includes the fields **ISBN**, **Author ID**, **Book Title UnitsInStock**, and **UnitPrice**, sorted in ascending order by **UnitsInStock**, then open the **History Stock Analysis query** in Datasheet view
   The query displays just the fields you need.

2. Select all of the columns in the History Stock Analysis query, then click the **Copy button** on the Access Standard toolbar

3. Start Excel, open the file **INT F-2.xls** from the drive and location where your Project files are stored, then save it as **History Overstock Analysis.xls**
   An Excel worksheet opens, identifying the history units in stock at the end of previous fiscal years.

4. Click the **Sheet2 tab**, rename the sheet tab **2003 Stock**, click **cell A1**, click the **Paste button** on the Excel Standard toolbar, then AutoFit columns as necessary to see all the data
   Compare your screen to Figure F-3. The green error indicators in the upper-left corner of cells indicate that the numbers were pasted into Excel as text instead of numbers. To calculate formulas in Excel, numbers need to be in a numerical format.

5. Convert the data in **columns D** and **E** to **numbers**
   Now you can perform calculations.

> **QuickTip**
> To calculate the value for each book in the worksheet, multiply the UnitsInStock by the UnitPrice.

6. Calculate the total value of each book in column F, type **TotalValue** in cell F1, then AutoFit column F

7. Calculate the total number of units in stock in **cell D42**, then calculate the total value of all units in stock in **cell F42**

8. Copy the data in **cells D42** and **F42**, then paste the values into **cells B8** and **C8**, respectively, on the History Overstock worksheet
   The calculation results from the 2003 Stock worksheet now appear on the History Overstock worksheet.

9. Create two charts of the data in the History Overstock worksheet, using Figure F-4 as a guide: one showing the units in stock and the other showing the value of the units in stock, for the four years represented in the worksheet
   Compare your results with Figure F-4.

10. Close the History Stock Analysis query data sheet window and the KC Stock List database, then exit Access, *but do not exit Excel*

FIGURE F-3: Results of the Access query copied into Excel

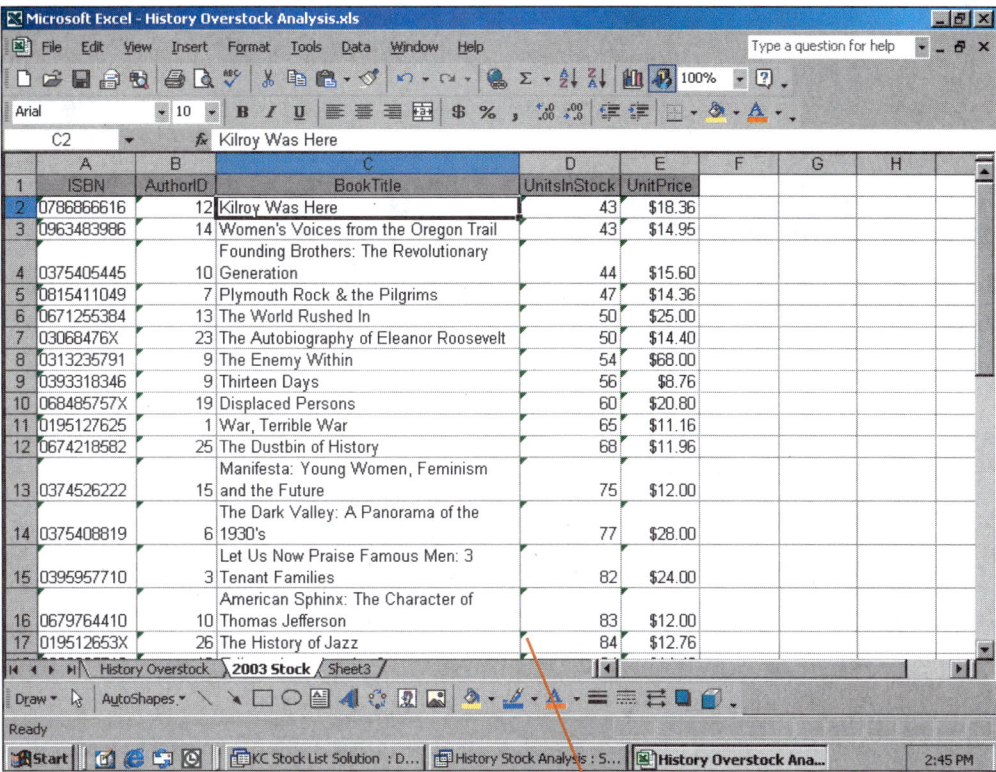

Error indicator

FIGURE F-4: Charts created from data

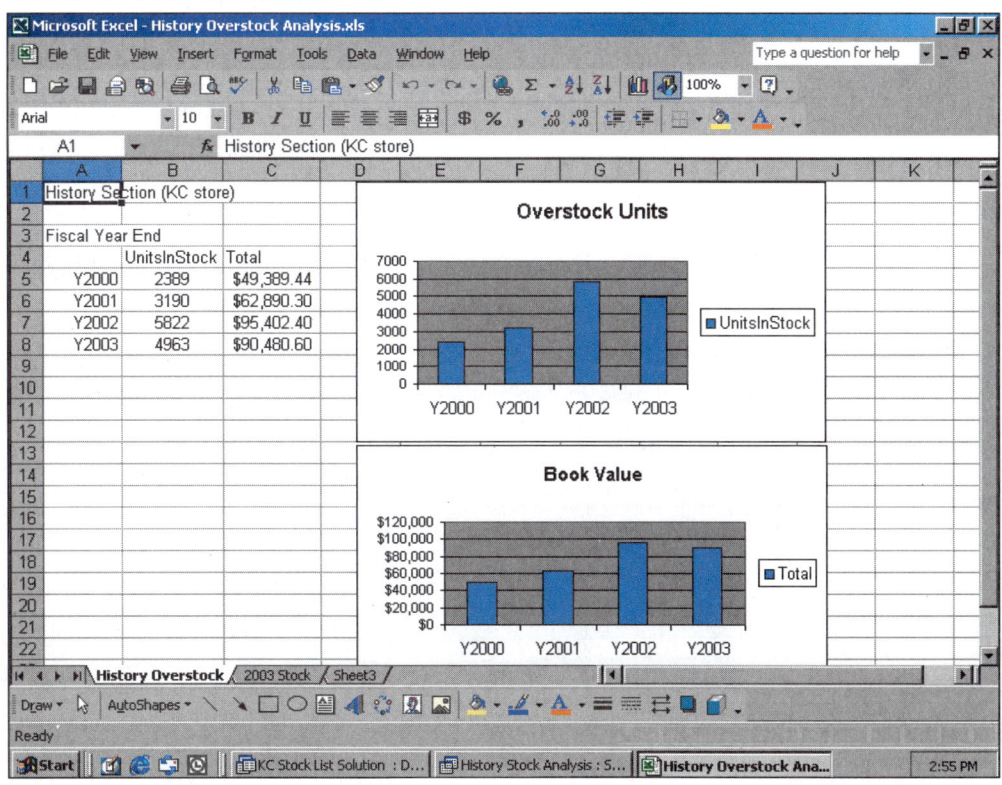

INTEGRATING WORD, EXCEL, AND ACCESS

Embedding an Excel Chart into a Word Document

As you have learned, you can embed an entire Excel worksheet in a Word document by using Word's Object command on the Insert menu. You can also embed partial information from an Excel worksheet, such as a chart or specific data, by selecting the information and then copying and pasting it into your Word document. Embedding an Excel chart into a Word document enables you to take advantage of all of Excel's functionality from your Word document, allowing you to create a professional-looking chart. Andrew decides to include his charts showing the overstock at his store in a memo to Maria.

1. Click the chart containing the data on overstock units, then click the **Copy button** on the Standard toolbar

2. Click the **Word program button** on the Windows taskbar, open the file **INT F-3.doc** from the drive and location where your Project Files are stored, then save the document as **KC Store Memo 2.doc**

3. Click in the space directly below **History section unit overstock**, then click the **Paste button** on the Standard toolbar

   The chart appears in the document, as shown in Figure F-5. The chart is not embedded at this point because Word gives you the choice of embedding the chart or just inserting a picture of the chart. If you embed the chart as a picture, you will not able to open the chart from Word and edit it in the future.

4. Click the **Paste Options button** at the bottom of the chart, then click **Excel Chart (entire workbook)**

   The Excel chart is embedded into the document. If you want to edit an Excel chart after you've embedded it, you can double-click the chart to open it. Your Word document will remain open, but Excel's toolbars and menus will appear for you to use. Because the chart is embedded, rather than linked, any changes you make to the chart in Word will not affect the chart in Excel.

5. Embed the chart containing the data on the value of the overstock units from the History Overstock worksheet into the KC Store Memo 2 document below the line **Total overstock value**

   Compare your screen with Figure F-6.

6. Add your name as a footer in your document, then save and print it

7. Close all files, then exit Excel and Word

FIGURE F-5: Chart showing History overstock

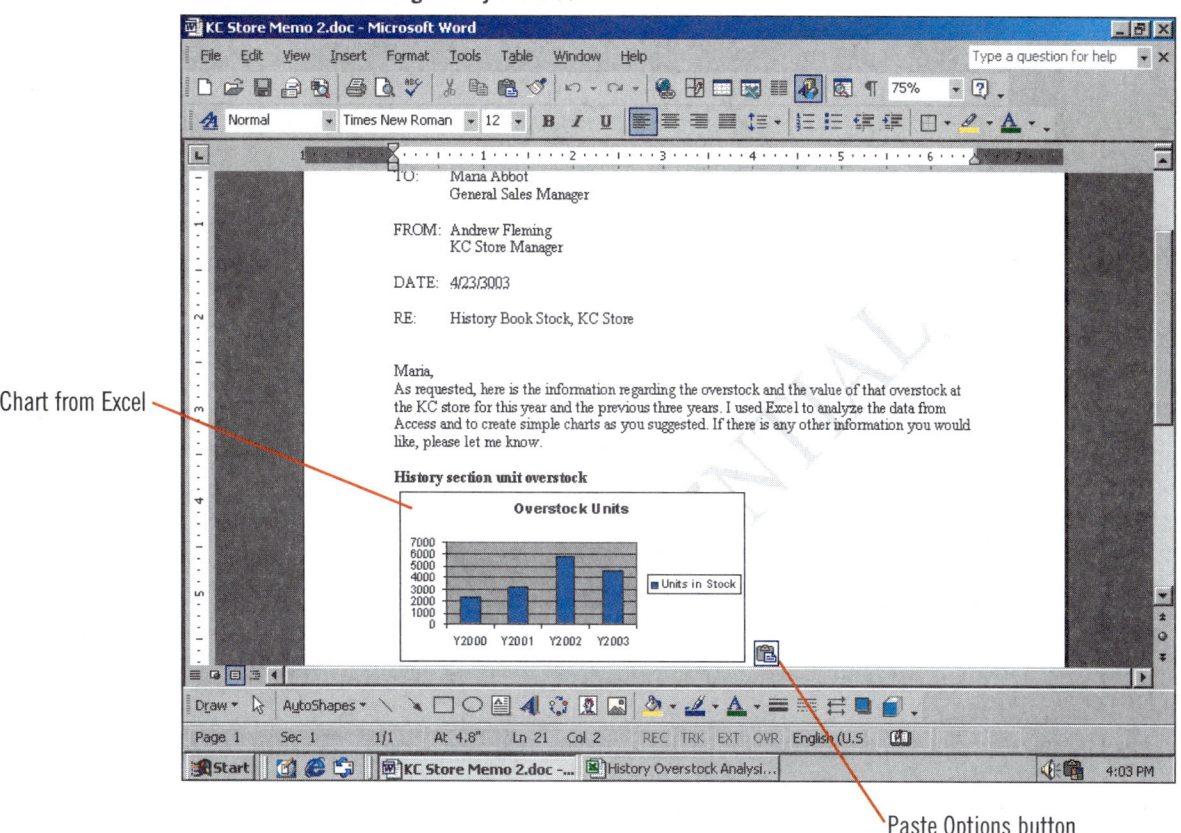

FIGURE F-6: Word document with embedded Excel charts

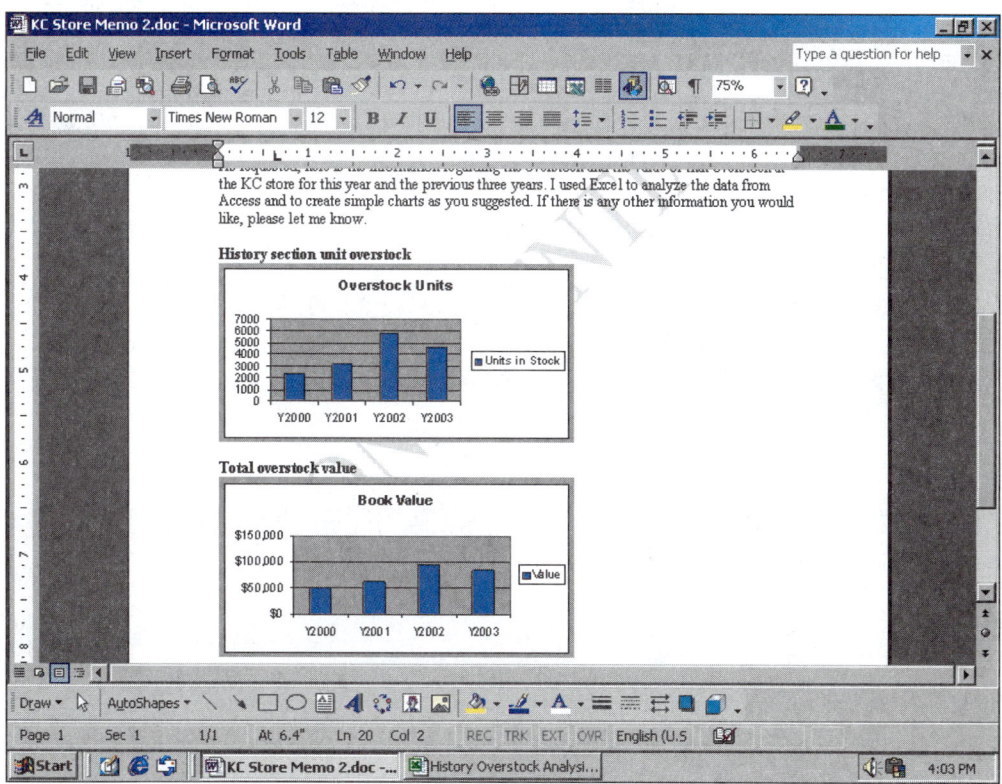

INTEGRATING WORD, EXCEL, AND ACCESS INTEGRATION F-7

Integration Practice

▶ Independent Challenge 1

As the new owner of your own flower shop in Spain, Tonia's Flowers, you need to generate a weekly inventory report to help you decide how much new inventory to order. The quickest way to do the inventory report is to create a query in Access, then analyze the data in Excel.

a. Start Access, open the Tonia's Flowers.mdb database from the drive and location where your Project Files are stored, then add at least five new items to the Product Line table.

b. Create a query named In-Stock Items that sorts products in ascending order by the Units On Order field. Make sure your query includes fields that identify the product name, the number of units in stock, the number of units on order, the unit price, and the lead time. Add a criterion that retrieves only those products for which eight or more items are in stock.

c. Copy the results of the In-Stock Items query to a new Excel workbook, then save the workbook as **Stock Report.xls** to the drive and location where your Project files are stored.

d. Calculate the sum of all products in stock, then calculate the value of all the products on order.

e. Include your name on the footer of the worksheet, then save and print the Excel worksheet.

f. Close all open files, then exit Excel and Access.

▶ Independent Challenge 2

You work for a trade consulting company, XEO Business Systems. You have just been assigned a research project to analyze the latest U.S. government information on retail trade. To complete the project, you will create a query in Access and then use Excel to analyze the data. You will finish the project by embedding the Excel data in a Word document.

a. Open the Access database U.S. Trade Analysis.mdb from the drive and location where your Project Files are stored, then open the Trade by State table.

b. Create a query called Trade by State Query that includes fields from the table that identify the state, industry description, payroll, sales, and sales rank. Sort the query results by the sales rank in ascending order.

c. Copy the query results to a new Excel workbook, then save the workbook as **State Trade Analysis.xls** to the location where your Project files are stored.

d. Use AutoFilter to determine the data for each of the five sales rankings, then create a chart for each sales ranking. Save your changes.

e. Create a Word document named **Top State Trade Analysis.doc**. Include your name in the footer. Enter some basic text describing the data you created in Excel. Insert all five charts in your document.

f. Save and print the Word document. Close all open files, then exit Word, Excel, and Access.

Integrating

Word, Excel, Access, and PowerPoint

Objectives

- Create a PowerPoint presentation from a Word outline
- Embed a Word table and Excel worksheet into a presentation
- Insert Access data into an Excel worksheet
- Analyze Access data in Excel
- Insert Excel data in a Word document
- Import Excel data into a PowerPoint presentation

With Microsoft Office, you can create professional-looking, integrated PowerPoint presentations using not only PowerPoint's built-in tools, but also the formatting and data analysis tools available in Word, Excel, and Access. Because PowerPoint is a part of Microsoft Office, you can exchange files or data easily between PowerPoint and Word, Excel, and Access. Maria Abbott, MediaLoft's general sales manager, needs to prepare a store evaluation presentation using information she has compiled for the Kansas City store. You will help Maria develop her PowerPoint presentation using information from Word, Excel, and Access.

Creating a PowerPoint Presentation from a Word Outline

When you want to use content from an existing Word document in a PowerPoint presentation, you can simply send the information to PowerPoint using the Send To command from Word. This approach can save you a lot of time because you need not retype or copy the information into PowerPoint. If the Word document is formatted with styles, each level 1 heading becomes a title for an individual slide, and all headings below each level 1 heading become subtitles or bulleted lists. Even if you don't have an existing Word document, you might prefer to create presentation outlines in Word and then send the outline to PowerPoint. In this lesson, Maria uses a Word outline to create a PowerPoint presentation. She then applies a design template to the entire presentation.

Steps

1. Open Word, then open the document **INT G-1.doc** from the drive and location where your Project Files are stored
   A Word document opens.

2. Click **File** on the menu bar, point to **Send To**, then click **Microsoft PowerPoint**
   A new PowerPoint presentation opens, displaying the text from the Word document.

3. Save the new presentation as **KC Store Evaluation.ppt**

4. Click the **Outline tab**, then examine the slides
   Compare your screen with Figure G-1.

5. Click the **Slides tab**, open the Slide Layout task pane, then modify the layout of your slides appropriately
   You may need to change a slide's layout, for example, so that the slide can accommodate a picture or chart.

   QuickTip
   If you don't find a suitable PowerPoint design template, create one or modify an existing template. If you modify a template, make sure that you rename the template and save it as a presentation template to the location where your Project Files are stored.

6. Click the **Slide Design button**, then select a **design template** of your choice
   As you look through the design templates, keep in mind that the template you choose may affect where large objects, such as charts and tables, appear on your slides. Figure G-2 shows a slide with a template applied.

7. Save your changes, click the **Word program button** on the Windows taskbar, close the file INT G-1.doc, *but do not exit Word*

FIGURE G-1: Word outline inserted into presentation

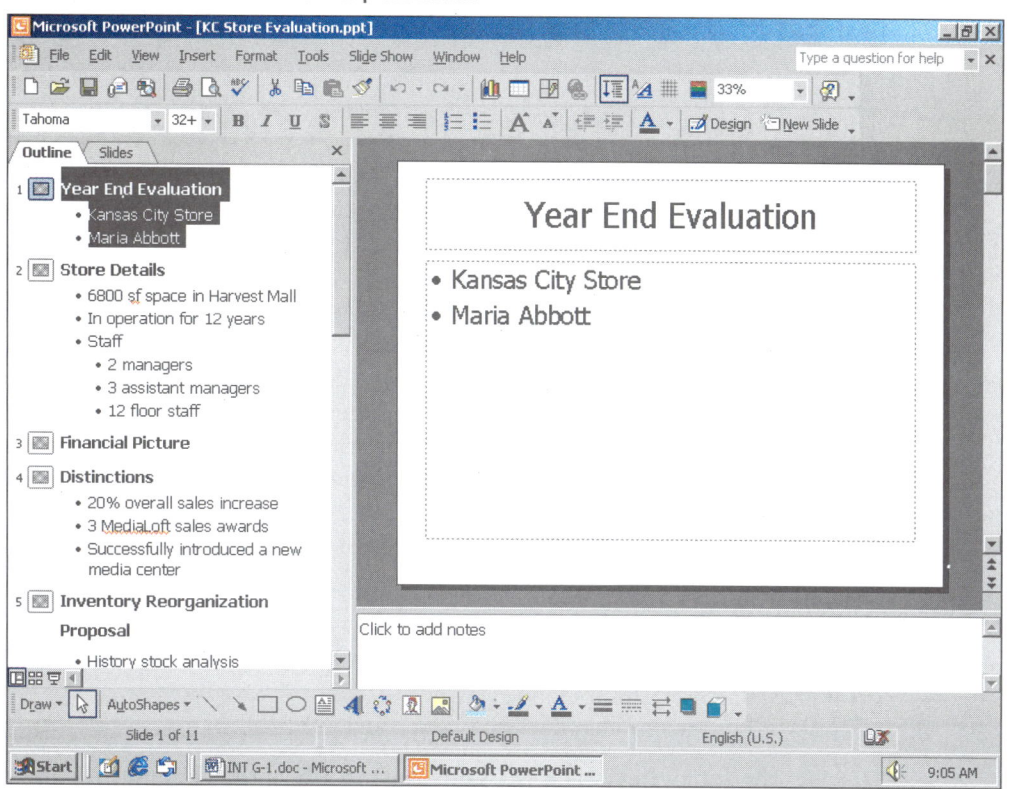

FIGURE G-2: Presentation with new design template

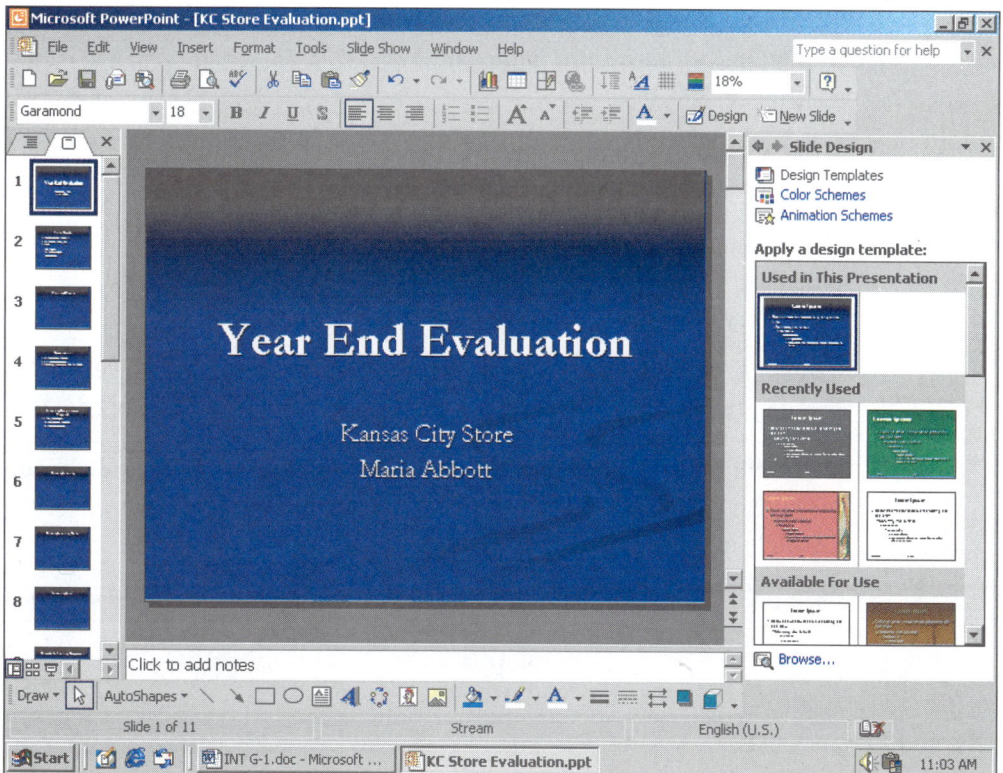

Embedding a Word Table and Excel Worksheet into a Presentation

After changing the design of your slides, you can add objects and change formatting as needed. When you insert content or an outline from another source, such as a Word document, the text or data may not fit the slide design or have the appropriate appearance. Therefore, you may need to change the slide layout or the content on the slide to achieve the desired look. At this stage, you can also decide whether to add data from other programs, such as Excel, to help communicate your message. ✐ Maria continues working on her presentation by embedding an object on the Slide Master, and then embedding an Excel worksheet and a Word table.

1. In Word, open the document **INT G-2.doc** from the drive and location where your Project Files are stored
   The Word document identifies the overstocked inventory by store in a table.

2. Select the table, then click the **Copy button** 📋 on the Standard toolbar

3. Click the **PowerPoint program button** on the Windows taskbar, click the **Slide 9 thumbnail** in the Slides tab, click **Edit** on the menu bar, then click **Paste Special**
   The Paste Special dialog box opens. The Paste Special command allows you to paste the Word table into PowerPoint as an embedded object. Since it's an embedded object, you can double-click the table to open it up in Word to edit or format the content.

4. Click **Microsoft Word Document Object** in the list, then click **OK**
   The table is embedded in the slide.

5. Resize the table appropriately, then center it on the slide
   Your slide should look similar to Figure G-3.

6. Start Excel, then open the file **INT G-3.xls** from the drive and location where you store your Project Files
   The History Overstock worksheet opens.

7. Select the range A3:C8, click 📋, switch to Slide 8 of the PowerPoint presentation, then use the **Paste Special** command to embed the partial worksheet

8. Resize the worksheet, format it using PowerPoint's formatting commands, then save your presentation
   Your slide might look similar to Figure G-4.

9. Close both the INT G-3.xls workbook and the INT G-2.doc document

FIGURE G-3: Slide showing Word table embedded in slide

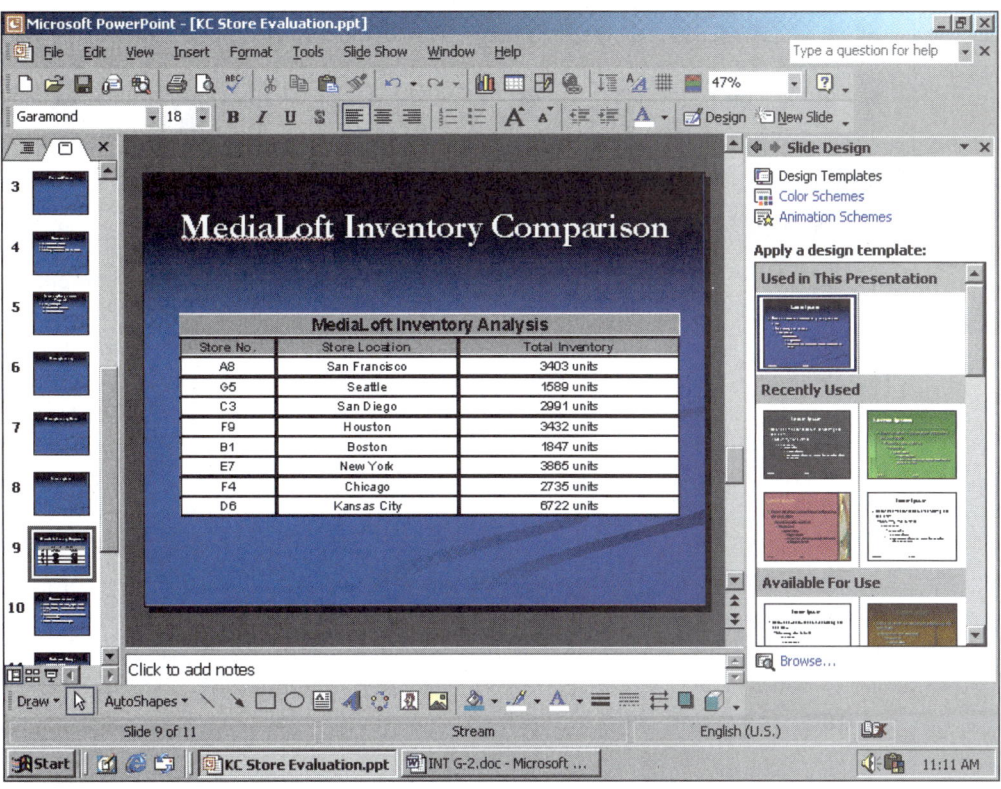

FIGURE G-4: Excel worksheet embedded in slide

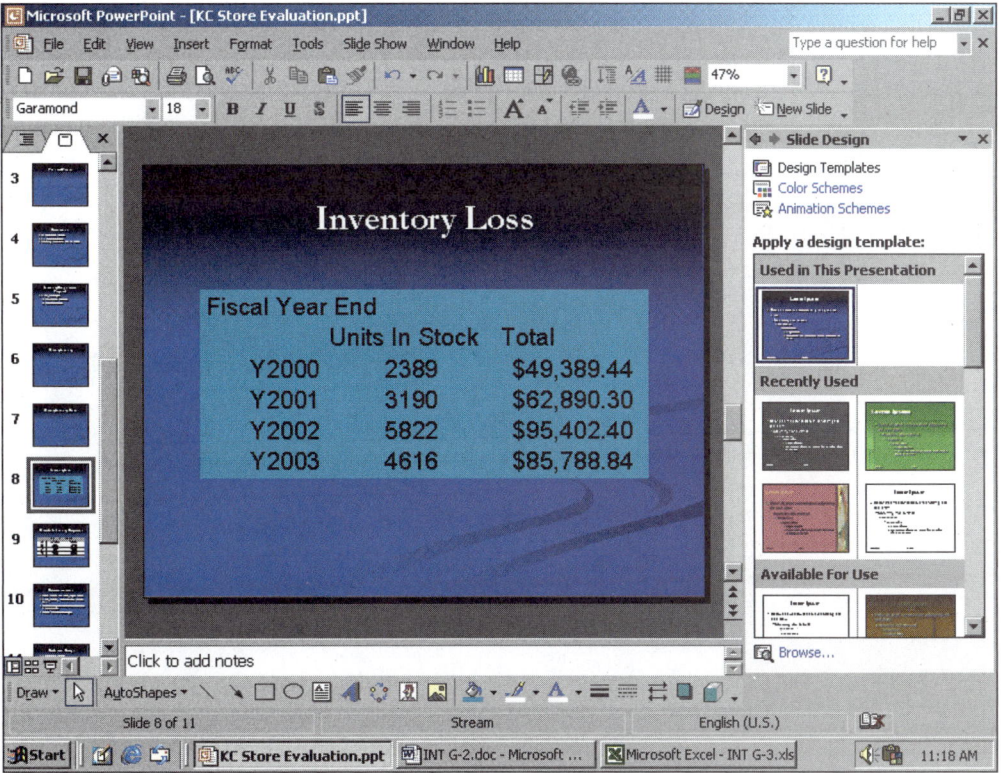

Inserting Access Data into an Excel Worksheet

You can import data from an existing Access database into a PowerPoint presentation. To get just the information needed, you retrieve and organize the data in Access, export the information into Excel for analysis and formatting, and finally import the information into the PowerPoint presentation. In this lesson, you'll create a select query in Access and export the data into a new Excel workbook. ✏️ To emphasize the inventory problem at the Kansas City store, Maria decides to incorporate data from Access into her presentation. To get the appropriate information, Maria first creates a select query in Access, then exports the results of the query to an Excel worksheet so she can analyze the information.

Steps

1. Open the Access database **KC Stock List-IG.mdb** from the drive and location where you store your Project Files

2. Create a query named **History Inventory** using the following fields: **AuthorID**, **BookTitle**, **ISBN**, **UnitsInStock**, and **UnitPrice**
   You might want to review the table in Datasheet view.

3. In Datasheet view, sort the results of the query in ascending order by AuthorID, then save the results
   Compare your screen with Figure G-5.

4. Analyze the History Inventory query with Excel
   An Excel worksheet and workbook, named History Inventory opens, displaying the data from the Access query.

5. Save the Excel workbook as **History Inventory List** to the drive and location where your Project Files are stored
   Your screen should look similar to Figure G-6.

6. Save and close KC Stock List database, then close Access

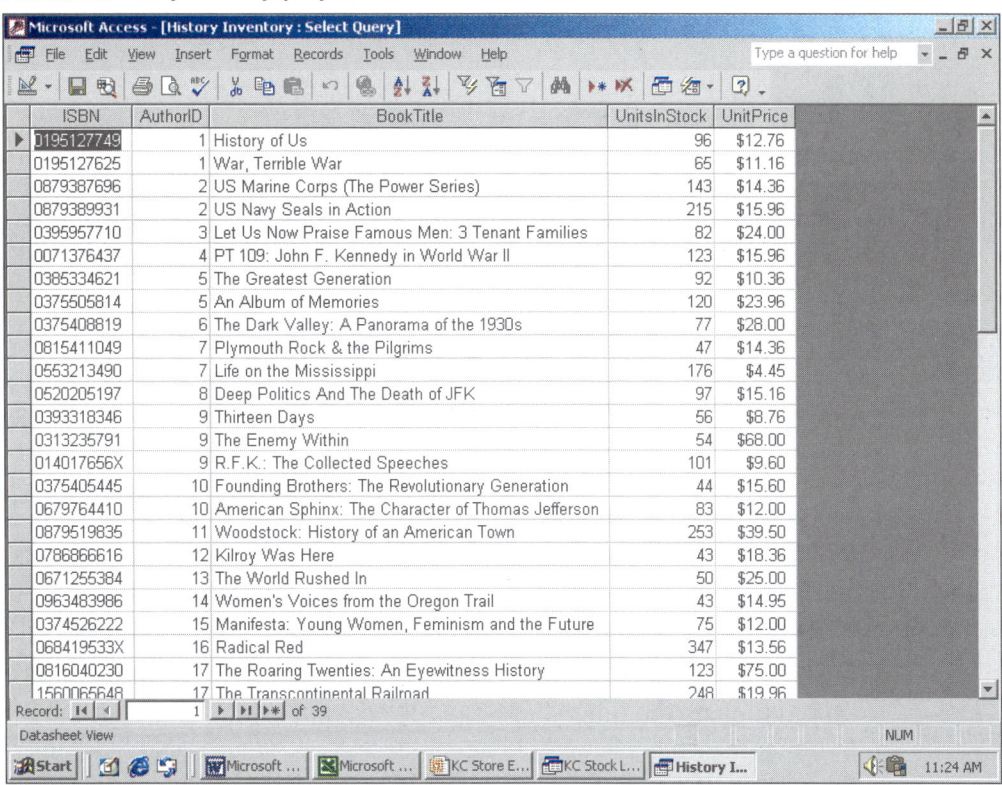

FIGURE G-5: History Inventory query in Datasheet view

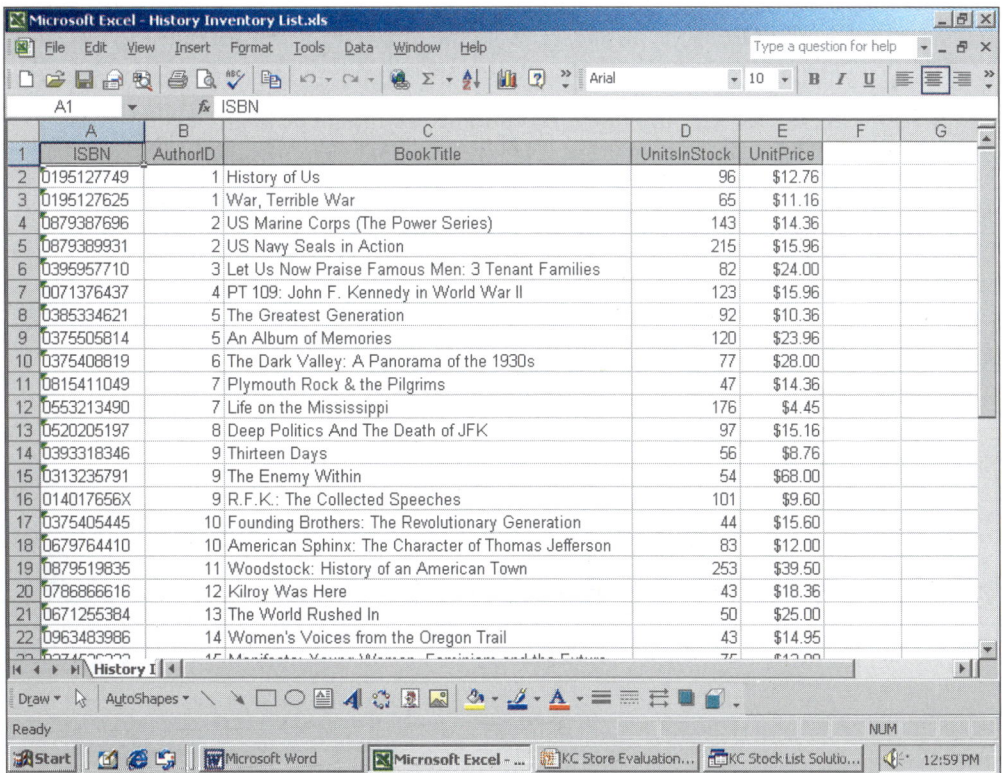

FIGURE G-6: Excel worksheet showing imported Access data

Analyzing Access Data in Excel

When you import data from an Access database into an Excel workbook it may need to be modified for others to understand it. Using Excel's analyzing and organizing features, you can format the data, filter the data, and perform calculations. Importing Access data into Excel can be very helpful when you want to use the Access data in a PowerPoint presentation. In this lesson, Maria hides a column of data that it is not necessary to view, calculates new data, filters and copies data to new worksheets, and then embeds data into her PowerPoint presentation.

1. **Hide the Book Title column, then add two columns to the worksheet, titled Total and 35%**
   The worksheet should have a total of six columns containing data.

2. **Calculate each book's total value in the Total column, then calculate a 35% increase for each book in the 35% column**
   Use Excel formulas to calculate all of these figures. 40 rows of data won't fit on a slide, so you will need to divide the data in half so you can embed it into the PowerPoint presentation.

3. **Create a new worksheet titled Top 20, filter the top 20 items in the Total column, then copy and paste the filtered data and the column headings to the Top 20 worksheet**
   Be sure to copy the column headings in the first row of the History Inventory worksheet to the new worksheet.

4. **Create a new worksheet titled Bottom 19, filter the bottom 19 items in the Total column on the History Inventory worksheet, then copy and paste the filtered data and the column headings to the Bottom 19 worksheet**
   Figure G-7 shows how the second new worksheet might look.

5. **Copy the data in the Top 20 worksheet, click the PowerPoint program button on the Windows taskbar, click the Slide 6 thumbnail in the Slides tab, click Edit on the menu bar, click Paste Special, then link the worksheet to the slide**
   The data from the worksheet is linked to the PowerPoint presentation.

6. **Follow the same procedure to link the data in the Bottom 19 worksheet to Slide 7 of the presentation**

7. **Format the linked worksheet objects using PowerPoint's formatting commands, to make them easier to view, then save your work**
   Figure G-8 shows a formatted linked object.

FIGURE G-7: Excel worksheet showing filtered data

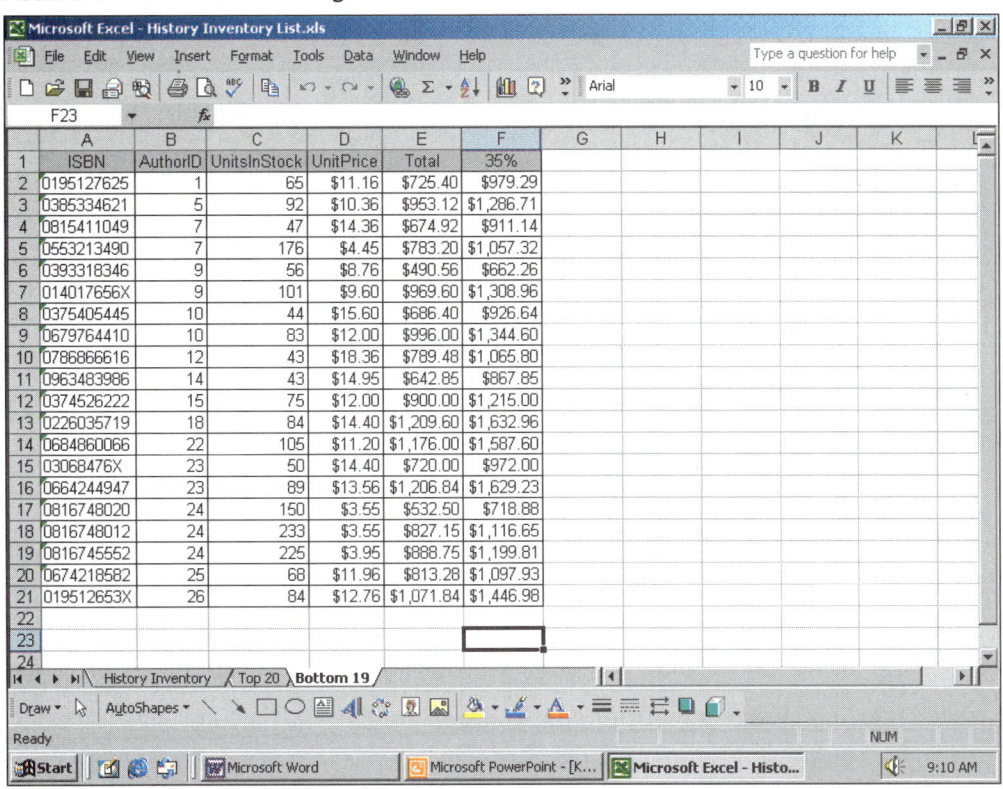

FIGURE G-8: PowerPoint slide showing linked worksheet

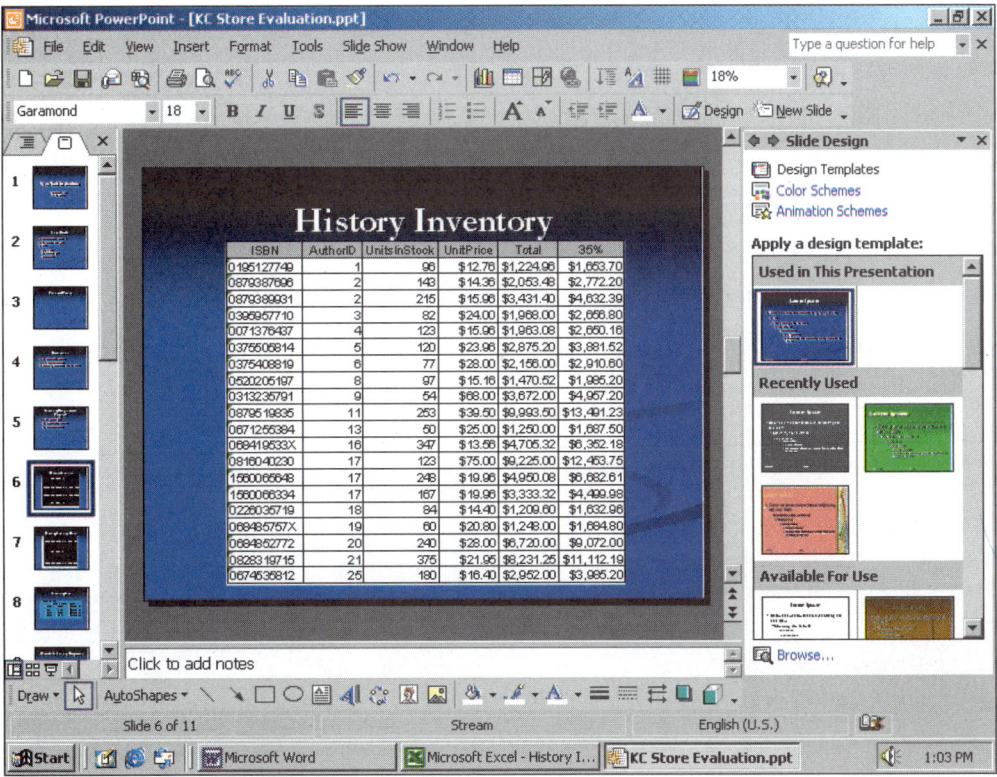

Inserting Excel Data in a Word Document

Trying to explain Excel data in a Word document can be difficult, especially when there are complex calculations involved. A visual object, such as a worksheet or a chart, can really enhance the message of a document and make all the difference in communicating the correct information. ➤ Maria needs to send her boss, the VP of sales, a memo regarding the inventory data from the Kansas City store. She decides to insert the Excel worksheet directly into her Word document.

Steps

1. Click the **Excel program button** on the Windows taskbar, then click the **History Inventory tab**
   The History Inventory worksheet appears.

2. Calculate the total sum for column F in cell F42, calculate the sum total for column G in cell G42, then format both cells using the **Bold button** on the Formatting toolbar

3. Unhide the BookTitle column, select the data in the worksheet, then click the **Copy button** on the Standard toolbar
   The data in the worksheet is selected.

4. Open the Word document **INT G-4.doc** from the drive and location where you store your Project Files, then save it as **Memo to VP**
   The Word document opens.

5. Place the insertion point in the space between the paragraphs, then click the **Paste button** on the Standard toolbar
   The data from Excel is inserted in the Word document, as shown in Figure G-9. The table needs to be modified to fit in the Word document.

6. Delete the AuthorID and the UnitPrice columns, then adjust the width of the BookTitle column so that the book titles fits on one line
   Compare your screen to Figure G-10.

7. Format the table using Word formatting commands

8. Include your name in the footer of the document, then save and print the document

FIGURE G-9: Data from worksheet pasted in Word document

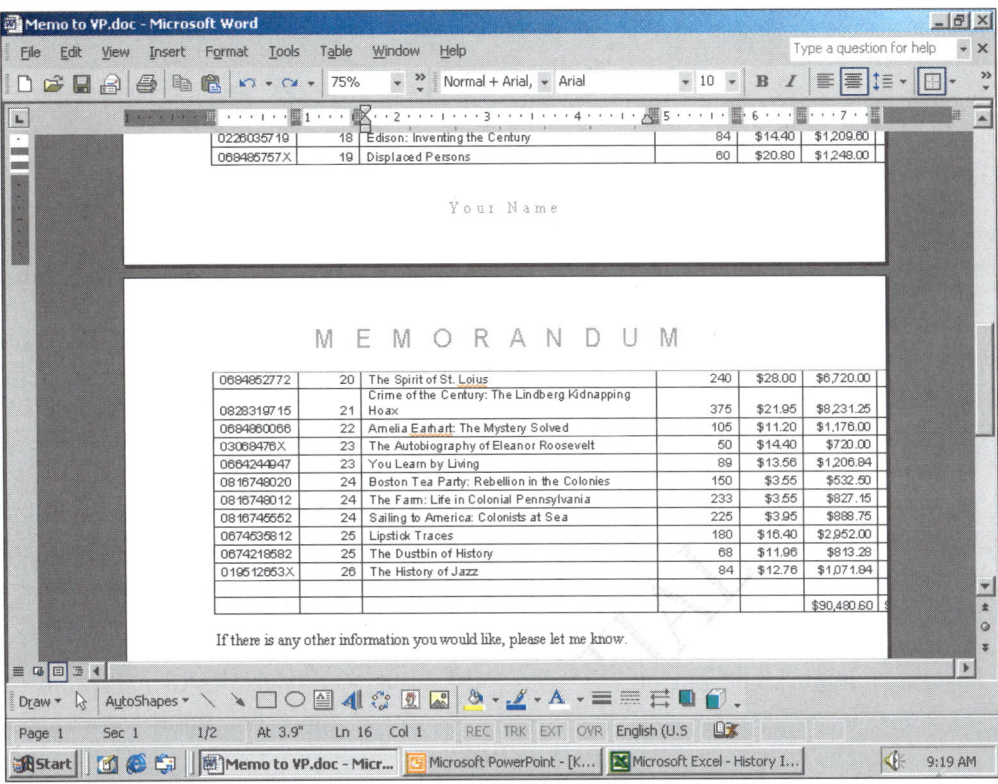

FIGURE G-10: Formatted table in Word document

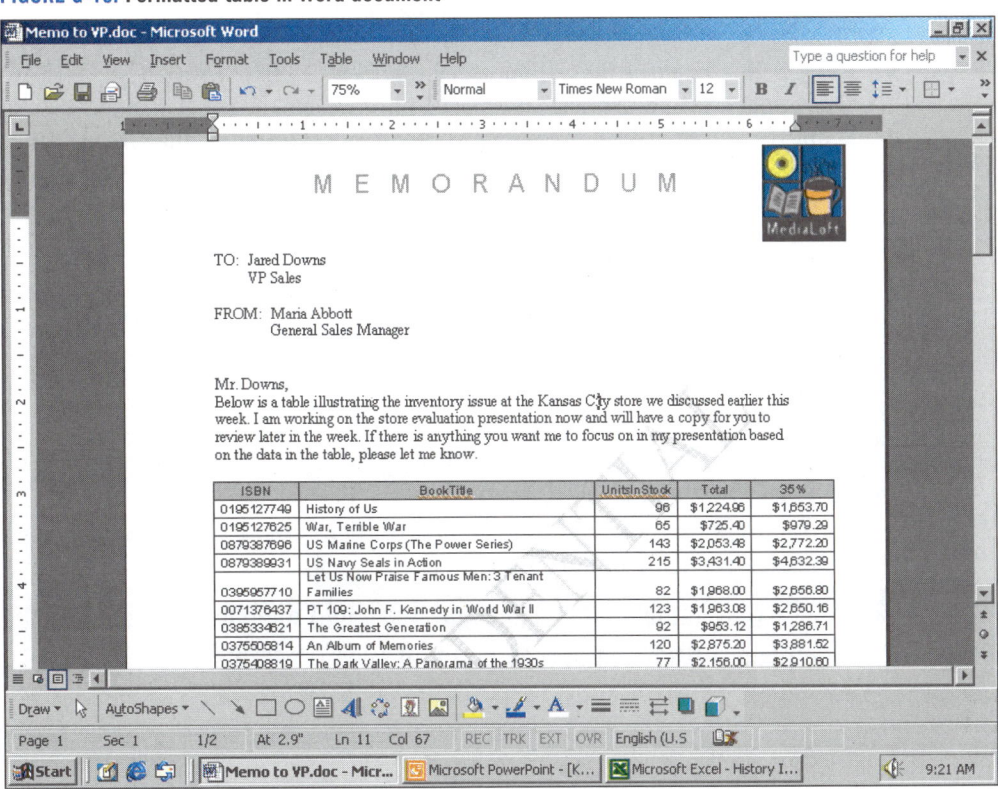

INTEGRATING WORD, EXCEL, ACCESS, AND POWERPOINT

Importing Excel Data into a PowerPoint Presentation

An easy way to create a chart in PowerPoint is to import existing data from Excel using Microsoft Graph. Once you import data into Microsoft Graph and create a chart for your presentation, you don't need to use Excel to change or modify the chart. Maria finishes her work by importing data from Excel into Microsoft Graph and then embedding the chart in a new slide. She evaluates the presentation to verify that it's organized and complete, then creates handouts using Word.

1. Click the **PowerPoint program button** on the Windows taskbar, click the **Slide 3 thumbnail** in the Slides tab, then click the **Insert Chart button** on the Standard toolbar
   A new chart appears on the slide with default data.

2. Clear the default data in the datasheet, click the first cell in the datasheet, click the **Import File button**, locate the Excel workbook **INT G-5.xls** from the drive and location where your Project Files are stored, then click **Open**
   The Import Data options dialog box opens.

3. Click the **Range option button**, type **A1:D5**, then click **OK**
   The data from the workbook appears in the datasheet.

4. Format the Graph datasheet and chart as needed
   Experiment with the chart's type and 3-D view to determine the best format. Figure G-11 shows an example of how your chart might look.

5. Review the presentation, then make changes as necessary
   You might use clip art, drawn objects, photographs, animated movies, digital movies, or sound to enhance your presentation. Remember, however, that movies and photographs greatly increase the presentation's file size. If necessary, change an object's appearance to better fit with the slide color scheme or slide design. Make sure that the content of the presentation flows logically and is complete. You may need to add or remove some content to complete the presentation.

6. Finish the presentation by checking for spelling errors, then set custom animations, slide timings, and interactive settings for the presentation slides
   Figure G-12 shows an example of how your presentation might look.

7. Send the presentation to Word to create linked handouts, then save the document as **KC Pres Handouts**
   Use the Send To command on the File menu in PowerPoint to create a link between your presentation and a Word document.

8. Include your name on the slides and notes and handouts, save and print the presentation and the handouts, then close all open programs
   You may need two disks to save the entire presentation.

FIGURE G-11: Microsoft Graph datasheet showing imported Excel data

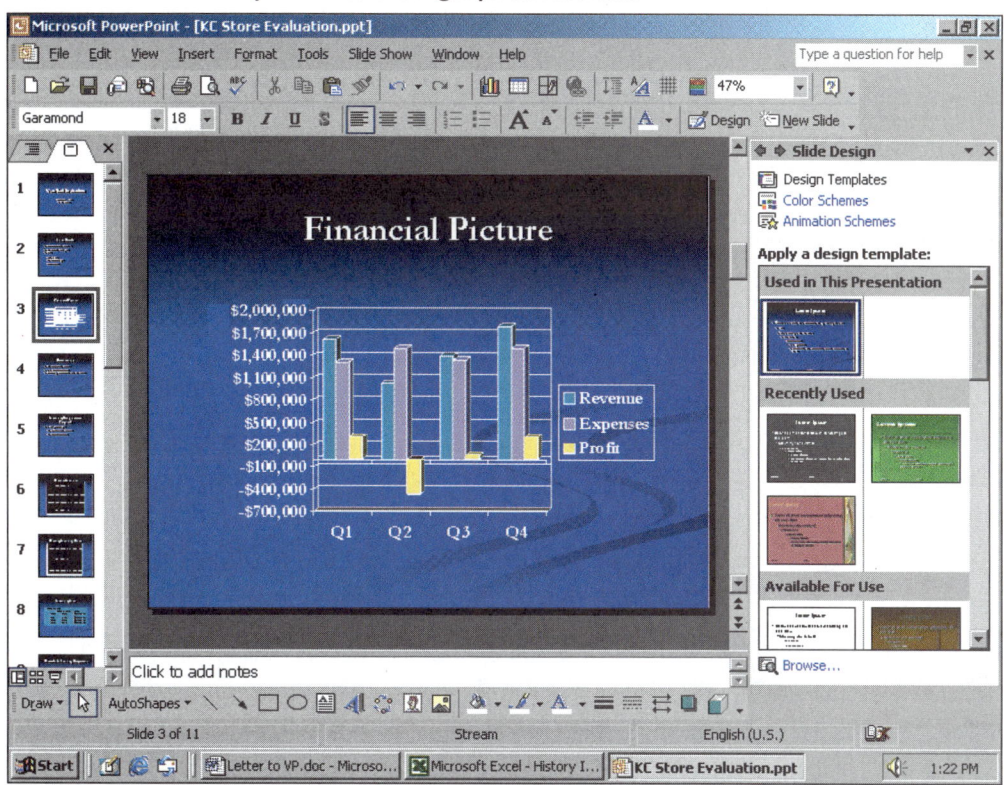

FIGURE G-12: Final presentation

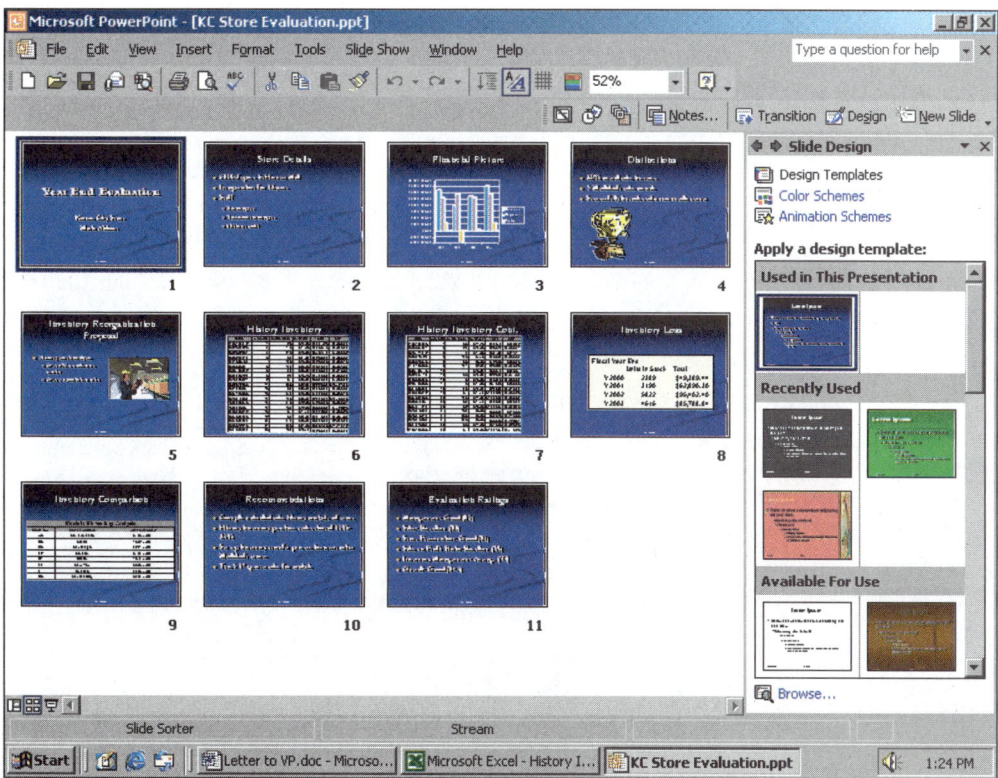

Integration | **Practice**

▶ Independent Challenge 1

As a marketing analyst at Davis Press, a publishing company, you have been asked to research a marketing strategy for a new sports magazine that will compete with periodicals such as *Sports Illustrated*. You decide to use PowerPoint to develop a presentation to illustrate your research findings and marketing recommendations.

To help you complete this independent challenge, a partially completed Word document is provided. You will complete the Word outline and then use it as the outline for a new PowerPoint presentation. Assume the following information to be true as you work on the outline and create the presentation:

- The name of the new magazine is *AllSports*.
- Currently, only three magazines have some of the features that the new *AllSports* magazine will offer.
- *AllSports* should appeal to both men and women aged 25–50.
- *AllSports* should include articles on major sports, such as football, baseball, and basketball, as well as sports such as gymnastics, tennis, and fishing.
- The magazine will focus on sports analysis and the people behind the sports.

a. Open the Word document INT G-6.doc from the drive and location where your Project Files are stored, then save it as **AllSports Outline**.
b. Review the partially completed Word document, then replace the italicized text with your own content.
c. Add information to the Word outline that strengthens your presentation.
d. Create a presentation using your completed Word outline, then save it as **AllSports Magazine**. Consider what kind of results you want and how you need to adjust the text in PowerPoint.
e. Preview the presentation and plan the design of each slide. Change the slide layout, if necessary.
f. Apply a template or a shaded background. Customize an existing presentation template or create one of your own.
g. Add or create objects to enhance the slides in your presentation. Analyze each slide to see whether an object might enhance the impact of the text on that slide.
h. Open the Word document INT G-7.doc from the location where you store your Project Files, then save it as **AllSports Table**.
i. Use your own information to add one or more magazine examples and two more categories to the table.
j. Format the table, then embed it into your presentation. Your presentation may look similar to Figure G-13.
k. Spell check the presentation, then set slide show animations and transitions to the slides of your presentation.
l. Include your name as a footer on slides and notes and handouts in the final presentation, then save and print your presentation slides. Close PowerPoint and Word.

FIGURE G-13

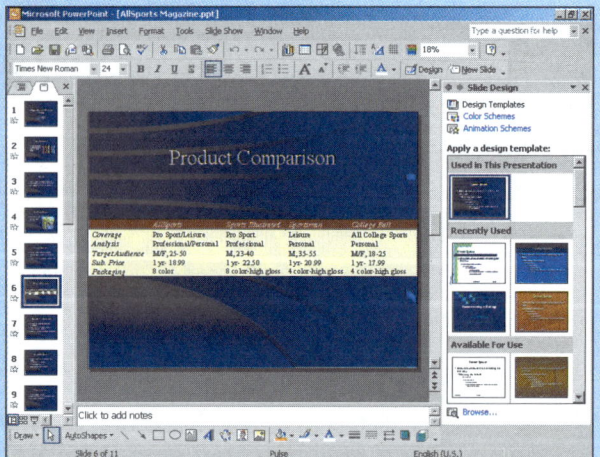

▶ INTEGRATION G-14   **INTEGRATING WORD, EXCEL, ACCESS, AND POWERPOINT**

Practice

▶ Independent Challenge 2

You are the controller for Health & Goodness Inc. (H&G), a distributor of dried foods. Vomar Ltd., an international food wholesaler located in Madrid, Spain, is purchasing H&G. You need to give a detailed presentation to the chief financial officer at Vomar on the revenue generated by all of H&G's clients during the last quarter. The information you present will help determine the relevant issues regarding the sale.

In this independent challenge, you will analyze an Excel worksheet, then embed the charts that you create into a PowerPoint presentation. Your presentation should be at least 10 slides long. Use the Excel worksheet provided to help complete your presentation.

a. Open the Excel worksheet INT G-8 from the drive and location where your Project Files are stored, then save it as **H&G Sale**.
b. Review the partially completed Excel worksheet. You'll need to create a separate chart for each client.
c. Create an analysis of the data on a separate worksheet that shows the total value for each product.
d. Create similar analyses of the worksheet data that enable you to design charts showing each client's total product revenue as well as the total revenue from all clients.
e. Format each chart appropriately using Excel's formatting tools.
f. Open a new PowerPoint presentation, then save it as **H&G Financial Review**.
g. You may want to use the AutoContent Wizard to help with the basic content of your presentation. Consider the results you want to see in PowerPoint and how you might design the slides of the presentation. Remember, this slide show is primarily a financial presentation showing revenue figures taken from Excel worksheets.
h. Preview the presentation and plan the design of each slide. Change the slide layout, if necessary. If you used the AutoContent Wizard in Step g, change the sample text.
i. Apply a template or shaded background, if necessary. Customize an existing presentation template or create one of your own.
j. Switch to Excel and embed each chart in a different slide for your presentation. Figure G-14 shows an example of an embedded Excel chart in the presentation.
k. Add or create objects to enhance the slides of your presentation as necessary. Analyze each slide to see whether an object might enhance the impact of the text on that slide.
l. Spell check the presentation, include your name as a footer on the slides and notes and handouts, then save your changes.
m. Print your final presentation slides, then close PowerPoint and Excel.

FIGURE G-14

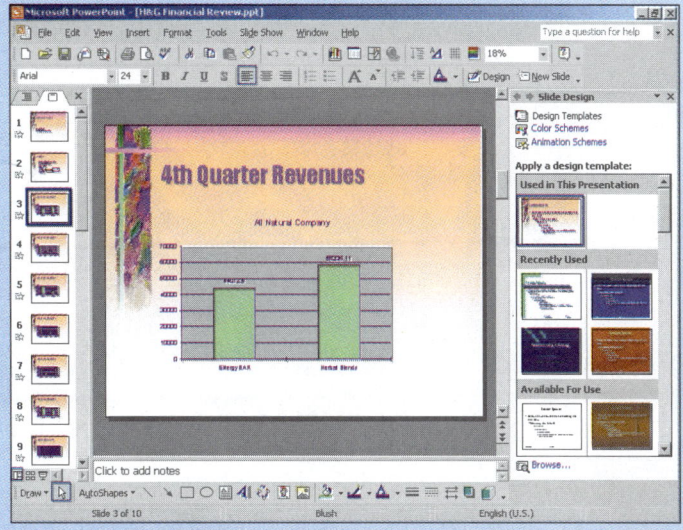

Integration | Practice

▶ Independent Challenge 3

One of your jobs at XEO Business Systems, a trade consulting company, is to research government census data and then present your findings. You have already compiled much of the information you need; now you need to focus on creating a presentation using your research information. To complete the project, you will download information from the Internet, then create an Excel chart. You will finish the project by creating a PowerPoint presentation, then embedding six Excel charts into the presentation.

   a. Connect to the Internet, then use a search engine to locate Web sites that have information on the 2000 census population figures for the states of California, Florida, New York, Pennsylvania, and Texas. If your search does not produce any results, you might try the following link: www.census.gov.
   b. Identify the total population for each state.
   c. Open the Excel workbook INT G-9 from the drive and location where your Project Files are stored, then save it as **Census 2000**. The workbook identifies the top five retail sales producing states in the United States. The charts in the workbook identify the top five sales categories for each of these states.
   d. Create a new worksheet called **Population**, enter the information you retrieved from the Internet, then create a chart.
   e. Create a new presentation called **Trade Data**, then enter information that summarizes the data in the Census 2000 workbook.
   f. Embed all six charts from the Census 2000 workbook as pictures, using the Paste Special command into your presentation.
   g. Format the Excel charts in PowerPoint if needed, then add concluding text to the last slide in the presentation. Include appropriate information to reinforce the message of the presentation.
   h. Add an appropriate design template, customize the color scheme, and adjust the placeholders on the master views as necessary.
   i. Set slide transitions, slide timings, and custom animations as necessary. Include your name as a footer on the slides and notes and handouts in the presentation.
   j. Spell check, save, and print your presentation slides and the Population worksheet.

Project Files List

Read the following information carefully!

It is very important to organize and keep track of the files you need for this book.

1. Find out from your instructor the location of the Project Files you need and the location where you will store your files.

- To complete many of the units in this book, you need to use Project Files. Your instructor will either provide you with a copy of the Project Files or ask you to make your own copy.
- If you need to make a copy of the Project Files, you will need to copy a set of files from a file server, stand-alone computer, or the Web to the drive and folder where you will be storing your Project Files.
- Your instructor will tell you which computer, drive letter, and folders contain the files you need, and where you will store your files.
- You can also download the files by going to www.course.com. See the inside back cover of the book for instructions on how to download your files.

2. Copy and organize your Project Files.

Floppy disk users

- If you are using floppy disks to store your Project Files, the list on the following pages shows which files you'll need to copy onto your disk(s).
- Unless noted in the Project Files List, you will need one formatted, high-density disk for each unit. For each unit you are assigned, copy the files listed in the **Project File Supplied column** onto one disk.
- Make sure you label each disk clearly with the unit name (e.g., Word Unit A).
- When working through the unit, save all your files to this disk.

Users storing files in other locations

- If you are using a zip drive, network folder, hard drive, or other storage device, use the Project Files List to organize your files.
- Create a subfolder for each unit in the location where you are storing your files, and name it according to the unit title (e.g., Word Unit A).
- For each unit you are assigned, copy the files listed in the **Project File Supplied column** into that unit's folder.
- Store the files you modify or create for each unit in the unit folder.

3. Find and keep track of your Project Files and completed files.

- Use the **Project File Supplied column** to make sure you have the files you need before starting the unit or exercise indicated in the **Unit and Location column**.
- Use the **Student Saves File As column** to find out the filename you use when saving your changes to a Project File that was provided.
- Use the **Student Creates File column** to find out the filename you use when saving a file you create new for the exercise.

PROJECT FILES 1

Unit and Location	Project File Supplied	Student Saves File As	Student Creates File
Introducing Office XP	(No files provided or created)		
Integration Unit A			
Lessons	INT A-1.doc	Manager Memo.doc	
			Manager Sales.xls
Independent Challenge 1	INT A-2.xls	Chamber Statistics.xls	
	INT A-3.doc	Chamber Consultants.doc	
Independent Challenge 2			Population Projections.xls
			Population Analysis.doc
Integration Unit B			
Lessons	MediaLoft-IB.mdb		
	INT B-1.doc		Survey Form Letter.doc
			Survey Letters.doc
			Customers.xls
Independent Challenge 1			Student Records.mdb
			Student Info.xls
			Student Info.doc
Independent Challenge 2	MediaLoft-IB.mdb		
			Funding Letter.doc
			Pleasantown Letters.doc
Integration Unit C			
Lessons	INT C-1.ppt	Company Status.ppt	
	INT C-2.doc		
	INT C-3.xls		
	Cafe Profit.xls		
			Handouts for Status Meeting.doc
Independent Challenge 1			Office Review.ppt
	INT C-4.doc		

Unit and Location	Project File Supplied	Student Saves File As	Student Creates File
Independent Challenge 2	INT C-5.xls	Statistics.xls	
			Stat Outline.doc
			Bureau.ppt
			Bureau Handouts.doc
Independent Challenge 3	INT C-6.doc	Cover Letter.doc	
	Nomad.tif		
	Customer Data.mdb		
	INT C-7.xls	Tour Type.xls	
			Tour Evaluation.ppt
	INT C-8.doc		
Independent Challenge 4			Rail Tours.doc
			Royal Tours.ppt
			Royal Tours Data.xls
Integration D*			
DISK 1			
Lessons			Welcome.htm Welcome_files folder and related files
	Mloft.jpg		
	INT D-1.doc	Vacation.htm Vacation_files folder and related files	
	INT D-2.mdb	Health Plans.htm Health Plans_files folder and related files	
	INT D-3.xls	Bonus.htm Bonus_files folder and related files	
	INT D-4.ppt	AR Presentation.htm Annual_files	

Unit and Location	Project File Supplied	Student Saves File As	Student Creates File
DISK 2			
Skills Review	Mloft.jpg INT D-5.doc INT D-6.mdb INT D-7.xls INT D-8.ppt TOC.htm Employee.htm	TOC.htm TOC_files folder and related files Survey.htm Survey_files folder and related files Sales Reps.htm Sales_Reps_files folder and related files Division Sales.htm folder and related files Eastern Presentation.htm Eastern_files folder and related files	
DISK 3			
Independent Challenge 1	INT D-9.doc INT D-10.mdb INT D-11.xls INT D-12.ppt	Grapevine Home.htm Gravepine Home_files folder and related files Donations.htm Donations_files folder and related files Programs.htm Programs_files folder and related files Financial Report.htm Grapevine Annual Report.ppt	
DISK 4			
Independent Challenge 2	INT D-13.doc INT D-14.mdb INT D-15.xls INT D-16.ppt	Oil Spill Home.htm Oil Spill Home_files folder and related files Press Release.htm Press Release_files folder and related files Prevention Programs.htm Prevention Programs_files folder and related files Oil Spills by Company.htm Oil Spills by Company_files folder and related files Oil Spill Presentation.htm Oil Spill Presentation_files folder and related files	

Unit and Location	Project File Supplied	Student Saves File As	Student Creates File
DISK 5			
Visual Workshop			Cafe Home.htm
			Daily Specials.htm
			Contact.htm

*Because the files created in this unit are large, you will need to organize the files onto 5 floppy disks if you are completing all the exercises. Copy the files as outlined above, and label each disk clearly (e.g., Integration Unit D Disk 1).

Unit and Location	Project File Supplied	Student Saves File As	Student Creates File
Integration Unit E			
Lessons	INT E-1.doc	Advertising Report.doc	
	INT E-2.xls	Q3 Ad Costs.xls	
	INT E-3.xls		
	Q3 Expenditures Worksheet.xls		
Independent Challenge 1	INT E-4.doc	Lysander Budget Memo.doc	
	INT E-5.xls	Lysander Budget.xls	
Independent Challenge 2			Computer Budget.xls
			Computer Memo.doc
Integration Unit F			
DISK 1			
Lessons	KC Stock List.mdb		
	INT F-1.doc	KC Store Memo.doc	
	INT F-2.xls	History Overstock Analysis.xls	
	INT F-3.doc	KC Store Memo 2.doc	
DISK 2			
Independent Challenge 1	Tonia's Flowers.mdb		
			Stock Report.xls
Independent Challenge 2	U.S. Trade Analysis.mdb		
			State Trade Analysis.xls
			Top State Trade Analysis.doc

*Because the files created in this unit are large, you will need to organize the files onto 2 floppy disks if you are completing all the exercises. Copy the files as outlined above, and label each disk clearly (e.g., Integration Unit F Disk 1).

Unit and Location	Project File Supplied	Student Saves File As	Student Creates File
Integration Unit G			
DISK 1			
Lessons	INT G-1.doc	KC Store Evaluation.ppt	
	INT G-2.doc		
	INT G-3.xls		
	KC Stock List.mdb		
	INT G-4.doc	Letter to VP.doc	
	INT G-5.xls		
			KC Pres Handouts.doc
DISK 2			
Independent Challenge 1	INT G-6.doc	AllSports Outline.doc	
		AllSports Magazine.ppt	
	INT G-7.doc	AllSports Table.doc	
Independent Challenge 2	INT G-8.xls	H&G Sales.xls	
		H&G Financial Review.ppt	
Independent Challenge 3	INT G-9.xls	Census 2000.xls	
		Trade Data.ppt	

*Because the files created in this unit are large, you will need to organize the files onto 2 floppy disks if you are completing all the exercises. Copy the files as outlined above, and label each disk clearly (e.g., Integration Unit G Disk 1).

Glossary

Absolute link A hyperlink that contains a fixed Web page address.

Data source The file that contains the data to be used in a mail merge.

Destination file The file into which you paste, link, or embed data from another file.

Destination program The program used to create the destination file.

Embed To paste an object into a file while maintaining a connection to the source file; you can edit an embedded object in the destination file by double-clicking it to open the source program.

Embed To paste an object into a file while maintaining a connection to the source file; you can edit an embedded object in the destination file by double-clicking it to open the source file.

Filter A program built into the Office suite that converts data from one program into a format that can be read by another program.

Hyperlink An object or link (a filename, word, phrase, or graphic) that, when clicked, "jumps to" another location in the current file or opens another PowerPoint presentation, a Word, Excel, or Access file, or an address on the World Wide Web.

Hypertext Markup Language (HTML) The formatting language used to describe Web pages.

Integration The ability to use data created in one Office program in a file created in another Office program.

Link (verb) To paste an object into a file while maintaining a connection to the source file; when you edit the source file, the changes are automatically updated in the destination file.

Link A "live" connection between a source file and its representation in a destination file; when one is updated, the other is updated automatically. Can also refer to a hyperlink (see also *Hyperlink*).

Object An item in a document that can be manipulated. Objects are drawn lines and shapes, text, clip art, imported pictures, and embedded objects.

Main document In a mail merge, the document into which you are merging the data source.

Merge Combining data from one file with data from another file to create a new file.

Merge fields In a mail merge, placeholders in the main document that are replaced with data from the data source during the merge.

Multitask The ability to open several programs and files at once and then to switch back and forth among them.

Publish To post Web pages on an intranet or the Web so people can access them using a Web browser.

Relative link A hyperlink that gives another Web page's address in relation to the current page.

Source file The file from which you copy the data you are going to paste, link, or embed in the destination file.

Source program The program used to create the source file.

Style A named collection of character and paragraph formats that are stored together and can be applied to text to format it quickly.

Tags HTML codes that describe how the elements of a Web page should appear when viewed with a Web browser.

Integration

Theme A set of Web page formats, including backgrounds and styles, that are named and stored together; can be applied to a Web page to format it quickly.

Web browser A software program used to access and display Web pages.

Web page A file saved in HTML format that can be viewed using a Web browser.

Web publication A group of associated Web pages.

Web server A remote computer running Web server software

Index

A

absolute links, INTEGRATION D-16
Access 2002, OFFICE A-2, OFFICE A-8–9
   analyzing Access data in Excel, INTEGRATION G-8–9
   converting objects to static or dynamic Web pages, INTEGRATION D-11
   copying datasheets into Word documents, INTEGRATION F-2–3
   copying datasheets to Excel, INTEGRATION F-4–5
   creating Web pages from tables, INTEGRATION D-10–11
   exporting tables to Excel, INTEGRATION B-6–7
   exporting tables to Word, INTEGRATION B-7
   inserting Access data into Excel worksheets, INTEGRATION G-6–7
   merging data between Word and, INTEGRATION B-2–5
applications. *See also specific applications*
   compatibility, OFFICE A-2
   integrating. *See* integration; *specific applications*
   multiple, opening, INTEGRATION A-4–5
   open, switching between, INTEGRATION A-5
appointments, managing, OFFICE A-16

B

business productivity software, OFFICE A-2

C

chart(s). *See* Excel 2002
clip art, OFFICE A-10
comments, Word documents, OFFICE A-4
compatibility of programs, OFFICE A-2
copying
   Access datasheets into Word documents, INTEGRATION F-2–3
   Access datasheets to Excel, INTEGRATION F-4–5
   Word data into Excel, INTEGRATION A-6–7
copying and pasting, INTEGRATION A-2
creating Web pages, INTEGRATION D-4–5
   from Access tables, INTEGRATION D-10–11
   converting Access objects to static or dynamic Web pages, INTEGRATION D-11
   from Excel workbooks, INTEGRATION D-12–13
   from PowerPoint presentations, INTEGRATION D-14–15
   from Word documents, INTEGRATION D-8–9

D

database(s), OFFICE A-8. *See also* Access 2002
database management systems, OFFICE A-8–9
destination files, INTEGRATION A-2, INTEGRATION C-2
destination programs, INTEGRATION C-2
documents. *See also* Word 2002
   creating Web pages from, INTEGRATION D-8–9
   creating with Word, OFFICE A-4–5
dragging and dropping, INTEGRATION A-2

E

editing
   Excel worksheets in PowerPoint, INTEGRATION C-10–11
   hyperlinks, INTEGRATION D-16
electronic spreadsheets. *See* Excel 2002
e-mail, INTEGRATION A-2, OFFICE A-16
embedding objects, INTEGRATION C-2, INTEGRATION C-3
   editing embedded objects, INTEGRATION C-2
   Excel charts into PowerPoint slides, INTEGRATION C-6–7
   Excel charts into Word documents, INTEGRATION F-6–7
   Excel worksheets into presentations, INTEGRATION G-4–5
   Excel worksheets into Word documents, INTEGRATION E-4–5
   integration, INTEGRATION A-2
   Word tables into presentations, INTEGRATION G-4–5
eServices, INTEGRATION A-2, INTEGRATION A-3
Excel 2002, OFFICE A-2
   analyzing Access data in Excel, INTEGRATION G-8–9
   copying Access datasheets to, INTEGRATION F-4–5
   copying Word data into, INTEGRATION A-6–7

Index

creating Web pages from workbooks, INTEGRATION D-12–13
embedding charts into PowerPoint slides, INTEGRATION C-6–7
embedding charts into Word documents, INTEGRATION F-6–7
embedding worksheets into presentations, INTEGRATION G-4–5
embedding worksheets into Word documents, INTEGRATION E-4–5
exporting Access tables to, INTEGRATION B-6–7
importing Excel data into PowerPoint presentations, INTEGRATION G-12–13
inserting Access data into worksheets, INTEGRATION G-6–7
inserting Excel data in Word documents, INTEGRATION G-10–11
inserting hyperlinks to Excel files in Word documents, INTEGRATION E-6–7
linking charts to Word documents, INTEGRATION E-2–3
linking worksheets to PowerPoint slides, INTEGRATION C-8–9
updating worksheets in PowerPoint, INTEGRATION C-10–11
exporting, INTEGRATION A-2
  Access tables to Excel, INTEGRATION B-6–7
  Access tables to Word, INTEGRATION B-7
  PowerPoint presentations to Word, INTEGRATION C-12–13

F

field(s), merge, INTEGRATION B-4, INTEGRATION B-5
file(s)
  destination, INTEGRATION A-2
  source, INTEGRATION A-2
filter(s), INTEGRATION A-2
formatting Web pages, INTEGRATION D-6–7
form letters, INTEGRATION B-4–5
frames, Web pages, INTEGRATION D-15

G

Graph, importing Excel data into PowerPoint presentations, INTEGRATION G-12–13
graphic images, OFFICE A-10

H

HTML (Hypertext Markup Language), INTEGRATION D-1
  tags, INTEGRATION D-4
hyperlinks, INTEGRATION E-6, OFFICE A-14
  absolute, INTEGRATION D-16
  editing, INTEGRATION D-16
  to Excel files, inserting in Word documents, INTEGRATION E-6–7
  integration, INTEGRATION A-2
  publishing, INTEGRATION D-17
  relative, INTEGRATION D-16
  updating, INTEGRATION C-11
  Web pages, INTEGRATION D-16–17
Hypertext Markup Language (HTML), INTEGRATION D-1
  tags, INTEGRATION D-4

I

images, OFFICE A-10
importing, INTEGRATION A-2
  Excel data into PowerPoint presentations, INTEGRATION G-12–13
Insert Hyperlink dialog box, INTEGRATION A-2, INTEGRATION A-3, INTEGRATION D-16, INTEGRATION D-17, INTEGRATION E-6, INTEGRATION E-7
inserting
  Access data into Excel worksheets, INTEGRATION G-6–7
  Excel data in Word documents, INTEGRATION G-10–11
  hyperlinks to Excel files in Word documents, INTEGRATION E-6–7
  Word outlines into PowerPoint presentations, INTEGRATION C-4–5
Insert Object dialog box, INTEGRATION C-8, INTEGRATION C-9
integration, INTEGRATION A-1–7, INTEGRATION B-1–7, INTEGRATION C-1–13, OFFICE A-2, OFFICE A-14–15. *See also* embedding objects; exporting; importing; linking objects; *specific programs*
  destination file, INTEGRATION A-2, INTEGRATION C-2
  Office applications with Internet Explorer. *See* Web pages
  opening multiple programs, INTEGRATION A-4–5
  source file, INTEGRATION A-2, INTEGRATION C-2
  uses, INTEGRATION A-2
  Word and Excel, INTEGRATION A-6–7
Internet. *See* Web entries; World Wide Web (Web; WWW)
Internet Explorer, INTEGRATION D-1–17, OFFICE A-12–13
  integrating Office applications with. *See* creating Web pages
  Web pages. *See* creating Web pages; Web pages

J

journals, OFFICE A-16

L

letters (correspondence), form, INTEGRATION B-4–5

Index

link(s), INTEGRATION E-2. *See also* hyperlink(s)
linking objects, INTEGRATION C-2, INTEGRATION C-3
  editing linked objects, INTEGRATION C-2
  Excel charts to Word documents, INTEGRATION E-2–3
  Excel worksheets to PowerPoint slides, INTEGRATION C-8–9
  integration, INTEGRATION A-2
  updating Excel worksheets in PowerPoint, INTEGRATION C-10–11
  updating links, INTEGRATION C-11

▶ M

mail merge, INTEGRATION B-2–5, INTEGRATION B-4–5
Mail Merge Wizard dialog box, INTEGRATION B-2, INTEGRATION B-3
main document, INTEGRATION B-2, INTEGRATION B-3
Match Fields dialog box, INTEGRATION B-4, INTEGRATION B-5
merge fields, INTEGRATION B-4, INTEGRATION B-5
merging data between Access and Word, INTEGRATION B-2–5
Microsoft programs. *See specific program names*
multitasking, INTEGRATION A-4–5

▶ N

names of Web pages, INTEGRATION D-3

▶ O

object(s), INTEGRATION E-1
  embedding. *See* embedding objects
  linking. *See* linking objects

Object dialog box, INTEGRATION E-4, INTEGRATION E-5
Office Clipboard, INTEGRATION A-2, INTEGRATION A-3
Office XP, OFFICE A-1–16. *See also* Access 2002; Excel 2002; Internet Explorer; Outlook 2002; PowerPoint 2002; Word 2002
  compatibility and integration, OFFICE A-2
  components, OFFICE A-2
  online collaboration, OFFICE A-2
online collaboration, INTEGRATION A-2, OFFICE A-2
opening multiple programs, INTEGRATION A-4–5
outlines, Word, inserting into PowerPoint presentations, INTEGRATION C-4–5
Outlook 2002, INTEGRATION A-2, OFFICE A-2, OFFICE A-16

▶ P

Paste Special dialog box, INTEGRATION E-2, INTEGRATION E-3
  embedding objects, INTEGRATION C-7
pasting, INTEGRATION A-2
personal information managers, OFFICE A-16
pictures, OFFICE A-10
planning Web publications, INTEGRATION D-2–3
PowerPoint 2002, OFFICE A-2, OFFICE A-10–12
  creating presentations from Word outlines, INTEGRATION G-2–3
  creating Web pages from presentations, INTEGRATION D-14–15
  embedding Excel charts into slides, INTEGRATION C-6–7
  embedding Word tables and Excel worksheets into presentations, INTEGRATION G-4–5
  exporting presentations to Word, INTEGRATION C-12–13
  importing Excel data into presentations, INTEGRATION G-12–13
  inserting Word outlines, INTEGRATION C-4–5
  linking Excel worksheets to slides, INTEGRATION C-8–9
  updating Excel worksheets in, INTEGRATION C-10–11
presentation(s). *See* PowerPoint 2002; slide(s)
presentation graphics programs, OFFICE A-10. *See also* PowerPoint 2002
program(s). *See also* applications; integration; *specific programs*
  destination, INTEGRATION C-2
  source, INTEGRATION C-2
publishing
  hyperlinks, INTEGRATION D-17
  on Web, INTEGRATION D-1
Publish It with MS Word feature, INTEGRATION B-7

▶ R

relative links, INTEGRATION D-16
reminders, OFFICE A-16

▶ S

Send to Microsoft Word dialog box, INTEGRATION C-12, INTEGRATION C-13
slide(s), OFFICE A-10, OFFICE A-11
  embedding charts into, INTEGRATION C-6–7
  linking worksheets to, INTEGRATION C-8–9
slide shows, OFFICE A-10
Sort dialog box, INTEGRATION B-6, INTEGRATION B-7
source files, INTEGRATION A-2, INTEGRATION C-2
source program, INTEGRATION C-2

Index

spreadsheet programs, OFFICE A-6. *See also* Excel 2002
styles, INTEGRATION C-4
   Web pages, INTEGRATION D-6
switching between open programs, INTEGRATION A-5

▶T

table(s)
   Access, OFFICE A-8
   creating Web pages from, INTEGRATION D-10–11
tags, HTML, INTEGRATION D-4
tasks, managing, OFFICE A-16
themes in Web pages, INTEGRATION D-4
tracking feature
   contacts, OFFICE A-16
   Word, OFFICE A-4, OFFICE A-5

▶U

updating links, INTEGRATION C-11

▶W

Web. *See* World Wide Web (Web; WWW)
Web browsers, OFFICE A-12. *See also* Internet Explorer
Web pages, INTEGRATION D-1
   content, INTEGRATION D-5
   creating. *See* creating Web pages
   formatting, INTEGRATION D-6–7
   frames, INTEGRATION D-15
   hyperlinks, INTEGRATION D-16–17
   naming, INTEGRATION D-3
   planning Web publications, INTEGRATION D-2–3
   style, INTEGRATION D-5
Web publications, planning, INTEGRATION D-2–3
Web servers, INTEGRATION D-1
what-if analysis, OFFICE A-6
Word 2002, OFFICE A-2
   copying Access datasheets into, INTEGRATION F-2–3
   copying data into Excel, INTEGRATION A-6–7
   creating documents, OFFICE A-4–5
   creating PowerPoint presentations from Word outlines, INTEGRATION G-2–3
   creating Web pages from documents, INTEGRATION D-8–9
   embedding Excel charts into documents, INTEGRATION F-6–7
   embedding Excel worksheets into documents, INTEGRATION E-4–5
   embedding Word tables into presentations, INTEGRATION G-4–5
   exporting Access tables to, INTEGRATION B-7
   exporting PowerPoint presentations to, INTEGRATION C-12–13
   inserting Excel data in Word documents, INTEGRATION G-10–11
   inserting hyperlinks to Excel files in Word documents, INTEGRATION E-6–7
   inserting outlines into PowerPoint presentations, INTEGRATION C-4–5
   linking Excel charts to documents, INTEGRATION E-2–3
   merging data between Access and, INTEGRATION B-2–5
word processing programs, OFFICE A-4. *See also* Word 2002
workbooks. *See* Excel 2002
worksheet(s), OFFICE A-6–7. *See also* Excel 2002
   building, OFFICE A-6–7
worksheet cells, OFFICE A-6
World Wide Web (Web; WWW), OFFICE A-12–13. *See also* Web *entries*
   publishing on, INTEGRATION D-1